ROCK

HARDWARE

A BALAFON BOOK
AN IMPRINT OF OUTLINE PRESS LIMITED

ROCK HARDWARE

A BALAFON BOOK
First British Edition 1996

Published in the UK by Balafon Books,
an imprint of Outline Press Ltd.
115J Cleveland Street, London W1P 5PN, England

Published in the United States by Miller Freeman Books
600 Harrison Street, San Francisco, CA 94107
Publishers of 'Guitar Player' and 'Bass Player' Magazines
Miller Freeman, Inc. is a United News and Media Company

US ISBN 0-87930-428-6

REST OF WORLD ISBN 1-871547-35-0

Printed in Hong Kong

Creative Director: Nigel Osborne
Editorial Director: Tony Bacon
Design: Paul Cooper
Editor: Paul Trynka

Print & Origination by Regent Publishing Services

96 97 98 99 00 5 4 3 2 1

Contents

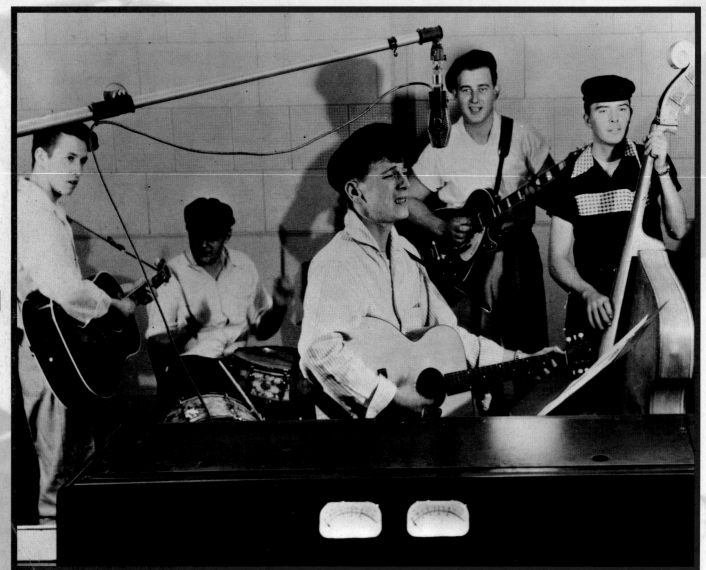

Although rock music is without doubt the most talked-about art form of this century, the mechanics of this art form are invariably overlooked, as stories of sex and drugs take precedence over the rock'n'roll. Yet while cultural upheavals such as the Second World War and major social changes of the 1940s played their part in the creation of this radical form, countless technical innovations combined to influence and arguably to define the sound of rock music.

In some cases, influential instruments predated the existence of rock'n'roll – the Hammond Model A organ, or the Fender Telecaster, for example. Elsewhere, the hardware was developed specifically for this new sound. The story of how these pioneering instruments were adopted by the music's innovators, and how they went on to change the sound of rock, is one of the most fascinating aspects of the music's history.

In the following pages you will read how the hardware of rock music has evolved – and how it has changed music in the process. Each of the succeeding chapters illustrates one vital strand of the music's development. Whether it's the evolution of the modern drum kit or the advent of the huge PA systems that amplified the epochal rock festivals of the late 1960s, each aspect of this story throws new light on the history of rock. Crucially, this is also the story of the players who used this technology to make some of the most influential sounds of all time. This book offers a unique insight into the development of rock music, in some cases crediting significant unsung heroes, in others offering new explanations of how rock's most celebrated figures achieved their fame. From pioneering bluesmen distorting their harmonicas through tiny amplifiers to modern producers using digital technology in search of sonic perfection, Rock Hardware is the story of the people and the instruments that helped to make this music special.

Guitars & Amps

"When I was at school, rather than paying attention I was dreaming about guitars. They were magical to me. I think the only way you could really appreciate the impact of the guitar is to do a little bit of work, to go back and examine its history."

ERIC CLAPTON, GUITARIST

The Electric Guitar

In social and cultural terms, the electric guitar is the most significant instrument of the 20th century. It revolutionized the way music was made, allowing small combos with just four or five musicians to play or record, rendering the big bands of the 1930s and 1940s effectively redundant, opening up the musical scene, and thus paving the way for rock'n'roll, and all the musical developments that came in its wake. Yet while the electric guitar had arrived in pretty much its present format by the early 1950s, it would take guitarists nearly two decades fully to realize the potential of this radical new instrument.

The roots of the solidbody electric guitar derive from the lap steels and early Rickenbacker Electro Spanish guitars of the 1930s, but the instrument as it's now known was born in a few short years at the beginning of the 1950s. Some would argue the new instrument actually grew up and matured there and then. Without doubt, a quick glance within any modern guitar store reveals a basic line-up of instruments – Fender Telecasters, Stratocasters, Gibson Les Pauls and their many lookalikes – which would have been familiar to any retailer whose history stretches back to the 1950s.

The Rock'n'Roll Decade

Popular music was in a state of radical flux in the years following WWII. By this time musicians had been experimenting with electric instruments for several years: early exponents of the

The appeal of the electric guitar derived both from its musical potential, and its visual impact. This 1950s photograph provides compelling evidence, if any were needed, that electric blues pioneer T-Bone Walker was fully aware of both qualities.

electric guitar included the celebrated Charlie Christian, featured guitarist with Benny Goodman, and T-Bone Walker, a friend of Christian's and pioneer of electric blues guitar. Robert Lockwood Junior, guitarist with Sonny Boy Williamson II, was a crucial trailblazer for the electric guitar, via the King Biscuit Time radio show, broadcasting regularly out of Helena, Arkansas, from 1941. By now the electric lap steel was extremely popular in country music (lap steels, or Hawaiian guitars are played on the lap or on a stand, and pitched by means of a bottleneck or slider – the pedal steel is a more sophisticated version which allows the tuning to be controlled by means of pedals). The electric lap steel effectively paved the way for the conventional electric guitar within country music, where it was used by many celebrated outfits including Bob Wills And His Texas Playboys. It was the popularity of the lap steel that prompted California inventor and radio repair-man Leo Fender to enter the musical instrument business, and ultimately to design an electric guitar which dispensed with the clumsy hollow body of the archtop electrics produced by Gibson and other manufacturers.

Whereas Gibson's rich guitar-making heritage ironically prevented the Kalamazoo-based company from taking the radical steps envisioned by their upstart rivals, Leo Fender's pragmatic approach meant that his first attempt at an electric guitar would become definitive. Fender's 1940s lap steels formed the basis for his first solid electric, the Broadcaster. The guitar's simple ash body and maple neck were chosen for the reasons of the wood's ready availability. Fender's concentration on production efficiency defined other aspects of the guitar's construction: the 'bolt-on' neck, achieved with four machine screws, allowed for simple replacement of faulty components, but also simplified manufacture. The component parts could be fabricated separately, and only joined together after they'd been finally sprayed and polished. First produced in 1950, to be renamed the Telecaster by August 1951, this guitar established a bench-mark for production-scale solidbody electric guitars. The Telecaster has remained in production ever since with little significant alteration. As Leo Fender was to prove with the Precision bass and the Stratocaster, he did indeed get it right first time.

We'll probably never know exactly what influence a Californian inventor Paul Bigsby (who later developed the Bigsby tremolo) was to have on the development of the electric solidbody. According to George Fullerton, Leo Fender's assistant from 1948, "Leo did see Paul Bigsby's guitar, and I'm sure that was an influence to Leo to get something going on his own."

Although the Bigsby-Travis solidbody guitar was only produced in very small numbers, many of its design characteristics would reappear on later production guitars: the single-cutaway shape was similar to the Gibson Les Paul, the headstock was similar to that of the Fender Stratocaster; the through-neck – a lap steel with body 'wings' – would appear on Rickenbacker's Combo 400 and Gibson's Firebird.

■ Bigsby Travis guitar
Designed: circa 1948

The influence of this solidbody Bigsby-Travis guitar, sketched out by country star Merle Travis and built by California inventor Paul Bigsby, belies its one-off status. The through-neck, single cutaway styling and through-body stringing would be echoed in many subsequent electrics, while the headstock design is uncannily close to 1954's Fender Stratocaster. Ultimately, the guitar's significance lies less in its much copied design details, than in the fact that its example helped inspire Leo Fender to commence mass production of solidbody electrics.

■ Fender Stratocaster
Introduced: 1954

Fender's Stratocaster in many respects completed the development of the electric guitar, with its emphasis on a pure tone, sonic versatility, ergonomics and tuning stability.

■ *Fender amplifiers utilized generic designs but were just as significant as guitars in the company's growth. By the launch of the Stratocaster in 1954, featured on the cover of that year's price list (right), Fender's amplifier range featured seven models.*

FENDER ELEC
PRICE LI

Order From

FENDER SALES, Inc.
308 E. 5th Street   Santa Ana, Calif.

The Solidbody Takes Off

The electric guitar was already an unqualified success by the time Fender launched the Telecaster. Industry heavyweights Gibson had many successful electrified models within their line, including the ES-350, ES-175, the up-market Super 400CES and a host of budget models, but all were based on traditional hollow body designs. Ironically, given its hollow body heritage, Gibson was the first major manufacturer to realize the potential of Fender's radical new guitar. As Ted McCarty, who'd joined Gibson in 1948 and became President in 1950, puts it: "I watched him [Fender], and watched him, and said we've got to get into that business." But when Gibson introduced the Les Paul 'gold-top' model in 1952 it was far from a token Telecaster copy. Both guitars were single-cutaway, solidbody, twin pickup instruments, but compared to the plank-like Telecaster the Les Paul was an inspired progression from Gibson's archtop tradition, in looks, construction and choice of materials. Where Fender utilized indigenous woods, Gibson chose Central and South American mahogany for the neck and body, Brazilian rosewood for the fingerboard and maple for the distinctive carved top. Gibson used a traditional glued-in or set neck joint with a small traditional heel as opposed to the angular 'heel' of the Telecaster. Where Fender chose the longer 25.5″ scale length, Gibson retained their nominal 24.75″ (actually slightly shorter at approximately 24.6″). Each of these differences created a guitar that sounds, feels and plays quite differently. Although refinements such as the humbucking pickups, Tune-O-Matic bridge and stop tailpiece

were yet to be added to the Les Paul, in these two years the two 'opposites' of the electric guitar were created; distinct but definitive examples which many others would imitate. But whereas the Les Paul would ultimately prove to be Gibson's definitive solidbody electric, Leo Fender's trump card, the Stratocaster, appeared in 1954. A development of the Telecaster, the Strat retained the same basic construction but the body was significantly altered to the now iconic double cutaway or '"twin horn" shape. The sleek new body featured a deep ribcage contour plus a forearm contour on the front that created, as Fender called it, "comfort contouring." Other aspects of the Telecaster were similarly completely re-thought; the advanced tremolo and three single-coil pickups gave the Strat a more versatile tone and playing potential. There were happy accidents too, as when some players discovered that the 3-way lever switch could be jammed in two extra 'in-between' positions – giving neck and middle pickup or bridge and middle pickup – which created a totally unique sound, lighter and less direct than the individual pickups. The component-style construction was taken a stage further too; the Strat's pickups and electrics, with

Fender's Telecaster, introduced in its Broadcaster guise in 1950, arguably bore more relation to earlier Fender electric lap steels than to existing conventional hollow body electrics made by Gibson and others. It fully illustrated Leo Fender's genius for generating a market where no proven player demand existed.

Gibson Les Paul

Introduced: 1952

Gibson's Les Paul, the second solid body electric ever produced, presented an inspired alternative to the Telecaster, but early versions were handicapped by the unwieldy 'wrap under' bridge and tailpiece design. This drawback was corrected with a new bridge/tailpiece in 1953.

the exception of the unique dished jack socket, could all be loaded onto the pickguard; consequently body, neck and now the electrics could all be assembled separately. Though Leo couldn't have foreseen the impact of this construction method, it means today that components can be made and stockpiled not just in different corners of the factory but on different continents. This cost-effective production – compared to the fixed neck and carved top of the Les Paul – means that the bolt-on electric is still today the cheapest way of building an electric guitar; the main percentage of lower priced, 'entry-level' guitars are bolt-ons.

Leo Fender's second electric guitar would come to represent the summit of his achievements. As Don Randall, head of Fender's sales operation recalls, "The Stratocaster started out from a marketing standpoint, to move into a more expensive product than the Telecaster. There was no way we could have foreseen how influential Leo's guitar would become."

Cool Jazz and Hot Blues

As the electric guitar evolved, so players learned how to harness the potential of this radical instrument. By 1953, Charlie Christian's influence meant that many jazz players were using Gibson's mellow-voiced hollow body instruments, but their blues-playing counterparts were much quicker to pick up on the potential of the solidbody. The advent of the solid electric coincided with the arrival of a whole new generation of electric blues artists – Muddy Waters, Clarence 'Gatemouth' Brown, Guitar Slim, B.B. King and many others – who used the Telecaster or Les Paul to create totally new sounds which would become a vital part of the tonal palette of 1960s rock music. Their groundbreaking tones would be achieved despite the intentions of the first generation of amplifier designers, who were primarily concerned with using simple, well-known circuits to make amplifiers which would be obedient rather than

The Early Years

1932: *Adolph Rickenbacker, Paul Barth and George Beauchamp produce the first electric guitar: a lap steel nicknamed the Frying Pan. It is soon followed by a conventional hollow body guitar version.*

1935: *Gibson develops its electric lap steel, the EH-150. A year later Gibson launches the conventional, 'Spanish' ES-150. The first two recordings using the new electric guitar are Andy Kirk's* 'Floyd's Blues,' *with Floyd Smith on electric Hawaiian guitar, and Jimmie Lunceford's* 'Hittin' The Bottle,' *with Eddie Durham on amplified archtop.*

1936: *Epiphone enters the electric guitar market. Other electric manufacturers now include National, Kay and Vega.*

1939: *Charlie Christian joins Bennie Goodman, and plays electric guitar on songs such as* 'Rose Room.' *He becomes the electric's first champion, influencing blues and jazz players.*

1941: *Les Paul builds "the Log," at the Epiphone factory.*

1945: *With partner Doc Kauffman, Leo Fender produces electric lap steels out of his shop at Spadra Road, Fullerton.*

1948: *Merle Travis designs a radical solid electric guitar with California inventor Paul Bigsby.*

■ *Early electric guitars found their most fervent champions in the blues field. Clarence 'Gatemouth' Brown used various Gibson hollow body guitars including the Gibson L-5 shown here, but defected to the more practical solidbody Telecaster within months of its launch.*

characterful. For jazz players such as Barney Kessel or Tal Farlow, the amplifier's role was to project the guitar's natural sound to a wider (and perhaps noisier) audience, without adding or subtracting anything. In this pre-distortion, pre-channel-switching era, all the sustain, harmonic richness and tonal variation had to come from the player and the instrument alone. This allowed the player's technique to shine through, but it severely limited the range of sounds.

In the late 1940s and early 1950s, all amplifiers relied on vacuum tubes (or valves), consisting of metallic electrodes within a sealed glass or metal tube. The tube manufacturers allowed free use of basic circuits published in their 'applications manuals', and many early amp brands – including National, Gibson, Supro, Premier and Fender – started out using these circuits. Hence, many amplifiers used essentially similar circuits, and models promoted as being for one specific instrument – say, lap steel, accordion or electric-Spanish guitar – would usually contain near-identical electronics. Output power was typically 5 – 20 watts. However, as the new generation of bluesmen started exploring the limits of amplified sound, they discovered that the P90 pickups of the Les Paul feeding the tube amps of the day caused a crunchy, distorted overdrive which intensified the richness and sustain, giving the guitar a more demanding and urgent voice – but one which also blended perfectly with harmonica and nicotine'n'whiskey-tinged vocals. The input signal would overload the preamp circuitry; high volume settings would then add power amp distortion, aided by a struggling loudspeaker that contributed its own compression and tonal 'fingerprint'. High-energy bluesman Buddy Guy's stinging and raunchy sound typified this approach. Guy plugged his Stratocaster into an early Fender 4x10 Bassman combo, lodging the pickup switch in 'in-between' position, winding up the volume and hitting the strings hard. This approach is now regarded as classic, but in the 1950s it was not a mainstream sound; in fact, most white audiences and record-buyers remained ignorant of the sound of a heavily distorted guitar until the Cream/Hendrix heavy rock phenomenon of the mid 1960s. And amplifier manufacturers resolutely ignored the possibilities of controllable distortion until that era. Five per cent distortion? Get that thing repaired!

■ **Gibson ES-350**
Introduced: 1948

The Gibson ES-350 represented the state of the art in the electric guitar before Fender's arrival. Its ply top reduced feedback, the two pickup layout offered versatile tonal options, while 1955's thinline version was especially practical. Together with the lower-priced ES-175, the ES-350 was a leader in the jazz guitar market; it would later become a favorite of Chuck Berry.

11

1950: *Leo Fender designs the first production solidbody electric guitar: the Fender Broadcaster.*

1951: *The Gibson guitar company uprates its design efforts for hollow body electric guitar under the supervision of new president Ted McCarty. Key models in the electric range include the pressed top ES-175 and ES-350, plus the arch top Super 400CES and L-5CES.*

Solids and Semis: the second generation

While the Tele and Strat featured pretty much their current configuration on their launch, the original 1952 Les Paul had some growing up to do. The first gold-top Les Paul used two existing Gibson P90 single-coil pickups. The upmarket Les Paul Custom of 1954 featured a new pickup, designed by Gibson engineer Seth Lover to be louder than the P90, and nicknamed the 'Alnico' after the oblong alnico (an alloy of aluminum, nickel and cobalt) magnets. Another important advance featured on the Custom was the new Tune-O-Matic bridge

■ B.B. King has become synonymous with the ES-335 and ES-355; King cites the combination of light weight and excellent top fret access as the main reasons for his championing of the design. King started out using a variety of Gibson archtops and a Fender Esquire before switching to the ES-335 in 1958, and the up-market ES-355 the following year, although in this circa-1963 photo he is using the hollow-body ES-330. Other bluesmen including Freddie King used the ES-335 in King's wake.

designed by Ted McCarty, offering individual string length adjustment for superior intonation; this bridge appeared on the 'gold-top' model the following year. Around 1956 Seth Lover designed the Gibson humbucking pick-up design, which was fitted to both models of Les Paul in 1957, and many other Gibson models the following year. With its nickel silver cover and single row of adjustable polepieces, the humbucker utilized two coils arranged to minimize hum pickup from external sources. This humcanceling concept had originally been patented in 1936, and was also featured on Rickenbacker's Combo guitars of 1954, on Gretsch's Filtertron pickups designed by Ray Butts, and on the revised Fender Precision bass guitar of 1957. However, the Gibson humbucker became regarded as the milestone design. Its powerful but smooth tone was more rounded than the P90 and much fatter sounding than Fender's single-coils. Early examples, later termed PAF, for their 'Patent Applied For' stickers, are highly sought-after – original examples now change hands for hundreds of dollars and over 90 per cent of humbucking pickups made today are based on the PAF.

Fender may have kick-started the solidbody revolution, which was soon joined by other companies, including Gretsch with its clearly Les Paul-inspired Duo-Jet design of 1953, but Gibson went further than most in exploiting the concept. The flat-fronted, single pickup Les Paul Junior, which appeared in 1954, cost just $99.50, a bargain compared with the $225 Les Paul, the $189 Telecaster and the $249 Strat. The Jr. was joined by the beige-colored Les Paul TV – that this author at least believes has nothing to do with television but was Gibson's stab at a Telecaster clone, at least in terms of color and cosmetics – and twin pickup Special in 1955.

By 1958 the Les Paul's sales were dropping and the decision was made to change the gold-top finish to a more conservative sunburst. This revealed the often spectacular figure of the maple tops and created, arguably, the most desirable electric guitar of all time. Produced between 1958 and 1960, the 'Sunburst' helped inspire a modest improvement in sales, but not enough to prevent the model's demise at the end of 1960, at which point it was replaced by the double cutaway design later named the SG.

■ Gibson ES-335
Introduced: 1958

A pioneering example of semi-solid construction, the ES-335 fused Gibson's hollow-body heritage with the newly established solidbody

format in a supremely ergonomic package. When the now more celebrated Les Paul was discontinued in 1960, the ES-335 remained a mainstay of Gibson's electric guitar line.

ES-335 retained the larger body outline although in a revolutionary new symmetrical double-cutaway shape. The thinline guitar was built from pressed maple laminate – like most of the post-war Gibson archtops – but featured a solid center block which minimized the top's movement, thereby substantially eliminating feedback and giving the Tune-O-Matic bridge, tailpiece and pickups a solid mounting. It also meant that the neck could join the body at the 19th fret so top fret access, even compared to the then single-cutaway Les Pauls, not to mention existing archtops, was superb. The ES-335 remains a masterpiece of design, combining disparate existing styles to create a uniquely new instrument. Gibson's final 1950s fling was the development of the so-called 'modernistic' designs: the Flying V and Explorer. Seen at the time as a joke in extremely poor taste, they proved that the electric solidbody did not have to echo the shape of its hollow body cousins. Launched by Ted McCarty to prove that the company was "not a bunch of fuddy duddies," the guitars perhaps proved their point, but were a commercial failure. Meanwhile, the company's customers were quick to spot the potential of Gibson's truly revolutionary ES-335, which immediately became a staple of jazz and blues guitarists, as well as later rock players such as Eric Clapton.

Though the impact of the solidbody was significant, players' tastes did not change overnight. For many the new, small solid-bodies just didn't look, or feel right even if the lack of feedback and sustaining sound made more practical sense. It was with these thoughts in mind – to achieve the tone and playability of a solidbody but with the appearance and feel of a 'real' guitar – that Ted McCarty came up with the thinline semi-solid Gibson ES-335 – one of the most versatile instruments of the era, and arguably Gibson's finest, most original design. Gibson had experimented with its first hollow 'thinline' electric acoustics in 1955; the

■ Gibson Les Paul Jr.
Introduced: 1954

Gibson president Ted McCarty expanded the Les Paul line with upmarket and budget versions from 1954. The Les Paul Jr. retailed at

$99 and became one of Gibson's best-selling instruments of the time. It was joined in 1955 by the Les Paul TV, which with its pale 'limed' mahogany finish echoed the cosmetics of Fender's Telecaster.

■ Gibson Les Paul 'Sunburst'
Introduced: 1958

With the addition of Ted McCarty's Tune-O-Matic bridge and stud tailpiece, Seth Lover's humbucking

pickups, and a cherry sunburst finish, the Les Paul reached an evolutionary peak – which failed to prevent its replacement by the twin-cutaway SG-style solid in 1960.

■ **Gibson Flying V**
Introduced: 1958

The Flying V was a commercially ill-fated attempt to rival Fender's reputation as innovators. But as the first example of how the solidbody guitar could assume just about any shape that took the designer's fancy, it would later boast many imitators.

The Race For Power

Although the Fender company is primarily thought of as a guitar manufacturer, its amplifier designs were crucial to the musical development of country, rock'n'roll and blues, as the firm's designs began to gain a distinctive voice which helped to shape the sound of the guitar. Throughout the 1950s, an era synonymous with the company's distinctive Tweed (i.e. linen-covered) combos, and into the early/mid-1960s Tolex (cloth-backed vinyl) era, Fender's informal tie-up with various West Coast country-style guitar pickers paid dividends. Well known players such as Jimmy Bryant and Speedy West, Bill Carson (later an employee), Dick Dale and Eldon Shamblin, as well as purely local players, contributed to this soundshaping process, either feeding back information on the latest prototype or by visiting the Fullerton factory. Over these years, there were modifications to almost every aspect of the designs, including the tone circuitry, tube types, speaker configuration, style of tremolo and output stage bias arrangement. Compared to early designs, the late-1950s Fenders became models for how guitar amplifiers should sound: louder, punchier, and more attacking, with a fully-developed presence, a well defined bass end, and more control over the final tonality. Ironically, at volume these amplifiers were also more likely to attain that tube generated distortion to make a guitar crunch nicely, while the rectifier tube(s) in the power supply added a forgiving quality by 'sagging' when the amplifier was pushed hard. It's ironic because Leo Fender certainly aimed to avoid distortion in his amps, which – like early Marshalls – were advertised as being distortion-free. In fact by the mid 1950s crunchy and distorted amp sounds were becoming more and more prevalent; Telecaster user James Burton was getting a tasty edge on his early recordings with Dale Hawkins; Guitar Slim, and Howlin' Wolf sideman Willie Johnson, were overdriving their amplifiers in similar fashion. By 1958, Gibson's humbucking pickup had arrived and was capable of overdriving virtually any amp. But on the inward looking California music scene, clean was beautiful, half volume was plenty, and single-coils were quite powerful enough, thank you. Clarity and good tone were the order of the day, complemented by tremolo (rhythmic volume fluctuation) and later by spacey-sounding spring reverb – a key element in surf music. Although these are admirable qualities – and the Fender amps of this period are now worth a fortune – they're not the whole story; it's fascinating to consider what sort of amps Fender might have built if he'd visited Chicago more often, befriended a few 'race' acts, and realized the appeal that

Solidbodies: the Golden Years

1952: Gibson produces the Les Paul model, with trapeze bridge and two single-coil P90 pickups. It is the only solidbody competitor to Fender's newly renamed Telecaster.

1953: Francis 'F.C.' Hall takes control of the Rickenbacker company and recruits Roger Rossmeisl to design a line of solidbody models. Gibson fits a stop-bar bridge tailpiece to the Les Paul model.

1954: Fender launches its top-line model, the Stratocaster. Rickenbacker introduces the Combo 600 and Combo 800. Gretsch enters the solidbody market with the Chet Atkins 6121, which costs nearly $100 more than its Gibson or Fender equivalents. The 6121 is in fact semi-solid, with extensive body routing, while the Les Paul-style contoured top is pressed maple ply,

■ *The Fender Bassman amplifier was designed for the comparatively rigorous task of amplifying the company's pioneering bass guitar. By the late 1950s it was in demand for six-string use by the likes of Buddy Guy.*

Life After Les Paul

As the 1950s drew to a close Gibson was apparently at a loss to find a strong direction for its solidbodies. It seemed convinced, however, by the virtues of the double-cutaway body outline – probably inspired by the Stratocaster – as shown by the change in shape of its successful but short-lived Les Paul Juniors and Specials. By late 1960 the single-cutaway Gibson Les Paul was replaced by the all-mahogany, thinner-bodied, double-cutaway and pointed horned SG/Les Paul, known today simply as the SG. Although this move has been judged a mistake in retrospect, the

■ *Smaller vintage Fender combos, such as the Champion and Princeton shown in the advertisement on the right, are now treasured for the ease with which they distort. Somewhat ironically, this was one characteristic which Leo Fender was attempting to minimize at the time.*

SG has been in production ever since and can hardly be called a failure. Keeping similar hardware and electronics to the previous models, the SG's double-cutaway design and 22-fret neck-to-body join meant the guitar was more manageable, with excellent access to the upper frets, while the light weight meant that guitar was regarded as infinitely more comfortable for players than its weightier predecessor.

Fender, too, did not remain idle: the Jazzmaster appeared in 1958 as its top-line solid with a new single-coil pickup design. The guitar was designed, as the name implies, to give a fuller and richer sound – more Gibson-like, in fact – with advanced electrics and a new tremolo. Though overshadowed in retrospect by the Strat, the Jazzmaster stayed in production until 1980; the similarly-styled Jaguar (in production from 1961-1975) with its shorter scale length and brighter voiced pickups, with at least partial metal screening to reduce hum pickup, again enjoyed initial success as the most expensive Fender solid – but longterm it proved a disappointment. Gibson's 1963 Firebird was a fairly disastrous attempt at a radical design. The 'space-age' reverse body design owes plenty to the Jazzmaster's off-set shape and signals Gibson's first use of a through-neck. By 1965, although the name was the same, the shape was entirely different, as the Firebirds changed to a conventional, and far less stylish non-reverse style with standard glued-in neck. Along with the SG, this ugly ducking remained Gibson's main electric solidbody throughout the early 1960s.

the Bassman combo, later to form the basis for Marshall's early designs, had in the blues clubs. It's also significant that once modern silicon rectifiers (solid-state diodes) became available, from around 1960, Fender started to dispense with tube rectifiers in his medium and high power amps. This gave a stiffer power delivery that satisfied the engineers, but left guitarists with ringing ears if they turned up the wick for a crunchy edge. Tellingly, Fender's Bassman reissue has interchangeable tube/solid-state rectifiers. And bargain hunters should note that small Fenders – particularly the Champ and Princeton Reverb – missed out on these 'improvements' altogether.

15

rather than the solid maple of the Gibson. Gibson launches an upmarket solidbody, the black Les Paul Custom or 'Fretless Wonder,' and a budget model, the Les Paul Jr.

1955: *The more practical Tune-O-Matic bridge and stop tailpiece combination fitted to the Les Paul Custom on its launch appears on the standard model. Gibson introduces the two pickup slab-body Les Paul Special, and the Les Paul TV, which echoes the cosmetics of the*

Telecaster. By now several companies including National and Kay produce popular solidbody electrics.

1956: *Seth Lover invents the Gibson 'humbucking pickup'; it is fitted to the Les Paul the following year. Fender introduces two 'student' models, the Duo-Sonic and Musicmaster.*

1957: *Fender launches the Jazzmaster; with its warmer sound and rosewood fingerboard, it is aimed at Gibson fans*

1958: *Gibson launches the ES-335, the Flying V and the Explorer, changes the standard finish on the Les Paul Model to sunburst to create a guitar generally termed the Les Paul Sunburst, and redesigns the Les Paul Special and Jr./TV in a double cutaway configuration.*

1960: *Gibson's Les Paul line is completely revamped, with all guitars changing to a similar all-mahogany double cutaway design. The guitar is renamed the SG in 1961.*

The Brits are Coming

By 1960, the electric guitar's reputation as the premier instrument of popular music was by no means fully established; much of the first wave of American rock'n'roll had been superseded by vocal groups and insipid teenage balladeers; only the influence of mainly instrumental bands such as The Ventures in the U.S., and The Shadows in the U.K., kept the new instrument in the limelight. It would be the British response to the groundbreaking generation of blues and rock'n'roll acts which established the electric guitar as an intrinsic part of rock music, as bands such as The Beatles, The Rolling Stones, The Who and The Animals suddenly brought rock'n'roll songwriters like Chuck Berry into fashion – and also brought a similar revival in the fortunes of previously obscure American guitar manufacturers such as Gretsch and Rickenbacker.

Rickenbacker's Bakelite Hawaiian and Spanish electrics from 1935 are seen by many as the first solidbody electrics (even though the Bakelite construction was semi-solid to reduce weight). However, it wasn't until 1954 that Rickenbacker produced anything that could be called a conventional electric Spanish guitar, with the Combo 600 and 800. With the company's antiquated horseshoe pickup design, and unconventional styling, these guitars must have appeared relatively old-fashioned on their launch. However, these early instruments boasted some groundbreaking features, such as the through-neck construction of 1956's Combo 400. Despite this feature, and the new 'tulip' shape, compared to Fender and Gibson the guitar looked comparatively bizarre. By 1957 the Combo series had changed to the now familiar 'sweeping crescent' body shape. Just three years later an unknown guitarist obtained a Rickenbacker guitar of this shape in Hamburg,

probably influenced by Jean 'Toots' Thielemans, a Belgian jazz musician best known for his harmonica playing. The guitarist was John Lennon; and Rickenbacker had its meal-ticket.

Lennon's guitar, a model 325 from the Capri series which was launched in 1958, was semi-solid. Rickenbacker preferred 'hollow body': the body was routed out from the back leaving a solid center body section, and then sealed by an additional back piece. This construction was used to reduce the guitar's weight – a idea copied by Fender later with their Telecaster Thinline. Though the 325 was a three pickup, short scale guitar, the Capri line included the full-scale twin pickup 330 and the more deluxe-spec'd 360, the 'soon-to-be-classic' 1960s Rickenbackers. In 1963 Rickenbacker developed what was if not the first electric 12-string then certainly the most high-profile. When an early example was presented to George Harrison it was referred to as the "beat boys' secret weapon" and was, of course, featured on *A Hard Day's Night*, there and then becoming synonymous with The Beatles' janglesome sound; the Rickenbacker 12-string subsequently became a staple of every band since that time, from The Byrds to REM, who needed that classic, ringing jangle tone.

Although Gretsch also received a huge unpaid endorsement from George Harrison's initial use of the Les Paul-inspired Duo Jet, and subsequent use of a Chet Atkins Country Gentlemen, like Rickenbacker its highly idiosyncratic designs were achieved at the expense of versatility. Always synonymous with rockabilly and country styles, thanks to the likes of Chet Atkins, Duane Eddy, Eddie Cochran, and latter day rockabilly Brian Setzer, Gretsch guitars featured many neat design features, thanks to the imaginative design skills of players like Jimmie Webster and Chet Atkins – not to mention the electronic skills of Ray Butts: the 1951 introduction of the Melita Synchro-Sonic bridge with

16

■ **Rickenbacker 360-12**
Introduced:1963
Rickenbacker provided the definitive electric 12-string thanks to high-profile use by George Harrison, whose guitar is pictured here, and Roger McGuinn. Although the fretboard is cramped, this guitar is lighter and better balanced than many of its imitators.

■ The Beatles were responsible for popularizing a huge range of equipment following the success of their 1964 US tour. Rickenbacker and Gretsch guitars, and Vox amplifiers, benefited from the consequent exposure. Unsurprisingly, Vox and Rickenbacker based much of their advertising around the mop-top connection.

individual string intonation occurred before Gibson's Tune-O-Matic, while Ray Butts' Filtertron humbucker appeared at the same time as the Gibson PAF but had been in existence some time before. However, the company's ultimate success relied only marginally on these design innovations, for it would be the George Harrison connection which single-handedly revolutionized the company's profile. As Duke Kramer, head of Gretsch's Chicago operation points out: "You've got to remember that these were hand-made guitars – the way they were fitting necks, for instance, didn't lend itself to mass production. By the mid-Sixties it took a year to get a Gretsch guitar. They'd gone up from making maybe 50 guitars a week to 75 or so a day."

■ **Gretsch Duo-Jet**
Introduced: 1954
This black Gretsch Duo-Jet, owned by George Harrison, bears significant responsibility for the Beatles-inspired popularity enjoyed by Gretsch in the 1960s.

■ **Vox AC30**
Introduced: 1959
The first significant British amplifier design, the AC30 was used by every significant British beatboom group.

Vox And Marshall

At the same time as a new generation of British musicians was learning to play rock'n'roll, their compatriots were laying foundations for the 'British amp sound'. In 1956, a young British guitarist and electronics buff, Dick Denney, put the finishing touches to a home-made guitar amp in which he had tried to get away from the usual applications-manual circuits and hi-fi-type refinements. Denney had identified technical solutions which sounded right for electric guitar, and his opinion was clearly shared by others: within a year he was the Chief Design Engineer of Jennings Musical Industries, and by 1958 his 15 watt Vox AC15 combo – equipped with 12″ Alnico-magnet Celestion speaker – was wooing professional players. Soon the Shadows were touring with AC15s, and by late 1959 they were using Denney's newly-developed Vox AC30 30 watt 2x12 combo, effectively a double-AC15, intended to keep the responsive, toneful and sustaining sound of the original amp. Lead guitarist Hank Marvin teamed his Vox with an Italian-made, multi-head tape-echo unit, to obtain the distinctive rolling repeats featured on the Shadows' instrumental hits. (The widely available Watkins Copicat tape-echo was a popular alternative, and in the U.S.A. the Echoplex unit was influential.)

The slightly later Top-boost AC30 introduced a gutsy brilliant channel for lead work, and this combo was extensively used by the Stones, the Yardbirds and other influential blues-based groups. Another famous Vox connection: Jimi Hendrix is said to have written and rehearsed much of *Are You Experienced?* on a small Vox combo while staying at Chas Chandler's London apartment in late 1966. Most importantly, The Beatles recorded their first album using Vox amplifiers in early 1963 and went on to become the most visible endorsees any amp company could wish for. Vox provided amps and technical assistance; they also developed new models with the Beatles in mind, and used the Beatles' tours to road-test the gear. (Dick Denney reports an amusing incident at a pre-US-tour warm-up gig in Scarborough, where newly-fitted castors threatened to send the latest outsize speaker-cab rolling down the sloping stage towards three of the Fab Four; only the timely intervention of the designer prevented a national disaster... .) In the search for more volume and projection to compete with larger and ever-noisier audiences, 30 watts became 50, then 100, while 2x12 open-backed combos became 2x12 closed-back cabs and, later, 4x12s with horns.

More fundamental still to the sound of rock'n'roll was the development of the Marshall brand. In 1962, drum tutor and London shop owner Jim Marshall asked his service engineer, Ken Bran, to investigate the possibility of building a pro-standard amplifier based loosely on the Fender sound but with a thicker, more sustaining response. This all-British version of the Fender Bassman using British components – the JTM45 head – won fans quickly, and was soon being used by the Who's Pete Townshend and other professionals. Within a few years, Marshall had developed a strong identity, with 50 watt and later 100 watt

Jimi Hendrix arrived on the British rock scene in September 1966. Hendrix was inspired by Eric Clapton to use a Marshall stack, which he combined with a Sound City system for cleaner sounds. Pairing this set-up with a stock right-hand Stratocaster, Hendrix created sounds which Leo Fender had never envisaged, and single-handedly ensured the Stratocaster's long-term popularity.

Playing Dirty

1950: *Howlin' Wolf's Chess Hit, 'Moaning At Midnight,' features guitarist Willie Johnson using a searing over-amplified guitar sound.*

1951: *'Rocket 88' by Jackie Brenston, arranged by Ike Turner and produced by Sun's Sam Phillips, features a distorted guitar sound caused by a damaged amplifier. This Chess release will be cited by many as the first rock'n'roll record.*

1953: *Guitar Slim is the first guitarist to use a purposely distorted guitar sound, on his trendsetting Specialty single, 'The Things I Used To Do.'*

1958: *Link Wray popularizes the sound of the distorted guitar in the pop market with his powerful instrumental 'Rumble.' It will prove to have a profound influence on UK guitarist Pete Townshend.*

1965: *Eric Clapton has bought a Les*

heads sitting atop 4x12 cabs, either in half-stack (with one cab) or full-stack format (amplifier head with one slope-front and one straight-front cab). Now players could be heard in large venues or at outdoor festivals, in the days before big PA systems, and they also gained a stage backdrop and (crucially) fat tube distortion via powerful pickups.

From Beat To Rock

British rock music developed quickly from its celebrated arrival in the early 1960s. Much of the impetus came from The Beatles' constant redefinition of the limits of songwriting and recording; similar advances were brought about by the incestuous, competitive musical environment which saw a new generation of guitar players vying to outdo each other. The Yardbirds, a tightly-knit group of R&B fans from the Surrey art school scene, provided three of Britain's best-known guitar heroes in the form of Eric Clapton, Jeff Beck and Jimmy Page. Once Clapton, dissatisfied with The Yardbirds' pop leanings, defected to John Mayall's Bluesbreakers, he helped redefine the role of the lead guitarist. He also revolutionized the *sound* of rock guitar; partnering the obsolete Gibson Les Paul Sunburst with Marshall's 45 watt 1962 model combo amp, he revealed how the Gibson's powerful humbucking pickups could shift the Marshall into overdrive to give a creamy, sustaining sound. This potent combination alone meant that Clapton was able to expand on the legacy established by his blues influences such as Freddie King. In Cream, Clapton championed the use of multiple Marshall stacks, and others following his example included Deep Purple, Led Zeppelin and Free. In turn Jimi Hendrix, who had learned from the blues tradition at first hand on the US 'chitlin' circuit, built on the Marshall sound Clapton had established to create what was effectively a definitive vocabulary for rock guitar. Using virtually every facility of his factory stock Stratocasters to the full – wrenching at the vibrato, lodging the pickup switch in 'in-between' setting for chiming rhythm sounds, or cranking the output up for full-blooded distortion, Hendrix created sounds which even that celebrated visionary Leo Fender could not have envisaged. Hendrix's use of the Marshall stack, from late 1966 to 1970, helped establish Marshall as the definitive rock amp – even though the guitarist flippantly described his set-up as looking "like two refrigerators linked together." Because he favored a stock single-coil Stratocaster, though, Hendrix teamed his tube-powered stacks with an Arbiter Fuzz Face (for long, sustaining

Charlie Watkins' WEM Copicat would become the definitive U.K. delay-based effects unit from its launch in 1964. Its US equivalent was the Echoplex, while cheaper imported copies made in Italy were used by Hank Marvin and others.

This Marshall prototype for the JTM45 was based on the design of the Fender Bassman, but differences in the transformer and other components ensured a distinctive sonic blueprint which was emphasized in later Marshall heads.

distortion) and a Vox Wah-Wah pedal. The latter allowed him to sweep the tonal range with his foot – giving a voice-like quality – or select tonal extremes. So the Marshall was the solid foundation, but a lot of Hendrix's manipulation of texture/tone was done via hands and feet while playing. Over the latter half of the 1960s, Marshall was not the only British company making high quality stacks: the company's rivals included Hiwatt, designed by Dave Reeves, with the electronics manufactured by Harry Joyce; and Orange/Matamp, run by Cliff Cooper and Matt Mathias. Hiwatt and Orange gear has recently been reissued, while Joyce now makes amps under his own name.

Paul sunburst after seeing photographs of Freddie King with a Les Paul Model. He combines the Les Paul with a Marshall 1962 model combo during Jimmy Page-produced sessions for Andrew Loog Oldham's Immediate label. Pete Townshend combines his Rickenbacker 360 electric with a Marshall stack and the Link Wray-influenced powerchord for 'My Generation.'

1966: *Eric Clapton establishes the*

Marshall as the definitive rock amplifier via his guitar work on the UK Number One album Blues Breakers, with John Mayall. Jimi Hendrix buys a Marshall stack soon after his arrival in the UK in the fall.

1967: *Hendrix, Clapton and Townshend's use of the Marshall stack influences many US bands, including Blue Cheer and Detroit's MC5, to follow suit. The stack configuration will become standard for the rock guitarist.*

The End Of The Golden Era

By the mid-1960s there was a huge peak in demand for guitars made by Fender, Gibson, and many other companies. But in retrospect the golden age of the electric guitar was drawing to a close. Partly as a result of the need for new investment to help increase production, the Fender company was sold to corporate conglomerate CBS at the beginning of 1965. Gibson president Ted McCarty resigned as President of Gibson later the same year

after buying another company, Bigsby Accessories. McCarty's move coincided with a gradual fall in Gibson's sales, and by 1969 the parent company CMI was merged into what was to become, by 1974, Norlin. The changes undergone by Fender and Gibson were to have a dramatically damaging effect on the guitars produced, in terms of quality and design; it would take both companies nearly two decades before any substantial change occurred in their corporate fortunes. The changes were not felt only in the field of guitars; at the same time that Gibson and

Fender were introducing their gawkiest and ugliest guitars to date, Fender's amplifier range was taking a similar nose dive in an attempt to embrace the new solid state age. Fender was not alone. By the late 1960s, British amplifier company Vox had introduced transistorized amps, failing to realize how much the sound of its amplifiers relied on the vacuum tubes. Apart from any sonic considerations, reliability and manufacture of the earliest units was questionable; Steve Howe reflects the experience of many guitarists when he reports that "the worst decision of my amplification life was when I traded my Vox AC50 for a transistorized AC100 – it let me down night after night, blowing up, crackling and always going wrong." Ironically, at the very time that guitarists were discovering the virtues of 1950s guitars, and amplifiers based around 1940s technology, those same products were seemingly disappearing.

■ By 1971 the Fender Stratocaster had gained the notorious features of large headstock, three-bolt neck and bullet truss rod, all of which were damned by association with the generally indifferent production standards at Fender in the 1970s. Ironically, although these 1970s Strats helped create a demand for vintage instruments, prices of 1970s originals are on the increase.

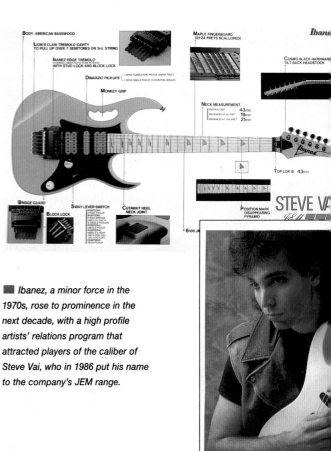

■ Ibanez, a minor force in the 1970s, rose to prominence in the next decade, with a high profile artists' relations program that attracted players of the caliber of Steve Vai, who in 1986 put his name to the company's JEM range.

Yamaha SG2000
Introduced: 1976

Yamaha's flagship electric was not devastatingly original, but boasted neat design touches and high quality workmanship which highlighted the indifferent quality of many contemporary Gibson electrics.

The Mesa Boogie amplifier kicked off the 1970s trend for high gain, high power combos. Boogie's compact amplifiers such as the late model Mk.II shown here pioneered three gain stages, channel-switching, on-board graphic eq and switchable power output.

The Rising Sun

Any big business can boast its share of copyists and derivative designs – and by the mid 1960s the electric guitar was certainly big business. By the end of this tumultuous decade, the American electric guitar was highly desirable but not particularly affordable, especially by the time it was exported to, for example, the UK and Europe. The difficulty experienced by Fender, Gibson and many others in satisfying demand for their product soon led to a growth in manufacturers replicating, to a greater or lesser extent, the American originals. In England companies such as Burns, Watkins and Vox produced derivatives of American design, in some cases providing a modicum of originality;

European makers such as Hofner, Framus and Hagstrom jumped on the bandwagon too.

But further east, in Japan, companies were springing up that would, by the late 1960s, begin to challenge the American big names. Cheaper labor and mass production techniques, plus an accurate eye for replicating designs, assisted the emergence of brands like Ibanez, Aria, Fernandes and Tokai, all of whom established their reputations and sales with copy guitars. The ascent of these companies, producing low-priced instruments of ever increasing quality, combined with Fender and Gibson's production problems, meant that by 1975 Japanese guitars started to become a convincingly credible option. Yamaha's SG2000, produced in 1976, was a potent illustration of Japan's emergence as a guitar making force. Although echoing Gibson styles, a sort of SG-meets-Les Paul, the SG2000 wasn't a direct copy, using for example a through-neck, and combining the carved maple top and twin humbucker layout of the Les Paul with a double cutaway design and excellent top fret access. With high-profile endorsements from players like Carlos Santana, the Yamaha SG became an important guitar. In some ways too it indicated a future design direction: the amalgamation of existing styles with a modicum of innovation to create a 'new' evolutionary instrument. Arguably, Paul Reed Smith worked along similar lines when he launched his production company in 1985. Rather than develop completely new designs to rival the classics from Fender or Gibson, Yamaha and Paul Reed Smith realized that the future lay in revising, rather than re-thinking, the designs of the best original instruments.

Customize with care

1. Brass Tremolo Bridge Unit FG-1301
2. Tremolo Arm – black finish FH-7400
3. Brass Tremolo arm knob FG-1200
4. DiMarzio 5-way Switch EP-1104
5. Brass knobs FG-1600
6. Inside panel shielded with copper shielding tape
7. 2 x DiMarzio strap buttons brass FG-1290
8. DiMarzio Strat-Trem body CBB-1002
9. Brass Screws FH-1000 (set of 24)
10. Brass Nut FG-1800
11. "Fender" Neckplate (Brass) FB-1000
12. Screws for above FH-1100
13. DiMarzio SDS-1 Pickup DP-113
14. DiMarzio FS-1 Pickup DP-110

■ By 1978, DiMarzio's extensive pickup range had been joined by retro-fit bridges and other hardware. Despite DiMarzio's advice to customize with care, many 1970s players unwittingly ruined their vintage instruments by replacing original hardware.

How to replace your pickups

The Vintage Phenomenon

Twenty years after Fender and Gibson produced their groundbreaking designs, a new generation of manufacturers and players were starting to analyze what made these early instruments so effective. Consequently the vintage collector's guitar market gradually became a reality. It was now inescapably obvious that current Fenders and Gibsons did not match up to their predecessors: a 1970s Strat, for example, now had a bigger, uglier headstock, the finish was thick polyester, there was the bullet truss rod adjustment and three-bolt neck, and horror stories of less than professional production. The story at Gibson was alarmingly similar; realizing the popularity of the Les Paul, the company chose to re-issue the comparatively unfashionable Les Paul Custom and 'gold-top', changing the latter into the Les Paul Deluxe in 1969. While successful in sales terms, the Deluxe's constructional changes and the use of small mini-humbuckers created a guitar that felt and sounded nothing like the classic 1958-60 Les Paul Sunbursts. Gibson had lost the plot too.

The loss of direction in the Gibson and Fender camps helped usher in a new generation of small U.S. guitar companies such as B.C. Rich, Dean and Hamer. Hamer were one of the earliest to exploit the shortcomings of contemporary Gibsons; their Sunburst guitar was essentially a high-class vintage-style hybrid, a double-cutaway Les Paul Special with a flat maple top and twin humbuckers. B.C. Rich were to take a more radical design path, but quality was uppermost in their original pieces. Historically these brands may have only marginally changed the design of the electric guitar, but they performed an equally valuable function, re-educating players into paying good money for beautiful and finely built guitars. It was in the mid-1970s that an unknown repairman, Paul Reed Smith, started building increasingly exotic one-offs, which were based, like Hamer's designs, on the Gibson double-cutaway Special. Smith's benchmarks were old guitars, especially Gibsons, and although he would not go into full scale production until the 1980s, by the mid 1990s PRS guitars had gained a reputation as some of the finest production instruments available. Appropriately, one of Paul's mentors is ex-Gibson President Ted McCarty, signaling Smith's intention of picking up the torch that Gibson had dropped so spectacularly in the 1970s.

Born To Boogie

In the amplification field, too, smaller companies set out to satisfy player's demands; demands to which the larger companies seemed increasingly oblivious. In the late-1960s, San Francisco store-owner Randy Smith arranged for a practical joke to be played on Barry Melton, guitarist with Country Joe & The Fish. Melton's Fender Princeton combo was coming into Smith's shop for some minor work. The joke consisted of ripping out the

Fuzz Facts

Since transistor technology made battery-powered effects units a reality in the early 1960s, fuzz-boxes (a.k.a. distortion-pedals) have been a fact of life. Portable and affordable, these units simply plug between guitar and amp, and can provide distortion textures from a crude, rasping buzz to long, smooth sustain.

Jimmy Page and Jeff Beck were two early enthusiasts; in the early-1960s, possession of a fuzz-box could be the difference between getting a gig, and not getting it... Influential products included the Vox Tone-Bender, with Roger Mayer's custom one-offs finding favor with players like Big Jim Sullivan and the aforementioned Page. In the US, the Maestro Fuzz-tone was an early example, with Hendrix later popularizing the Fuzz Face. Before that, distortion had been a hit-and-miss affair, with users of single-coil pickups at a natural disadvantage. Despite the inclusion of good distortion circuitry in electronic heart of this small amp, and building a hot-rodded Fender amp (effectively a 60 watt Bassman) onto the existing chassis, with the small speaker replaced by a large, high-power JBL. The idea was that the combo should look totally stock but sound loud, raunchy and sustaining, with a broad sound but good definition and fine tone. It worked; Carlos Santana, a talented local player hungry for sustain, soon had a crowd gathered outside the shop to hear his impromptu performance on the diminutive mutant. "Man, that little thing really boogies," he is reported to have said, establishing the Boogie brand name at a stroke. Around 200 mutants later, CBS Fender got wise and cut off the supply of replacement transformers, leading Smith to move seriously into manufacturing, with the establishment of MESA Engineering. Within a few years, MESA/Boogie's revolutionary 'cascading gain stages' – where one tube stage overdrives the next for smooth, saturated-preamp distortion, with the physical loudness set by a master-volume – was joined by foot controlled channel-switching, and a 5-band graphic EQ. Later Boogies would include a three-channel, footswitchable version, plus a revival of hot-running (but good sounding) Class A operation. Boogie's 'Simul-Class' circuitry has two sets of output tubes working together on a single chassis; one provides Class A tone, the other Class AB bulk power. More recently, the company's increasingly wide range of tube amps has incorporated models with switchable tube/solid-state rectification, plus some low-power, non-master-volume combos not unlike the original (unmodified!) Princeton, suggesting the wheel has now come full circle, while the combo-based approach has been modified with the advent of stacks, racks and pedals. Almost single-handedly through the 1970s and early-1980s, however, Boogie championed the cause of the small master-volume combo which could be miked-up through the increasingly sophisticated PA systems of the time. Other manufacturers followed suit, sometimes reluctantly; Marshall introduced master-volume models in 1975, and Fender were putting master-volume or switchable boost on most models by 1980, although it wasn't really until the Paul Rivera period (1981-85) that Fender took a systematic look at tube-distortion facilities.

Hot Rods And Add-ons

The re-evaluation of vintage instruments in the 1970s helped bring about a new, innovative sector of the industry, offering add-ons to existing guitars. Larry DiMarzio was the first to spot this opening, marketing the Super Distortion replacement pickup in 1975. This high output humbucker, based on a Gibson PAF, was designed to distort a tube amp for a natural crunchy tone rather than the fizzy artificial sound created by the fuzz-box. Other companies soon realized the potential of this 'hot-rodding' market; Mighty Mite, De Armond, and even Gibson saw the value of a hot humbucker. One name which would loom large in future years was Seymour Duncan who started rewinding pickups, then offered a small range of mainly vintage-like replacements by the later 1970s. Again, Duncan found a market by realizing many players were complaining that their new guitars didn't sound like the old ones. By 1978 DiMarzio pickups became a sales point for numerous guitar companies too: B.C. Rich, Dean and Guild all featured their pickups. The company soon moved into other replacement parts such as necks, bodies, bridges and tremolos, as did other small companies such as Boogie Bodies, Charvel, Mighty Mite and Schecter. Soon exotic wood bodies, brass bridges and nuts became fashionable. The key word was retro-fit – guitarists could build their own 'custom' instruments, or spruce up their existing axe by adding, for example, a PAF-style humbucker to a Strat. It was exactly this 'Frankenstein' approach that led a young guitar player, Eddie Van Halen, to make his own hot-rod Strat with its striped, hand-painted finish. Eddie's influence on guitar players from 1978 onwards was far-reaching, both in terms of playing, and guitar design and finishing – Eddie was almost single-handedly responsible for the early 1980s craze for graphic painted finishes.

■ Once derided as giving cheap, cheesy distortion, early fuzz pedals have now attracted the collecting fraternity. Both the Fuzz Face and Sola Sound (aka Coloursound) Tone Bender have been reissued, while the Electro-Harmonix Big Muff received a recent tribute via Mudhoney's Big Muff Superfuzz album.

many modern amps, the distortion pedal remains popular: it can give a two-channel head a footswitchable third channel, or broaden the scope of a vintage combo. Modern designs often include comprehensive EQ, so you can dial in your favored tonality – warm, thrashy, nasal – while some vintage reissue units are available with a choice of Germanium or Silicon transistors. Would sir prefer 1963 flavor, or 1968?

A new development is the all-singing, all-dancing preamp pedal, with switchable channels and speaker-simulated outputs for going direct-to-tape or into the PA. Some of these new pedals – like Mesa/Boogie's V-Twin and Hughes & Kettner's Tubeman – use tubes, and there's even a hand-wired Matchless preamp pedal. So the distortion box is alive and well, while the original 1960s units, or reissues featuring the now rare germanium diodes, gravitate towards nostalgic collectors with deep pockets...

■ *The use of alternative materials for guitar construction had begun back in the earliest days of the electric guitar. Rickenbacker's Model B electric of 1935 (main shot) was made of Bakelite using state of the art injection molding techniques. Similar aims of minimal resonance and production consistency inspired Dan Armstrong to attempt a similar approach for his 'Plexiglass' guitars of 1969.*

Catalog of Products

■ *Ned Steinberger's L-2 bass introduced the use of carbon graphite to the mass market. The guitar version, while less successful than its bass predecessor in terms of market share, went on to shift considerably more units.*

Fantastic Plastic

While some manufacturs were attempting to match 1950s specifications with their instruments, a few influential companies were investigating more radical techniques. The use of plastics for guitar construction stretched back to 1935, when injection-molding pioneer Adolph Rickenbacker had introduced his Bakelite-bodied guitars; National and Supro had utilized glass-fiber technology for their guitar bodies in the 1960s, while Dan Armstrong's famous see-through Plexiglass guitar, built for Ampeg from 1969 to 1971 was a graphic – if short-lived – reminder that the electric guitar could be made, seemingly, from any material in any shape. Travis Bean and Kramer used aluminum for neck construction, overlooking the fact that Rickenbacker had used it in the 1930s for their lap steels before deciding it was unsuitable due to the material's high coefficient of expansion. Subjected to changes in temperature, the guitars went radically out of tune. The most sensible alternative material choice, and one that is used increasingly in the 1990s, is carbon graphite-reinforced plastic. Modulus Graphite was the first company to patent the graphite neck, which was used on numerous high-end basses and guitars. A similar reinforced plastic was used by Ned Steinberger on his highly innovative headless – and virtually body-less – XL bass launched in 1981. Six-string guitars followed, while in the mid-1980s Steinberger introduced a wood-body guitar. The Steinberger bass and guitar helped popularize Rob Turner's EMG active pickups, low-noise units which incorporated a preamp and tone circuit within the pickup itself.

The last major technical advance of the 1980s involved the reinvention of Leo Fender's innovative Stratocaster tremolo unit. While Hendrix had demonstrated the potential of the unit, he had also shown that the Strat trem suffered tuning problems with heavy use. In 1979 guitarist Floyd Rose was granted his first patent for a guitar tremolo that locked the strings at both nut and saddle, enabling more drastic use of the tremolo arm, to the extent of motor-bike-style 'dive bombing.' On early versions the nut lock had to be un-clamped to re-tune, but by 1985 Rose had patented fine-tuners fitted to the bridge which simplified tuning. David Storey's tremolo design, patented in 1984 and manufactured by Kahler, used a ball bearing pivot, unlike the Floyd's twin-post knife-edge bearing arrangement. However, without the Floyd's fine-tuners, tuning newly fitted strings was more problematic.

Sign Your Name

By the start of the 1980s all the ingredients for the modern rock guitar were in place; it took the business vision of the Kramer company to combine the design ideas of Eddie Van Halen and Floyd Rose with the Kramer Baretta: a stripped down Stratocaster with single, slanted humbucking pickup, a simple volume control and bolt-on maple neck with either maple or rosewood 22-fret fingerboard. By 1988 Kramer was the best selling electric brand in the States both above and below $500, the Floyd Rose tremolo – its design licensed to several companies – was the essential fixture for virtually *any* electric guitar, and Eddie Van Halen's music was similarly all-pervasive.

Eddie Van Halen helped to usher in an era of player-designed or player-endorsed instruments, which the Japanese Hoshino company, owner of the Ibanez brand name, took to heart. Ibanez started to introduce more original designs in the mid-1970s, recruiting endorsees of that stature of Joe Pass, George Benson and Steve Lukather. In the late 1980s Ibanez upgraded its Artists Relations program, to challenge and eventually eclipse Kramer. The main weapon in the company's armory was what many regarded as the quintessential rock guitar, the RG550, along with its signature counterpart, the JEM Series, designed in conjunction with Steve Vai. Based on the by now familiar off-set double cutaway Strat-inspired body with a slim, bolt-on 24 fat-fretted neck, 1987's JEM Series models captured the mood of Vai's flamboyant appearance and guitar style. There was its monkey grip handle (for on-stage maneuvers), the day-glo colors of the JEM777, the floral finish and vine inlays of the JEM77, high output DiMarzio pickups and the 'lion's claw' tremolo routing that allowed for drastic up-bends with the Floyd Rose-licensed tremolo. Ibanez courted and captured the hot guitar players; Joe Satriani had his own model, fusionist Frank Gambale too. Vai even introduced the 7-string electric – not a new idea – with a lower B string and gave it mainstream exposure. The dominance of this virtuoso-endorsed modern rock guitar affected every manufacturer. Traditional companies such as Hamer produced graphic finish guitars with Floyd Rose, fat frets and high output humbuckers; Washburn too followed with its own interpretations of this style, while both Hamer and Washburn went to the extent of offering 36-fret guitars to accommodate two-handed tapping as practiced by E.V.H.

The third force in the modern rock guitar was that of Jackson guitars. Wayne Charvel had started a small parts company in the mid-1970s; employee Grover Jackson purchased the outfit in 1978 and expanded the range to include necks, bodies and custom guitars too – Steve Vai was a big customer pre-Ibanez. By 1981 the Jackson name debuted on a Flying V-inspired guitar built for Randy Rhoads; by 1982 Jackson had introduced the Soloist – the guitar that coined the name 'Superstrat'. The guitar's body was Strat-inspired, but smaller, with thinner horns, and neck-through-body or glued-in neck construction, 24 frets and the distinctive pointed, dropped 'beak' headstock. Jackson promoted the concept of made-to-order production instruments, allowing players to order numerous custom options – a facility now offered by all the major guitar companies. Huge expansion followed: the Charvel name was resurrected on a Japanese-made line in 1987. During the late 1980s Jackson/ Charvel was vying with Ibanez for the number two spot behind Fender as the USA's best selling guitar line. However, by the end of the decade Grover Jackson had left the company, later joining Gibson, Washburn and at the time of writing Rickenbacker.

On The Rack

The modular, D.I.Y. approach did not apply to the guitar alone, for over the same period a parallel movement spread through the field of amplification. Several innovative firms and products entered the amplification market, including ADA preamps, VHT and Rivera power-amps, and Rocktron, Digitech and Alesis effects-units.

From the consumer's point-of-view, the benefits offered by modular rack-based systems were three-fold. Players could purchase preamp, power-amp, effects units and speakers separately, mixing and matching the units as desired. The electronics could then be installed in a standard 19"-wide rack, which could be flight-cased to form a (relatively) portable, personalized sound system for guitar.

Secondly, the set-up would be in stereo, with two speaker-cabs giving a wide soundstage for dramatic chorus/echo; and a line-level stereo signal could be sent to the mixing desk, preserving your fully processed sound when playing big gigs or recording. Thirdly, the effects would be digital, of studio quality, while the main audio path would feature analog circuitry, including glowing tubes if required. Most significantly, all these functions could be coordinated by digital control circuitry, with settings stored in a programmable memory bank for instant recall via a dedicated footswitch or sophisticated MIDI foot controller. The possibilities of such systems are immense, though it's only recently that most guitarists have become

■ *Eddie Van Halen revolutionized both playing techniques and guitar design thanks to his technical wizardry on songs such as 1978's 'Eruption.' Van Halen's guitar style popularized the use of harmonics and extreme tremolo techniques, while his 'Frankenstein' red striped Linn Ellsworth/Kramer guitar inspired production models from Kramer and others.*

confident enough to program the average setup. As amplification technology advanced, transistor amplifiers improved: American company Peavey and Japanese rivals Roland both introduced credible solid-state amplifiers. As solid-state technology advances, the ultimate challenge is to make solid-state amps simulate the 'middle ground' in tube-amps, i.e. mildly crunchy textures which clean up when you play gently, and that fattening effect as the power-amp is pushed hard at volume. Already Marshall's Valvestate line and Peavey's TransTube models, plus some of Fender's new solid-state combos, are getting close, although the vacuum tube seems likely to be with us for some time yet.

■ *The Allman Brothers' Dickey Betts has become synonymous with the beefy, juicy sound of a Gibson Les Paul Sunburst; Betts' trademark sound helped inspire Paul Reed Smith's McCarty model, which Betts started using in 1994.*

looked as if Fender's very future was in doubt, but with the aid of a range of Japanese-made Fenders and re-issued US-built models the company survived. In 1986 Fender released the American Standard Stratocaster, subtly improving the tremolo system without altering the look of the guitar. A Telecaster version followed two years later and with increasing U.S.A. production, not to mention Japanese, Korean and increasingly important Fender Mexico

The Return To Retro

Ultimately, it would be a change in musical styles which saw off the 1980s rock guitar. However, even earlier in the decade some guitarists had begun a quest to find the lost tone sucked out of guitars and amplification in the pursuit of high performance. Floyd Rose tremolos – 'sustain drains' as some called them – irrevocably changed the sound of the guitar, as did high output pickups and complex electronics. Although guitarists in the alternative rock scene had long persevered with elderly Fender Jazzmasters or Gibson Les Paul Juniors, a significant move in the mainstream rock market came with the highly visible use of a vintage Les Paul sunburst by Guns N' Roses guitarist Slash. With a move back to basics, the Fender Strat and the Gibson Les Paul began to fight off their modern usurpers.

Fender's resurrection occurred after management changes which culminated in a buy-back from CBS in 1985. For a time it

operation, plus the establishment of the Signature Series guitars and the Fender Custom Shop – now a small guitar company in its own right – Fender were back. Now, in the late 1990s they are the biggest guitar company on the planet and the Stratocaster – 40 years old in 1994 – the world's best-selling guitar by a comfortable margin.

Gibson's fortunes, at a low ebb in the 1970s and early 1980s, enjoyed a similar resurgence as the Les Paul became more fashionable, and new management headed by Henry Juskiewicz addressed the company's production problems, instituting more accurate reissues of vintage Gibson guitars as well as new models such as the Nighthawk. Paul Reed Smith also profited from the increasing popularity of the vintage Gibson sound. Smith, like Floyd Rose had looked at the problems of the Strat's tremolo and designed and patented his own efficient system in 1984; its combination of vintage looks and sounds

The History Of The Tremolo

1935: Clayton Orr 'Doc' Kauffman's Vibrola appears on early Rickenbacker electrics.

1946-7: Paul Bigsby starts work on his vibrato, used on Gretsch and Gibson guitars from the early 1950s.

1954: Leo Fender rethinks vibrato design with fulcrum Stratocaster Synchronised Tremolo – the forerunner

of virtually all modern vibrato systems. He also institutes incorrect but now standard usage of 'tremolo.'

1958: Fender's Jazzmaster trem is lockable to cope with string breakage.

1964: The Burns Marvin is one of many guitars using a knife-edge pivot system derived from the Strat design.

1979: Floyd Rose granted a patent for his double-locking tremolo with string

locks at the nut and saddle.

1982: Alternatives to the 'locking' concept appear: Leo Fender updates his classic system for G&L, Paul Reed Smith patents his 'system' design two years later.

1984: David Storey patents single-locking Kahler tremolo.

1987: Fender revises Strat trem with

PRS McCarty Model
Introduced: 1994

Early PRS guitars such as 1986's Custom emphasized versatility; the

McCarty Model, endorsed by the ex-Gibson president, features a basic bridge design and bulkier neck heel in pursuit of a bigger tone.

Eric Johnson is an endorsee of Fender's American Standard Strat, but is also an enthusiastic user of all-original 1960s models. Johnson's trademark sound is obtained by using several amplifiers in parallel for a perfect combination of tones.

with modern engineering improvements became a model for many guitar designers. Smith's hybrid guitar design, which debuted in production terms with 1985's Paul Reed Smith Custom, offered the look of a 1958 Les Paul with an arched figured maple top, but with a double cutaway configuration that draws on the Strat's outline too. Smith designed his own pickups which, with the use of a 5-way rotary switch, enabled classic humbucking and single-coil, Strat-like tones. Originally just a 24-fret design, Smith's guitars have moved more toward the classic Gibson styles, especially with the McCarty Model, with PAF-like nickel covered pickups, 22 frets and his Stoptail wrap-over style bridge. As the name suggests, this model was introduced with the endorsement of the former Gibson president.

The Reissue Issue

Music Man, the company launched by Leo Fender and ex-Fender employees in 1974, had produced a potent successor to Leo's original bass guitars in 1976 with the StingRay bass. After Leo's departure following a boardroom dispute, and the company's purchase by the Ernie Ball outfit, Music Man produced a similarly effective reinterpretation of the Stratocaster. The Silhouette, launched in 1986, featured improved top fret access, a sturdier six-bolt neck-to-body join and 24 frets. The shorter headstock retains the typical Fender straight-line string pull with four tuners on the bass side and two on the treble, resulting in a less bulky headstock. The company even secured Eddie Van Halen as endorsee with his own-design guitar in the early 1990s. Reflecting the changing styles, the single-cutaway guitar featured a flat,

figured maple top, much removed from Eddie's 1980s flash.

Throughout the 1990s, practically every established guitar maker's design approach was simply to reissue anything approaching a 'classic' design. Those companies without 1950s or 1960s designs looked back to the 1970s or 1980s; Yamaha, Washburn and Ibanez both resurrected guitars from that period, as did U.S. maker Guild, while Hamer returned to its original 1970s roots with much more conservative, Gibson-esque solid-bodies. The quest for vintage tone and style is still paramount today. In some respects current design reflects a search for

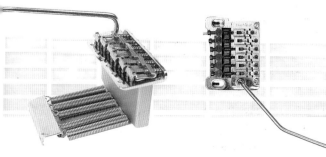

non-locking design for American Standard Stratocaster .

1990s: *Influence of Floyd Rose system diminishes in favor of simpler alternatives, and concentration on 'system' design, rethinking trem system, nut and tuners. Wilkinson trem, with Sperzel locking machine heads and friction reducing nut, becomes popular set up.*

Stevie Ray Vaughan (above) eschewed modern add-ons for his battered Strat, choosing instead to achieve a bigger tone by fitting heavy strings of up to .013 gauge.

28

improved ergonomics, exemplified by Bob Sperzel's 1980s locking machine head design, copied by Fender and produced by Schaller, or Trevor Wilkinson's intelligently designed hardware. In other respects, aged vintage instruments continued to dictate the agenda: the respected Seymour Duncan company, whose huge line of vintage pickups has eclipsed retrofit pioneers DiMarzio, has gone as far as marketing the Antiquity Series, pre-aged and corroded to look like 1950s pickups. In 1995 Fender did the same with its distressed Relic Series instruments, Custom Shop guitars which are battered and aged to look like 1950s originals, and marketed at a premium over pristine instruments.

The Tweed Look

By the 1990s, the retro trend resulted in a wealth of new vintage-flavor amps, some of them true reissues, others 'retro-modern' combos marrying vintage sound-flavors and cosmetics with modern channel-switching convenience and high-gain lead capability. More recently, an increasing number of small companies have sprung up to satisfy those purists who want to bypass printed circuit boards and opt for the uncompromising hand-wired construction of the 1940s and 1950s. Similarly, despite the advent of the effects loop on many modern amplifiers, allowing effects units to be connected at optimum levels, vintage style tremolo and reverb units which preserve all the character of 1950s originals are once again in demand.

Where the 1980s trend was for one amplifier which delivered several permutations of sounds, many professional guitarists now employ multiple-amp set-ups, using a switch-box to send their signal to one of several heads or combos; a common permutation is a Fender combo for clean-tones, Marshall head for crunch, and modern high-gain amp for lead work. Other players create a super-broad sound while retaining their hard-won tone by playing through several amps simultaneously; Stevie Ray Vaughan was a master of this approach, while Eric Johnson continues to achieve excellent tones from his multi-amplifier set-up.

Smashing Pumpkins' Billy Corgan is one of many 1990s musicians who eschew complex set-ups for a simple combination of Gibson and Fender guitars.

■ **Parker Fly**

Introduced: 1992

A brave attempt to bring genuinely new techniques to guitar design.

■ *The Rolling Stones' Keith Richards exemplifies the current fashion for battered, no-nonsense instruments.*

■ *While Marshall offers MIDI guitar preamps, it has also instigated a reissue program, which includes the JTM45 shown here.*

Where Do We Go From Here?

As the production electric guitar approaches its 50th birthday, we seem to have gone full circle. Those classic guitars produced by Fender, Gibson and others in the 1950s and early 1960s still predominate; Rickenbacker and Gretsch, once synonymous with the 1960s beatboom, enjoy renewed popularity, while the term 're-issue' is now almost as important as 'endorsed by.' Ken Parker and Larry Fishman's Parker Fly guitar, launched in 1993, is one of few current designs which continues the quest for innovation and new sounds. Its unusual construction is from lightweight tonewoods such as poplar and basswood, with carbon and glass fiber strengthening. Combined with the hybrid tonality of conventional DiMarzio magnetic pickups and Fishman piezo transducers for an acoustic tonality, the Parker Fly genuinely takes the electric solidbody to a new level.

While the Parker Fly represents a totally new approach to guitar design, one of the major efforts in the electric guitar industry is to ensure consistent production at ever-lower prices.

Favored locations have moved from Japan to Korea in search of lower costs; now the low-end manufacturers are forced to look further afield to Taiwan, Indonesia, India, and now China. Fender has its own factory in Mexico, which at just four hours from the California Custom Shop allows for close supervision by the parent company. Peavey established a high-tech manufacturing facility in the U.S.A. way back in '78, and although it too has been forced to source instruments and parts off shore, Peavey arguably has set a example for producing affordable guitars made in the U.S.A. There's no doubt that the duopoly established by Fender and Gibson in the 1950s remains; for both companies their offshore lines contribute to their massively influential position. Other manufacturers such as Paul Reed Smith continue to produce finely crafted instruments exclusively in the U.S.A. One thing is certain; despite its oft-predicted demise, the electric guitar remains the premier instrument in popular music, its only limitations being the imagination of those players who use it as a means of expression.

Keyboards

"The Hammond organ is not really your archetypal rock'n'roll instrument, and to try to make it one has been a very pleasurable battle in which I think I succeeded. But the piano is a much easier instrument to play in rock. I love playing rock'n'roll piano, because it blends much more easily."

JON LORD, DEEP PURPLE

While the guitar has become the most visible instrument associated with rock music, many other other profound influences have had their effect on its sound. Pounding piano players who were able to inspire rooms full of dancers with nothing more than the rhythm of their left hands, jazz organists who created timbres and riffs that are as hip now as they were 60 years ago, gospel players whose comping on piano and organ to the rhythm of clapped hands made music as close to the divine as we are likely to hear while in this mortal coil – these individuals brought to rock music something unique: the sound of keyboards.

The Hammond Organ and Leslie Speaker

Of the many keyboards used during the rock music era, few boast the mystique of the Hammond organ. Like Leo Fender's

Telecaster, Laurens Hammond's Model A was invented before the advent of rock'n'roll. Throughout the 1930s and 1940s various Hammond models were popular in small churches and chapels for traditional liturgical organ music, in nightclubs, restaurants and taverns for popular tunes, and on the radio; emotional high (and low) points of the popular radio soap operas were punctuated to such a degree with signature Hammond organ riffs that they are today still seen as a stereotypical part of the electric organ repertoire. It was the use of the Hammond organ by jazz greats such as Wild Bill Davis, Jimmy Smith and Larry Young and its place with the piano in the gospel groups that led it, by way of the blues and R&B, to early rock music.

One of the advantages of the Hammond organ in the early days of rock music was that it was electric and used amplifiers. An amp designed to be loud enough to fill a good sized church could, when pushed to its limit, compete with guitar combos such as Fender's Bandmaster. Of the many amplifiers and speakers used with the Hammond, those designed by Don Leslie were most often used in a rock setting. Dozens of different Leslie speaker models were available, but they all had one thing in common: at least one rotating horn, drum, or baffle through which the amplified organ sound was directed. (In later years a number of Leslie systems were developed which used electronic means to create the rotating speaker effect, but which are

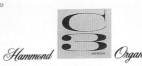

10

Hammond C-3 Series Organ

Here's an instrument of enormous power and beauty. Widely used in churches, schools, civic auditoriums, and institutions, its vibrant "cathedral" tone coupled with simple straight lines and closed cabinetry are perfectly matched for a dignified presentation of the complete range of organ music, as well as a magnificent variety of true church tones.

All of the exclusive Hammond features are here, including: "Touch-Response" Percussion, Harmonic Drawbars, separate vibrato controls for both manuals, and 18 "pre-set" combinations for readily changing the tonal qualities to exactly suit the organists' individual tastes. The majestic tones of the Hammond C-3 Series Organ and its incomparable versatility have justifiably earned it the title, "Music's Most Glorious Voice."

SPECIFICATIONS

DIMENSIONS: Closed without pedal keyboard—48½" wide, 25" deep, 38⅞" high; open and with pedal keyboard and bench—48¼" wide, 47" deep, 40" high.

WEIGHT: Complete with bench and pedal keyboard—450 pounds.

MANUALS: Swell and Great, 61 keys each.

PEDAL KEYBOARD: 25-note, rotating, detachable, flat lamp which illuminates the pedals.

TONAL CONTROLS: 9 pre-set keys and 2 sets of 9 adjustable harmonic drawbars for each manual; 2 adjustable drawbars (16' and 8') for pedals, 4 tablets controlling "Touch-Response Percussion."

EXPRESSION: One expression pedal controlling Swell, Great and Pedals; also equipped with normal and soft volume control.

MUSIC POWER OUTPUT: See section on Tone Cabinets, page 21.

Note: This model organ is also available as a self-contained instrument. See page 15.

Available in dark walnut and light oak finishes.

generally regarded as inferior in sonic terms.) These spinning baffles turned at a fast speed creating a tremolo/vibrato tibia effect or a slow speed creating an undulating chorale effect, intended to emulate the sound of a pipe organ in which the sounds of different pipes came from several directions. Rather than offering two speeds, several lower-priced Leslie speakers offered fast and off as the only options.

The most popular Leslies for rock music were the 145 and 147; both had a tube amp of around 40 watts R.M.S., a treble driver that pointed up into a spinning horn, and a 15″ bass speaker facing down into a rotating drum. The 147 had a larger cabinet and had, therefore, a greater bass response. The upper and lower rotors each had two motors, one for slow speed and one for fast. The upper horn was lighter and connected to the motors by a fairly tight belt, while the heavier lower rotor used a belt with lower tension. Hence, when switching between fast and slow speeds, the upper frequencies would change speed almost immediately, while the lower frequencies would change gradually.

As rock organ playing began to catch on, Leslie came out with a combo pre-amp for the 145 and 147, allowing those with portable combo organs (or even electric guitarists) to access the coveted rotating speaker sounds. The 145, 147 and all the other Leslie speakers at this time were designed for permanent placement in a home, tavern, or church, with bulky wood veneer cabinets and no carrying handles. As the Leslie company began to realize that more and more of these cabinets were being lugged around by rock bands, new models were introduced. The Leslie 900 was the best known: it put out about 100 watts R.M.S to compete with the increasingly-fashionable Marshall stacks, was covered with practical black, amplifier type vinyl, had handles and came apart into two sections for easier transportation, and featured a more road-worthy solid state amp.

The Hammond Sound
The heart of the Hammond's sound is provided by the spinning, notched metallic disks known as tone wheels. These tone wheels spin in a magnetic field creating a voltage that produces a sine-like wave. A key on the Hammond sounds up to nine of these waves at different pitches, each at any of eight volume levels. The level of each pitch is controlled by a drawbar. The fact that these waves are close to sine waves lets us look at the Hammond sound as a basic form of additive synthesis. While the envelope of these waveforms is set (key on, full volume – key off, zero volume), it is the variations in timbre within this organ-like envelope that help define the Hammond sound. The one place where the envelope varies is the percussion section. The Hammond percussion is an attack transient pitched at either 4' or 2$\frac{2}{3}$'. The player can choose one of two decay slopes for this sound; the fast setting gives a percussive, marimba effect, the slow setting a more chime-like sound. The percussion sound is available at two volume levels and is layered with whatever drawbar sounds are active.

Pulling out a Hammond drawbar is not necessarily analogous to pulling out a stop on a pipe organ. Any given pipe on a pipe organ can have a rich sound with many harmonics; the Hammond waveform was designed to have as few overtones as possible. However, few pipe organs have stops available at the Hammond's nine pitches. The fact that the waves produce by the Hammond are not true sine waves is seen by many players as the secret of its sound. Thanks to its mechanical origin, the tone wheel sine wave is slightly skewed, and this contributes to the instrument's sonic character. Listening to a modern electronic organ is a powerful demonstration of how pure sine waves lack the vitality of the Hammond's electro-mechanically produced sound.

■ *Jimmy Smith (far left with B3) took up the Hammond after hearing Wild Bill Davis, and became one of the instrument's best-known exponents via Blue Note albums including* Home Cookin' *and* Midnight Special.

■ *The Hammond A100 was essentially a Hammond B3 with built in amplifier and speakers. The tone wheels are concealed behind the lower aluminum panel, which also carries the potentiometers to adjust tonal balance.*

Of course, many organists found the new design cabinet lacked the warmth and richness of old designs such as the 147. Other new Leslies were introduced including small, single speaker systems that plugged into the speaker jacks of guitar amplifiers and huge, four speaker affairs that included built-in ultraviolet lamps to turn the psychedelic, fluorescent rotors into a self-contained light show.

The Combo Organ

The advantage of the Hammond organ, as we have seen, was its sound; powerful, rich and driving, it was perfect for pushing a rock song to higher levels of excitement. Unfortunately, the Hammond was also costly, bulky and heavy. Electronic organs that used vacuum tube oscillators had been around for almost as long as Hammond's tone wheel organs, but their sound was not as well suited to the needs of jazz, R&B and rock players. During the late 1950 and early 1960s, however, transistors began to be used in the place of vacuum tubes in electronic organs. It was now possible to build a more portable electronic organ, small enough to fold into a handy carrying case which could fit into the back seat of a car. As an added bonus, these instruments cost much less than even the smallest Hammonds. Bright and sassy, available in a rainbow of colors, portable and affordable, the combo organ perfectly represented the new rock ethos. For those who had taken a few piano lessons as a kid, there was no quicker way to become part of the wild new teenage music scene than to become the proud owner of a new combo organ.

The Vox Continental

Of the myriad of combo organs used in the 1960s the Vox Continental was destined to become the most famous. During the 1940s Tom Jennings founded Vox, which built large church organs in the U.K. through the 1950s. 1960 saw the release of the first Vox Continentals, which soon became popular with the new generation of British groups. The Continental was a visually striking instrument. Covered with a charcoal grey Rexine material with a bright orange top, featuring a gracefully curved chrome stand and a reverse colored keyboard (black naturals with white flats and sharps), the Continental looked superb on the color televisions that were just becoming the rage. The Beatles, The Dave Clark Five, The Animals, and many of the other wildly popular British groups of the early to mid 1960s used the Continental as well as Vox amplifiers and guitars. With this weight behind the Vox name, Jennings was able to sign a million dollar deal in November 1964 with the Thomas Organ Company of the United States. According to some reports, a fire at the Vox facility in England shortly after this led to Continentals being assembled at the Thomas plant in California for a brief time. Before long, Continentals as well as other Vox instruments were being made by Thomas in Italy.

With the popularity of the Continental, Vox expanded its line of combo organs in both directions. The lower-priced Jaguar looked very similar to the Continental but had an octave of 'reversed' colored bass keys (with white naturals and black flats and sharps) and voice tabs instead of drawbars. All Vox Jaguars seem to have been made in Italy, and their circuitry offered less tonal variations than the Continental, although the sound was somewhat similar. The Continental II (later re-christened the Super Continental) offered all the features of the Continental along with extra drawbars and a manual bass section in a dual manual package. While both of these instruments were produced in fairly large numbers, two other Vox organs were extremely rare. The logical issue of the Vox/Thomas union was the Continental Baroque, or V305. This instrument featured two five octave manuals, the bottom of which played the usual Continental sounds controlled by the usual drawbars; the top

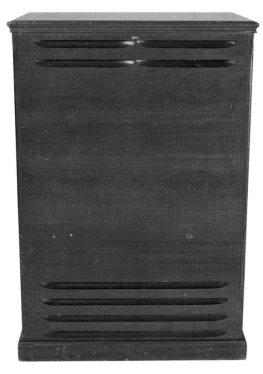

■ *Donald Leslie's 147 was the definitive rotary speaker. The back view shows both the rotary horn, visible at the top, and the black rotary drum, seen at the bottom, which directs the sound from the 15″ downward-facing speaker.*

The Animals' 1964 smash 'House Of The Rising Sun' was filled with Alan Price's Vox Continental arpeggios. The Continental's distinctive shrill sound derived from the square waves produced by its transistor circuitry, rather than the smooth sine waves produced by Hammond's tone wheels.

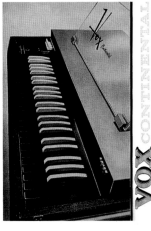

■ **Vox Jaguar**
Introduced: 1965

Appearing roughly five years after 1960's Continental, the lower-priced Vox Jaguar was made in Italy, and featured voice tabs rather than the Continental's drawbars.

manual played Thomas Organ special effects voices such as banjo, celeste and harpsichord. This organ was used by Paul Revere during the last days of the Raiders' fame. Perhaps the rarest Vox combo organ was the Junior which, with its three octave keyboard, resembles a cut-down Continental. Like the Baroque, the Junior has straight legs instead of the usual curving Vox stand and features a built-in amplifier and speaker system.

Elsewhere during the early 1960s combo organs were being built to challenge Vox's supremacy, particularly in the musical instrument building centers of Italy where master craftsmen had

been building organs for hundreds of years, constantly updating their craft to keep up with technological advances. As we have seen, later Vox organs were made in this country, but perhaps the most famous of the native Italian combo organs were those built by Farfisa.

The Farfisa Organ

The original Farfisa from the early 1960s was the Combo Compact. While the Vox organs were light and graceful, the Farfisas were sturdy and more workmanlike. Although never as popular with famous rock bands as the Vox, despite its occasional use by The Rolling Stones, the Farfisa was loved by garage bands all over the world. The popularity of the original Combo Compact led to a whole series of Farfisa organs: the Mini Compact was a small, 49 key version of the Combo Compact, the Mini Deluxe was a Mini upgraded to include a one octave bass section of grey colored keys. The Combo Compact Deluxe also offered extra bass keys as well as extra voices; the Duo Compact had all of these features plus two manuals and a separate preamp with an improved spring reverb. By 1968 Farfisa was offering a whole new line of organs. The FAST series had a white finish, grey keys with white flats and sharps, percussion along the line of Hammonds, and a completely new sound.

Other Italian organ builders were also making their mark in the combo organ world. Elka produced a line of Panther organs, also sold under names including Capri and Lo Duca; GEM and others were building organs sold under a variety of names. In the United States a couple of the major home organ makers as well

The U.S. Wurlitzer company was the first to bring an electric piano on the market. This 200 series, the second version of the piano, may be recognized by its molded plastic top, and was successful in both popular and educational markets.

The Thomas company was one of the leading U.S. home organ manufacturers, but despite its involvement with U.K. company Vox it would never crack the group market.

EXCITING NEW RANGE OF *Thomas* **TRANSISTOR ORGANS**

MODEL AR-2 FIESTA
The Fiesta is an exciting new full 44 note, two Keyboard organ with Repeat, Percussion, Twelve beautifully tab controlled organ voices, flutes, reeds, strings and diapasons. At the touch of a tab you can create banjo, mandolin and Marimba effects. A string bass pedal effect is at your command to add a new rhythmic dimension to your selection.
Clear, clean treble and full, rich organ bass is possible with the 75 watt all transistor Peak Power Amplifier.

as a couple of the big electric guitar makers decided to join in the combo organ fray. The Baldwin company, watching the rising popularity of rock band equipment, made an unsuccessful bid to buy the Fender company before buying the British Burns company in 1965. To complement the existing guitar line designed by Jim Burns, Baldwin added two combo organs, a solid body electric harpsichord, and a series of amplifiers. The first of these organs was the Howard, introduced in late 1965 or early 1966. Like many of its kind, it was built in Italy and its circuits were quite similar to those found in the Vox Jaguar and other Italian instruments. The Howard seems to have been made in fair numbers and examples of it are fairly common today. This instrument's brightly colored voice tabs, along with its push/pull coupler, called forth an array of raspy and raucous sounds that evoke perfectly the trashy garage band sound. Shortly after the Howard's debut, Baldwin introduced a combo organ under its own name. The Baldwin combo organ was designed and built in Arkansas, U.S.A., and this instrument was finished, like the Howard, in blue and black. Although very few of these instruments were built during its two year production run, they show up in working order more often than one might expect, in part (no doubt) due to their tank-like construction. The Baldwin's brightly colored tabs (which in purple, red, bright blue and yellow matched those of the Howard's) called up more traditional,

electric organ voices; its flutes are especially nice and the manual bass is rich and powerful.

One rather more distinctive Baldwin product was the Baldwin Electric Harpsichord. Based on the construction of a traditional harpsichord, the Baldwin, which came out in 1966, featured two pickups to amplify the sounds of the individual strings, plus a pair of switches, stereo outputs and two footpedals to offer a variety of splits and layering of sounds. Since each of the 57 keys plucked its own string, tuning problems kept many groups from bringing the Baldwin Harpsichord on the road; the Beach Boys did haul one around, but they also brought a piano tuner with them to get it ready for every gig. Although these instruments did not see a lot of road action, many were – and some still are – used frequently in the studio.

Wurlitzer, best known for its mighty theatre organs and its long line of electric pianos, came out with an innovative combo organ in the mid 1960s. Using integrated circuits, the 7300 was small and light. It used a system of drawbars similar to those of the Vox Continental, and in keeping with its space-age, streamlined appearance, the Wurlitzer's stand was a single pedestal that attached to the center of the underside of the instrument. Like the Baldwin organ, the Wurlitzer was well built and had a very pleasing sound. While neither achieved the level of fame of its European competitors, both are still seen in some circles as desirable and collectable instruments.

Of all the electric instrument builders in the U.S.A. during the 1960s, the Fender company, with its guitars, basses, amps, and Fender/Rhodes pianos, perhaps best represented the U.S. rock music scene. Like Vox in the U.K., Fender aimed to become a complete musical supplier, and combo organs were a logical addition to its line. The best known of the Fender combo organs, although nevertheless rare, was the Contempo. Finished in red and black with a tilting chrome stand and a wealth of voice tabs spread across its control panel, the Contempo was an impressive looking instrument. A flexible voicing structure as well as a pedal that controlled volume (up and down) and tone (side to side) gave the Contempo a good, if unusual, sound. The Contempo was made at the Fender plant in California, using a keyboard and some other components made by the Pratt-Read company. More rare is the Fender Starmaster. This writer could find no-one involved with Fender during the 1960s who had any recollection of this organ, which only showed up on the Fender price list for one year, and never made the catalogue proper. Evidently made of a green plastic material and supported on a wooden stand, the Starmaster is said to have been made in Italy, and badged with the Fender name.

The Gibson company made some of the most famous guitars of the 1950s and 1960s. The fame of the Gibson combo organ was the result of its use by only one famous keyboard player, Ray Manzarek of the Doors. Manzarek played a Vox in the early days of the Doors, the sound of that instrument being acceptable as well as its shape. The shape was important to Manzarek because the Doors relied on him to play not only the organ parts, but also the bass parts, by means of a Fender/Rhodes piano bass placed on the top left hand side of the Continental. As Continental production switched to Italy, Manzarek became dissatisfied with the relatively fragile new plastic keys. In his search for a replacement, he experimented with a Farfisa but found the top too rounded to support the piano bass; the flat-topped Kalamazoo K101, soon to be renamed the Gibson G101, was a perfect choice. Thus, the man who became perhaps the most photographed keyboard player of the late 1960s singlehandedly brought to the Gibson combo organ a level of fame it might never have achieved if its top had been rounded. The Gibson G101 was covered in pale green and grey material and loaded with special effects such as fuzz bass, wah-wah, pitch bend, and a percussive sustain effect that is featured on much of the Doors' *Absolutely Live*. A second Gibson combo organ, the

Gibson Stage Organ, was similar to the G101, but it was finished in black and orange, had two manuals, and, instead of having the familiar 1/4" jack output, was attached to its own amplifier by a kind of umbilical cord. The Doors were perhaps the most visible of Gibson organ users, but they certainly were not the only ones; The Mothers of Invention and enigmatic jazz master Sun Ra both used a Gibson combo organ as part of their distinctly individual sounds.

Electric Pianos

Although the sound of early rock'n'roll is filled with the conventional piano, the instrument has always had drawbacks

■ *While Wurlitzer and Rhodes pianos were popular in the U.S.A. German company Hohner enjoyed European success with its own electric pianos. In this 1965 shot, Manfred Mann is using the company's Cembalet.*

■ *This mid 1950s Wurlitzer Model 110 is the forerunner of the piano shown on the left. Although popular, 100 series Wurlitzers used fragile reeds that were prone to breaking or detuning.*

■ **Fender Rhodes 88**

Introduced: 1969

The Fender Rhodes was introduced in 73 key form, with the speaker cabinet doubling as the stand. The 88 key version appeared around the same time that Rhodes pianos switched to black plastic tops. By the late 1970s, Rhodes had attracted a stellar range of endorsees including Chick Corea and Herbie Hancock (catalog, left).

for group use; it is bulky, heavy, with its volume limited by its acoustic output. As on-stage volumes increased, piano players wanted a piano that could easily be amplified and was portable enough to be easily moved from job to job. The electric piano seemed to be the perfect answer. However, whereas the fact that electric organs didn't sound much like acoustic pipe organs was not a problem, electric pianos that didn't sound much like acoustic pianos were less satisfactory. Hence many rock players, used to the sound of an old upright, never saw the electric piano as a real replacement. However, every electric piano, while not having the sound of a real piano, had a unique

and desirable voice of its own. Thus, electric pianos were used on the road because of their portability and volume; in the studio where an acoustic piano would be available, they were used because of their distinctive sounds.

The Fender Rhodes

The name of Harold Rhodes is indelibly associated with the electric piano. During World War II Rhodes served in the United States Army Air Force, building his first pianos from bits and pieces of old B-17 Flying Fortresses. He used these (non-electric) instruments to help the morale of wounded airmen by teaching them to play the piano, an endeavor that earned him the Medal of Honor. By the late 1940s he had come out with his three octave, tube-amplified Pre-Piano, the first electric piano. It was his later 72 key instrument that attracted the attention of guitar and amplifier builder, Leo Fender. Although these two inventors often disagreed on how best to build an electric piano, their collaboration resulted in the Fender/Rhodes line of keyboard instruments. The first of these instruments to be produced was 1960's Fender/Rhodes Piano Bass: a 32 note instrument that produced electric bass sounds. With this instrument three piece groups could sound like four piece groups, and, although never wildly popular, the piano bass remained a steady seller into the early 1980s, even though production had ended by 1975.

As CBS negotiated to take over the Fender company, Rhodes commenced development of his full sized electric instrument. In 1964 the 73 key, Fender/Rhodes piano appeared. With its shiny, silver metal-flake fiberglass top and its speaker cabinet stand, it was a striking looking instrument, which was soon followed by other variations. During the mid to late 1960s, the Fender/Rhodes Celeste was available; this was a 37 key instrument that played the top range of the electric piano, in effect a treble version of the Piano Bass.

■ *Although Ray Charles' first hit, 'What'd I Say' was recorded with a Wurlitzer piano, Charles soon switched allegiance to Fender Rhodes, later declaring "I don't know any other keyboard that comes close to doing what the Rhodes does."*

At this time both the Piano Bass and the Celeste were also available in four octave versions. In the late 1960s the silver top was replaced with a black one, and in the early 1970s the piano was offered with the traditional amplifier stand or four screw-in legs. In the mid 1970s the name of these instruments was changed from Fender/ Rhodes to Rhodes, reflecting the fact that Leo Fender actually played a relatively minor role in their development. Before Rhodes piano production ended in 1981, a couple of last innovations were the new flat tops for stacking other instruments or music, and the 54 key stage piano. While large numbers of rock players used the Rhodes electric pianos, they may be best remembered for their contributions to the jazz/rock fusion movement. Pianists like Herbie Hancock and Chick Corea helped make the Rhodes sound a legitimate musical voice and not just an imitation of an acoustic piano.

Although Harold Rhodes built the first electric pianos, the first company to market them in large numbers was Wurlitzer. In 1954 the first model 100 electric pianos were produced in Corinth, Mississippi. The 100 series of pianos, which included the 110, 120, and 145, were made of fiberboard or wood and included a built-in tube amplifier and speaker system. Later models featured a solid state amp and a vibrato effect. It was the Wurlitzer 100 series that was heard on a couple of early electric piano hits: 'What'd I Say' by Ray Charles and Cannonball Adderley's 'Mercy, Mercy, Mercy' featuring Joe Zawinul. The Wurlitzer had a great sound, was small and portable, and had a nice piano feel and action. However, it went out of tune easily, and tuning was an intricate operation involving a file and a soldering iron. The 200 series of 1968 addressed this problem. Basically similar to the 100 series, the 200 pianos featured reeds

that would not go out of tune, as well as a new look with colorful vinyl tops and chrome legs. These pianos became very popular, not only with rock and jazz groups but as teaching tools in many educational institutions.

In 1958 Ernst Zacharias of the German company Hohner developed that company's first electric piano, the Cembalet. The Cembalet used rough-finished accordion reeds as a sound source, and the action was very simple. Pressing a key pushed a reed out of position and released it; the vibrations of this reed were then amplified. This design was not without problems and the action was prone to breaking. By 1962, a new Hohner electric piano had been introduced. The Pianet looked and sounded quite like the Cembalet and used the same accordion reeds. Its action, however, was quite unusual; each key on the Pianet was attached to a short metal rod with an adhesive pad of leather and foam at its end. Each pad rested on a reed, and as the key was depressed, the adhesive pad would pull the reed out of position. At a certain point, the reed would spring free and, as on the Cembalet, the vibrations would be amplified. Although these keyboards were developed for home use, they were embraced by rock keyboard players and the Cembalet and Pianet produced many of the rock piano sounds of the 1960s. Performers like the Beatles, Al Kooper in the Blues Project, Manfred Mann, the Zombies, Led Zeppelin (listen to 'Stairway to Heaven') and many others used them.

Herbie Hancock and Chick Corea both helped popularize the sound of the electric piano. Here Hancock, left, uses the Yamaha

CP80, essentially a portable grand piano with a pickup installed. Corea is using a Clavinet and a 1970s Fender Rhodes.

37

■ **Hohner Pianet**

Introduced: 1962

The Hohner Pianet used a distinctive action (see inset). Each key is attached to a foam and *leather pad. Hitting the key pulls the reed out of position, generating a note as the reed breaks free. Totally passive, the Pianet does not require a power supply.*

■ **Hohner Cembalet**

Introduced: 1958

The ancestor of the Pianet, the Cembalet used a different action which was prone to breakage.

Although, like the Baldwin Harpsichord, the Hohner Clavinet was not exactly an electric piano, it is simply too interesting an instrument to ignore. Zacharias looked for inspiration to the clavichord, a popular keyboard instrument from the late middle ages. What made the clavichord highly expressive was that its strings were struck directly by the keys, allowing velocity and aftertouch to affect its sound. In 1964 Zacharias produced an electrically amplified version of the clavichord, the Hohner Clavinet. Stevie Wonder, so the story goes, was looking for a keyboard that could make guitar-like sounds and came across the Clavinet; the rest was history. Wonder's funky, percussive chopping on the Clavinet, often accented with a wah-wah pedal, inspired a generation of keyboard players.

Like Laurens Hammond, Harold Rhodes and Ernst Zacharias, Jerome Markowitz of Allentown, Pennsylvania, was an active inventor who also came up with such devices as air raid sirens and bomb detectors. Around the time that Hammond was introducing his tone-wheel organ, Markowitz was developing a stable, vacuum tube oscillator for use in an electronic organ, designed to sound more like a traditional pipe organ than the Hammond. The Allen Organ Company's instruments soon became popular in settings such as churches, and recital halls where pipe organs traditionally would be found. In 1959, Allen began using transistors in its organs, and in the 1960s the Rocky Mount Instruments division of Allen started using this technology in a series of portable keyboard

instruments with the RMI name. Most of these were designed with rock band players in mind, although a few were apparently produced purely as novelty instruments. RMI's range included the Lark combo organ, the Explorer (which used weighted, mechanized key contacts called 'Flying Hammers' to create effects like guitar strums and mandolin tremolos), the electric Calliope, and the Rock-si-Chord (which created harpsichord and lute sounds), before striking gold with the RMI Electra Piano 300A in 1967, the first instrument to use purely electronic means to create a piano sound. Significantly, it was Jerome Markowitz, the Allen Organ Company and RMI, in conjunction with defence contractor North American Rockwell, who began in late 1968 to plant the seeds that would forever change the electronic music world. It was this unlikely coalition that began putting together the world's first digital musical instruments – and helped put in train a process which would eventually result in the loss of many treasured names in keyboard manufacture.

■ **Hohner Clavinet**

Introduced: 1964

Hohner's distinctive Clavinet was *inspired by the medieval clavichord, but would not really take off until its use by Stevie Wonder (right).*

■ *The RMI Electra Piano was the first instrument to use purely electronic means to create a piano sound, eliminating the tuning instability or reed breakage of electro-mechanical instruments. By 1967's standards the RMI offered a remarkably close approximation of an upright. The Rock-Si-Chord also produced harpsichord and lute sounds.*

RMI ROCK-SI-CHORD
from *Rock* to *Bach*

ROCKY MOUNT INSTRUMENTS, INC.

The Death Of The Electronic Piano

As electronics advanced, complex keyboards which relied on expensive-to-manufacture mechanical components gradually became regarded as obsolete or unfashionable. By the 1970s, the distinctive sound of the combo organ fell from favor, with the Hammond standing alone as the favored organ sound. Of course a few hardy souls still used their Farfisas and the like, and the Yamaha YC line of combo organs actually achieved quite a high level of popularity during the 1970s, while the late 1970s new wave and punk movements saw organists scouring pawn shops for old Vox Continentals and other now-treasured obsolete combo organs. Throughout the 1970s, the more esoteric electric pianos began to be discarded, including the Hohner Pianet (although a 1977 instrument that combined the Pianet and Clavinet in one box offered it a last gasp of popularity), the Wurlitzer (although it continued to be used in educational settings), and the RMI (although the world's first polyphonic digital synthesizer came out under the RMI name in 1974). The proliferation of polyphonic synthesizers and sampling keyboards in the 1980s ended the widespread use of even the Hammond organ and Rhodes Piano. The (in)famous ringing DX7 electric pianos and 8 operator drawbar organs, and the ubiquitous sample disks full of B-3 and DX7 piano samples gave players fairly accurate imitations of these instruments as well as Clavinets, synthesizers, and the ability to out-Mellotron the Mellotron with all kinds of strings and choirs. A generation of keyboard players grew up using Rhodes and Hammond, Vox and Hohner sounds, but never having played the actual instruments. In some cases the imitations began to become perceived as more real than the reality on which they were based; many a horror story has been told of young players used to a zinging DX7 'Rhodes' sound sitting down at the genuine article and complaining that it doesn't sound like the real thing. More recently, however, vintage keyboard instruments are being seen, understood, and appreciated for what they were and are. Authentic Farfisa organs, Wurlitzer electric pianos and Hohner Clavinets are being played by seasoned old-timers and psych-oriented new-comers alike, used along with the latest digital technology to create viable, exciting and innovative music.

Acoustic Guitar

'There are a lot of things you can do with an acoustic that you can't do with an electric. Some of the stuff we've done has seven, eight acoustics in there, they add a real breadth to the sound. A lot of the Stones stuff that people think of as electric is really acoustic."
KEITH RICHARDS, ROLLING STONES

Granted, the signature sound of rock music – from the throbbing bass rhythm of Chuck Berry to the pyrotechnic lead of Jimi Hendrix – is the electric guitar. But rock'n'roll did not start with an electric guitar. It started with an acoustic guitar.

Some might argue whether rock music begins with Elvis's first record, 'That's All Right,' or with earlier, more successful records such as Bill Haley's 'Rock Around the Clock,' which hit the pop charts six weeks before the release of 'That's All Right' or even with Jackie Brenston's 'Rocket 88,' a Number One R&B hit in 1951 and the record that Sam Phillips, who recorded both 'Rocket 88' and 'That's All Right,' says is the first rock'n'roll record. But rock'n'roll is more than music. It's an attitude. A culture. And rock culture does not begin with a western singer and his curly forelock, or with a wild sax solo and cranked-up guitars. Rock culture begins with the greasy ducktail and the sideburns. And the beginning of the beginning – the first sound on Elvis's first record – was an acoustic. Elvis kicks off 'That's All Right' strumming alone on his Martin D-18, setting the tempo and feel not only for bandmates Scotty Moore and Bill Black but for a revolution in music.

The acoustic guitar's historic moment alone in the spotlight lasted only a few seconds. After Elvis's first vocal line, Scotty Moore played his now-famous descending arpeggio on a Gibson ES-295, and the electric guitar overshadowed the acoustic forevermore. Overshadowed, yes; but replaced, no. The acoustic guitar has stayed mostly in the background but has remained an integral part of the beat of rock'n'roll.

Country Roots

Rock'n'roll music, as defined by Elvis, Bill Haley, Buddy Holly and Chuck Berry, came together from two roots: one black, one white. Blues, or 'rhythm & blues' as black music was labeled in Billboard magazine, went electric almost as soon as the electric guitar was invented. It was from the country side, or 'country & Western' as Billboard called it, that the acoustic guitar came into rock. It was exclusively a rhythm instrument, but a very important rhythm instrument. As it had been in dance bands and big band jazz music in the 1930s, the acoustic guitar in country music was an extension of the drum set; in many cases, such as Grand Ole Opry performances, the acoustic guitar was the drum set. The Opry did not allow drums onstage. Nor were there any drums on Elvis's early recordings for Sun Records. Elvis's D-18 was the rhythm. But it was a different kind of rhythm than any country, R&B or pop act had ever made. Where did it come from? That's the great unanswered question, whether you're concerned specifically with the rhythm guitar part or with the overall sound of 'That's All Right.' Up until that very moment, when the session was going badly and Elvis started fooling around, no one had heard him play guitar like that, much less sing like that. Scotty Moore hadn't. They had just met the Sunday before the session, when producer Sam Phillips sent Elvis over to Scotty's house to try to work up some material. "It was just the normal sing and strum thing," Moore recalled. Later, in the studio, it was as if someone had flicked a switch in Elvis. By Moore's recollection, "When we hit that groove, he put power into his playing."

Why did Elvis play an acoustic guitar instead of an electric? That's easier to answer: Probably not because he had any perspective on the acoustic guitar's past role in country or jazz,

■ *This 1942 Martin D-18 is the instrument that kicked off rock'n'roll, in the form of Elvis Presley's opening strums on 'That's All Right.' Elvis customized his guitar with stick on metallic letters, of which the 'S' has long since disappeared. The front and back shots of this historic instrument, recently sold for around $200,000 to a private collector, show belt buckle scratches and other damage incurred in Elvis's frenetic early performances.*

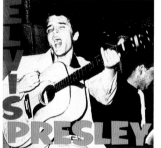

■ *Presley's D-18 provided the rhythmic pulse for his early Sun sides, and was later used as an improvized bongo; for live performances Presley protected the instrument with a tooled leather cover (right).*

manager Jim Denny when Elvis, Scotty and Bill arrived for their Opry appearance on September 4, 1954. Scotty recalled: "When we went in, he said, 'Where's the rest of the band?' And he'd heard the record!"

Setting the Style

If history were neat and orderly, Elvis would be remembered as an influential guitarist who established a new role for the acoustic guitar and set the standard for generations of rockers to come. But as it turned out, not that many people heard Elvis play guitar. 'That's All Right' sold 20,000 records, and none of Elvis's Sun singles ever made the national pop charts. In live performances his stage movements and the screams of the crowd made his guitar playing inconsequential, at least from an aural standpoint. The visual effect, however – Elvis's guitar stance, his guitar attitude – was as important as any sound the audience might or might not have heard. A young Bob Luman, then an aspiring country singer, described the experience: "He hit his guitar a lick and he broke two strings. I'd been playing ten years, and I hadn't broken a total of two strings... these high school girls were screaming and fainting and running to the stage, and then he started to move his hips real slow like he had a thing for his guitar... That's the last time I tried to sing like Webb Pierce and Lefty Frizzell." This was a guy with an acoustic guitar.

but simply because he had never played in a band. He had always just played by himself. It would have been ludicrous for him to have had an electric guitar.

And why was Elvis, a totally inexperienced guitarist, playing guitar on a master recording session? According to Moore, "Sam was too cheap to hire any extra musicians. That's the reason there only ended up being the three of us."

With no one else available to set the tone and the tempo, and certainly no way to put it into words (he couldn't very well have said, "Okay guys, let's make the first rock'n'roll record"), Elvis had to do it on his acoustic guitar. And he turned out to be the perfect musician for the job. "He had a good feel for rhythm," Moore said. "He didn't know all that many chords on the guitar, but he'd flog the fire out of one. It just came natural to him – had rhythm in his bones."

Between Phillips' production and Elvis's playing, the acoustic guitar took a quantum leap, from reinforcing the rhythm to filling in a broad tonal and rhythmic spectrum. The importance of the instrument is illustrated in a comment made by Grand Ole Opry

When RCA bought Elvis's contract from Sun, RCA hired guitarists for his sessions. His career skyrocketed in 1956 when his first RCA release, 'Heartbreak Hotel,' went to No. 1 on the pop charts, but with it, his importance as a guitarist evaporated. He did play acoustic guitar on a few RCA sessions, but in an entirely different way. "He'd beat out rhythm on the back of it, like playing a bongo or something," Scotty Moore recalled. That's Elvis, playing bongo-guitar on 'Don't Be Cruel' and 'All Shook Up.'

The Acoustic Strikes Back

Even before 'Heartbreak Hotel' effectively ended Elvis's career as an acoustic guitarist in March 1956, the acoustic guitar's role as the heartbeat of rock'n'roll had been seriously assaulted by Chuck Berry's electric guitar-driven 'Maybelline,' and subsequent hits 'School Day' and 'Rock And Roll Music.' Berry's simple rhythm lick became the very definition of rock'n'roll guitar, and he did it all on an electric. If the acoustic guitar were ever going to be relevant to rock'n'roll again, it would need a powerful boost. That boost came in 1957, from the country camp. The studio band on the Everly Brothers first hit, 'Bye Bye Love,' included Don Everly on acoustic guitar – a Gibson SJ (for Southerner Jumbo). Don's father, Ike Everly, was an accomplished country guitarist, and the brothers had grown up playing and singing in the family group. Their friend, country guitar great Chet Atkins, had shown Don an open-G tuning so he could play the country fiddle standard 'Black Mountain Rag,' but Don found new power in the open tuning: "You can sit in a bathroom and it makes you sound like an orchestra," he said. On 'Bye Bye Love,' he tuned to open-G, and every time the title line was sung he answered by running his hand far up the neck and playing a short rhythmic figure. The engineer on the session, Bill Porter, noticed Don's guitar fills and goosed them up in the mix every time they occurred. "The arrangement for 'Bye Bye Love' is a direct lift from a song I wrote called 'Give Me the Future,' ironically," Don recalled. "If that arrangement hadn't been on 'Bye Bye Love,' I don't think it would have done anything at all." Don's guitar work on 'Bye Bye Love' was prominent, but it was tame compared to his opening on the Everlys' next hit, 'Wake Up Little Susie.' Still in open-G tuning but starting seven frets up in D, Don hit the guitar with full, hard strums, playing a blunt chord progression – D, F, G, F, D – and changing chords against the beat. It was a jarring jolt of power – not the focused, cutting power of an electric guitar but a full, wide resonant force, a hurricane rather than a tornado. Where had it come from? "I was a big fan of Bo Diddley – that rhythm stuff," Don explained. "And I took that and interpreted it for country music. It was very helpful. Chet taught me the tuning and the chord progressions. Bo doesn't really use chords."

The Gibson SJ that Don Everly played represented Gibson's answer to Martin's D-18. Don Everly grew up in a Gibson family:

his father had always played Gibsons. Don was usually pictured with a J-200, and later his own Gibson Everly Brothers model, but he always wrote his songs on the SJ. Another seminal 1950s rocker, Buddy Holly, was always pictured with a Fender Stratocaster, but his songwriting guitar was a Gibson J-45. A year after Don Everly showed the potential of an acoustic rhythm guitar in a lead role, Eddie Cochran took the concept all the way, building entire records around the strummed acoustic. Although Cochran is always identified with a Gretsch electric, his signature sound on record was a Martin acoustic. After a debut single as a rather sickly Elvis copyist ('Sittin' in the Balcony'), he found his own voice in 1958 with 'Summertime Blues.' The rhythm guitar part was a single-string, reverb-laden line on an electric, sort of a bridge between Chuck Berry and the surf guitar sound

■ *C.F. Martin & Co of Nazareth, Pennsylvania, would prove the most potent influence on the flat-top guitar; the cosmetics and design of Martin instruments have been copied by every acoustic maker. Christian Friedrich Martin commenced making guitars in New York in 1833, moving to Pennsylvania six years later. Martin introduced its distinctive bracing, shown being crafted above, around 1850, to create essentially the first modern American flat-top.*

of the 1960s. The "lead" was a freely strummed acoustic. 'C'mon Everybody,' Cochran's 1959 single and the last before his death in a car wreck in 1960, followed the same formula.

Christian Friedrich Martin worked with Viennese guitar maker Johann Stauffer before emigrating to America. Stauffer's influence is obvious in early Martins: this 1830s example features Stauffer's distinctive headstock design.

The Everly Brothers were Gibson's first rock'n'roll-oriented endorsees. The Gibson Everly Brothers acoustic, shown left, was based on the Gibson J-185, fitted with oversized pickguards and an adjustable bridge reputedly designed by Ike Everly.

43

Martin OM-28
Introduced: 1930

Although the Martin Orchestra Model only remained in the range for three years, many of its features were incorporated into subsequent Martins, most notably the joining of the neck to the body at the 14th fret. This arrangement, suggested by banjo player Perry Bechtel, would become a standard configuration for flat-top guitars.

CF Martin Guitar Catalogue

Martin D-28
Introduced: 1931

The Martin Dreadnought, initially produced for the Boston company Ditson, was manufactured under Martin's own name from 1932 in D-18 and D-28 versions. The example shown here dates from 1951, and features the plain black-and-white binding introduced in 1947.

Gibson Nick Lucas Model

Introduced: 1928

The Lucas Model was one of Gibson's first flat-tops. This 1920s example's ivoroid fingerboard was custom-ordered.

Gibson J-200

Introduced: 1938

This large body flat-top was designed for country star Ray Whitley.

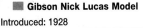

Gibson J-45

Introduced: 1942

This 1940s J-45 echoes Martin's dreadnought shape, but with 'sloping' shoulders.

The Folk Boom

As the 1960s began, the acoustic guitar's popularity grew beyond all imagination – but not in rock. It was the folk era of popular music. The Kingston Trio set the stage in 1958 with the soft strumming of 'Tom Dooley.' Peter Paul and Mary, probably the most influential act on the guitar playing masses of that era, fingerpicked classical-style nylon-string guitars. The 12-string guitar rose for a brief moment, and its power was displayed in such hits as the New Christy Minstrels' 'Green Green' and the Rooftop Singers' 'Walk Right In,' both in 1963. But when rock players such as George Harrison and Roger McGuinn discovered the 12-string it was in the electric format. After the 1950s the acoustic guitar might seem to show up only occasionally in rock music. There are plenty of examples of rock artists featuring acoustic guitars – from the Beatles' intricate fingerpicked 'Blackbird,' the Rolling Stones' ballad 'As Tears Go By' and Led

Zeppelin's FM radio perennial 'Stairway to Heaven' to MTV's *Unplugged* series in the 1990s. But is it rock'n'roll? By strict definition, no ballad can be rock'n'roll. If a song is performed in a manner suitable to acoustic guitar accompaniment, then it's probably not going to be rock'n'roll. Or so a rock purist's argument would go. But the argument is academic. The sound of the acoustic guitar continued to permeate rock'n'roll.

The early career of the Beatles – the only musical phenomenon to rival Elvis in terms of cultural influence – has a remarkable similarity to that of Elvis when it comes to the acoustic guitar. Like Elvis's first record, the Beatles' first, 'Love Me Do,' was built around an acoustic guitar with no electric guitar at all. George Harrison, the group's lead electric guitarist, played acoustic rhythm on a Gibson J-160E (a flat-top guitar that ironically was equipped with a pickup). John Lennon filled in lead parts on harmonica. As with Elvis, one has to ask, where did the whole idea of an acoustic guitar come from? Old photographs suggest that the Beatles never brought an acoustic guitar onstage, but on a business card for the Quarrymen (Lennon's schoolboy group) they claimed skiffle, country and Western music in their repertoire, so there was plenty of acoustic guitar in the music they grew up with. The acoustic guitar that Harrison and Lennon both bought in 1962 was an odd model, the Gibson J-160E. The J-160E was designed for the player who wanted the look of an acoustic flat top guitar but the sound of an electric, for its acoustic capabilities had been severely limited by a laminated top with straight-across "ladder" braces. This simple construction took away some of the volume and some of the rich tonality, but that may well have made the J-160E better for recording purposes. The Beatles and their producer George Martin obviously thought so, employing the J-160E to carry the rhythm on 'Love Me Do' and plugging it in to get an acoustic/electric blend for the rhythm of 'P.S. I Love You.' The Beatles made extensive use of acoustic guitars to give the rhythm a broader tonal range, as illustrated in their 1965 hits 'Eight Days a Week' and 'Help.' They moved on from the J-160E to other models. By 1965 Paul McCartney had bought an Epiphone Texan. Epiphone was by then owned by Gibson, and aside from some differences in ornamentation, the Texan was essentially a J-45. This is the guitar McCartney strummed on 'Yesterday.' By 1967, when the Beatles filmed a performance of 'Hello Goodbye,' Lennon was playing a Martin D-18.

The Rolling Stones' first hit, a remake of Buddy Holly's 'Not Fade Away' in 1964, sounded more than anything like an Eddie Cochran record, with the 'Bo Diddley' rhythm out front on an acoustic guitar. And like the Beatles' first record, the Stones used harmonica for lead (with electric guitar only coming in for a tribute-to-Buddy solo). A year later they hit No. 1 for the first time with 'Satisfaction,' best known for its distorted single-string lead

Bob Dylan helped trigger the folk boom, before teaming up with Paul Butterfield's electric band, and outraging the purists. Dylan has used various Martin and Gibson flat-tops; here, recording in the CBS studios circa 1963, he is using a well-worn late 1940s Gibson J-50.

electric guitar line, but successful as a record in part because of the hard driving acoustic rhythm guitar. With the Stones, as with the Beatles, the image of an electric guitar overshadows the acoustic reality. Their guitarist, Keith Richards, established what is now a classic rock'n'roll rhythm lick on electric guitar, alternating between the I and IV chords in an open tuning, and that's what comes to mind when you think of the Rolling Stones' music. But when you listen to it, as often as not the rhythm is powered along by an acoustic. On 'Street Fighting Man,' the archetypal Richards crunch comes from a multilayered acoustic guitar, compressed through a primitive cassette recorder. "I'd call that an electric sound," says Richards. "When I really learned how to use an acoustic, and investigated different tunings, it helped change the sound of the band."

One of the strongest influences on acoustic rock guitar goes almost unnoticed because his influence on electric rock guitar is so powerful. That influence is Jimmy Page, Led Zeppelin's guitarist. Page's crunching electric licks on 'Whole Lotta Love' and 'Black Dog' are as much a part of the rock guitar lexicon as

Always associated with electrics, The Beatles (above) used Gibson and Epiphone acoustics throughout their career, including the J-160E. This early Gibson attempt at an electric-acoustic features a magnetic pickup and heavily-braced top.

Chuck Berry's lead licks, a template for the generation of 'hard rock' guitarists to come. They created an overpowering image of Led Zeppelin as an electric guitar band, but surprisingly Page not only made wide use of the acoustic guitar, he did it in a way that was more intricate and more assimilated into a musical whole than either the Beatles or the Stones. Much of what was

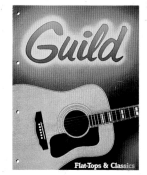

characteristic about Page's playing came from his acoustic influences, in particular that of Bert Jansch, who employed traditional English folk tunings (most notably the 'DADGAD' tuning). For Page, the acoustic guitar was often an instrument of coloration and ornamentation, the same as a keyboard. He used acoustics freely for lead, rhythm and everything in between. His acoustic filigrees on 'Over the Hills and Far Away' are a part of every young rocker's repertoire. And his acoustic accompaniment to 'Stairway to Heaven,' the anthem of FM-rock radio, is so well-known that many guitar stores have signs in their tryout rooms reading "No Stairway to Heaven."

Acoustic Punks

In 1966, anyone who thought the acoustic guitar would never again be out front in rock'n'roll came to a rude awakening, courtesy of 'Wild Thing' by the Troggs. It's hard to keep a straight face and talk seriously about this record. 'Wild Thing' is not the best of anything, in terms of style, music, lyric, performance or production. It's just a raw display of the power of an acoustic guitar – the 'Louie Louie' of the acoustic. Two months later Neil Diamond's breakthrough single 'Cherry Cherry' also illustrated the power of an acoustic guitar – but with infinitely more sophistication. Diamond's record harked back to the power-strumming of a decade earlier. Don Everly recalls one reviewer saying Diamond had taken the intro to 'Wake Up Little Susie' and made it into a whole song.

By the second half of the 1960s, there was more to the acoustic guitar in rock'n'roll than hard strumming. Paul Simon was instrumental in bringing the folkie fingerpickers and the rock strummers together. Although Simon once commented satirically in song – "Folk rock, whatever that is" – his recordings with Art Garfunkel, beginning with 'The Sounds of Silence' in 1965, defined the genre. Simon was a true virtuoso on acoustic guitar. On ballads, like 'Homeward Bound' (1966) or 'Scarborough Fair/Canticle' (1968), his fingerpicked licks were a signature part of the song. But when he wanted to rock, he stayed on acoustic, mixing picking and strumming together on hits like 'I Am a Rock' (1966) or 'Mrs. Robinson' (1968).

An early notion of what would become a full-scale movement for the acoustic guitar in rock'n'roll came in 1967 with Buffalo Springfield's 'For What It's Worth (Stop, Hey What's That Sound).' This anthem of the hippie culture had as its signature sound the harmonic tone of an electric guitar, but the beat was clearly set by an acoustic guitar. Two years later, one of the creative forces behind 'For What It's Worth,' Stephen Stills, introduced a new group that would push the acoustic guitar forward into a lead role in rock music. Vocally, he worked in tight harmony with David Crosby and Graham Nash but musically, the sound of Crosby, Stills and Nash was Stills' Martin D-28. The powerful sound of Stills' D-28 – full yet bright – came about as a mistake, according to Bill Halverson, who engineered the sessions.

Halverson had worked before on Buffalo Springfield sessions, as well as some Stills and Crosby demos, but he was unprepared for the music of CS&N. "They walked in without calling ahead for any setup or anything," Halverson recalled. "I asked 'What do you want to do,' and David said, 'Stephen is going to play some acoustic guitar.'" That turned out to be an understatement. Stills unpacked his pre-World War II 'herringbone' D-28; to a guitar player, a herringbone D-28 is the most powerful guitar ever made, but to Halverson, the "full and rounded" sound translates to "pretty dull, even with new strings." On the recording console he boosted the high frequencies and rolled off the low frequencies to reduce the D-28's inherent boominess. He also added compression, but still, he recalled, "It didn't sound very good at all." Before Halverson could make any more adjustments, Stills started playing. "I knew from my live recording days to punch 'Record,'" he said. "It was so loud, so bright and so over-compressed, my young career began to disappear before my eyes. He played for what seemed like an hour; it was seven-and-a-half minutes. All the guys in the booth are having a great time. I'm sweating, thinking it's over. At the end they come in, saying, 'It's wonderful, let's hear it back.' Stephen said, 'That's the best my guitar ever sounded. How'd you do it?' I just said, 'Thank you.'" Bass and drums were later overdubbed, but the only guitar on the song remained Stills' D-28. The song was 'Suite: Judy Blue Eyes,' the showpiece of Crosby, Stills and Nash's debut album and a hit single for them in 1969. Another song on the album, the catchy, alliterative 'Helplessly Hoping,' featured a solo fingerpicked guitar part that became a favorite of amateur musicians. It may be argued that these weren't really

This Ovation Collectors limited edition of 1990 uses spectacular maple for the top and headstock facing. The guitar also sports a complex computer-designed array of soundholes, which replace the usual central hole.

rock'n'roll recordings, but Stills was unarguably a rock musician, as respected on electric guitar as on acoustic. Moreover, his work blurred the lines between acoustic and electric in rock'n'roll. And, as Bill Halverson pointed out, "Hey, it's all rock'n'roll."

The Age Of The Powerstrum

As the 1970s dawned, power-strumming was reaching a peak of perfection. In 1970, George Harrison's post-Beatle debut, 'My Sweet Lord,' kicked off with the strongest acoustic strum since 'Wild Thing.' That same year the film *Woodstock*, chronicling the infamous 1969 rock festival, featured a stirring solo performance of the song 'Freedom' by Richie Havens, with an awesome display of open-E power-strumming on a Guild acoustic. Rod Stewart's 1971 breakthrough single 'Maggie May' was built around a crashing acoustic rhythm guitar. B.W. Stevenson's 1973 hit 'My Maria' featured the resonant bass strings of an acoustic guitar, hard-played by session ace Larry Coryell.

The acoustic sound was back in rock'n'roll. But there was a catch. It was never more obvious than in Crosby, Stills and Nash's performance of 'Suite: Judy Blue Eyes' in *Woodstock*. The powerful resonances of Stills' D-28 seemed to have been left in the recording studio. The notes were there but the sound was not. Onstage, the acoustic guitar was still a nightmare for a sound engineer. It was prone to feedback, so it could never be turned up loud enough. And the player had to stand still in front of the microphone; the acoustic guitar would never be a full-fledged rock'n'roll instrument until someone figured out how to free it from a microphone. There had been electrified flat-tops since the 1950s, such as Gibson's CF-100E and J-160E or Martin's D-18E and D-28E, but these had conventional electric guitar pickups installed on an acoustic guitar. Plugged in, they didn't sound like acoustic guitars anymore. They sounded like electrics – only worse. None of the natural resonance of the instrument came through the electro-magnetic pickup. The acoustic guitar needed amplification technology that picked up the natural tonality of the instrument.

Piezos To Go

The basic technology for this pickup had been discovered almost a century earlier, in 1880. Certain natural crystals, when pressed or squeezed, send out an electrical signal, called piezo-electricity after the Greek word for "press." By World War II this property could be induced into man-made ceramic materials. It seemed like a simple enough step to make a guitar bridge saddle out of this material and just plug it in. That's what Gibson did with a classical guitar, the C-1E in 1960. (It was a doomed model, since classical guitarists usually play seated and for that reason would be among those least in need of a pickup.) But the promise of easy amplification from piezo-electric materials was too good to be true. "It works without any engineering whatsoever," explained Larry Fishman, one of the leading designers and makers of pickups for acoustics. "You can take a piece and solder some wires to it, stick it on an instrument and you get a noise. I wouldn't call it a sound, but unfortunately that's where all the early applications were. They got a bad rap because they weren't properly engineered." The sound industry turned its focus to special microphones for acoustic guitars. Some were suspended inside the guitar through the soundhole; others were "contact" mikes, taped or glued directly to the top of the instrument. They were still prone to feedback at higher volumes, but delivered a

■ *Jimmy Page's foremost guitar influences were bluesman Hubert Sumlin, and folkie Bert Jansch. Led Zeppelin's mainly acoustic album* Led Zeppelin 3 *made heavy use of traditional English tunings associated with Jansch. Page's 1990s recordings with Robert Plant have again stressed his acoustic roots.*

■ *The Ovation Custom Legend (top) bears typical Ovation features of fiberglass bowl-shaped back, wooden top and built in pickup – all of which have been frequently copied. Ovation has since launched its own Korean-made Applause range.*

truer sound than the early piezo pickups. Consequently, when a new piezo-amplified classical guitar was introduced under the Baldwin and Gretsch brands in 1969 it went virtually unnoticed. Then in 1970 Glen Campbell, at the height of his career with hit records and a hit TV show, appeared on the *Tonight* show. Campbell was well-known for playing Ovation guitars, the new fiberglass-backed acoustic guitars, but for this performance he borrowed a guitar from country star Jerry Reed. It was one of the Baldwin electrics. The guitar industry as a whole may not have paid much attention, but Ovation head Charlie Kaman did. Campbell's endorsement was the lifeblood of the young company (Kaman had founded Kaman Aerospace in 1945 to build helicopters and diversified into guitars with Ovation, beginning in 1965) and Kaman was on the phone before the show was over, scrambling Ovation into action.

First, Ovation installed a Baldwin pickup in Campbell's Ovation. Then they licensed the Baldwin pickup for use in Ovations while engineer Jim Rickard developed and patented an improved piezo bridge pickup. When they brought it to market, two factors helped Ovation corner this new market for 'acoustic/electric' guitars. First, they built the pickup into their guitars rather than offering it as an 'after-market' accessory. Second, they designed the pickup for steel-stringed guitars – rock'n'roll guitars – rather than classicals. Compared to Ovation's built-in pickup, other systems, which required installation and a separate preamp, seemed unnecessarily cumbersome. Ovations already had a reputation for durability, and with easy plug-in capability, they quickly became the preferred guitar for performing musicians. The biggest threat to Ovation's dominance of the acoustic/electric market came in 1975 from the Japanese-made Takamine guitars – conventional wood-body guitars with excellent electronics. But Takamine was really no threat at all. Ovation owned part of Takamine and was the exclusive distributor in the U.S., so Ovation was able to actively promote rather than fight the newcomer. Like Ovations, Takamines proliferated in live performance venues, from cocktail lounges to the concert stages of such stars as Bruce Springsteen. The effects of Ovation and Takamine on the acoustic guitar world were profound. As the magnetic pickup had done for the electric guitar several decades earlier, the piezo pickup freed guitar designers from traditional acoustic construction. Some acoustic properties, such as natural resonance, were still important, but natural volume was no longer one of them. Acoustic guitars began to take on radical new shapes, with cutaway bodies and extra-thin bodies. Chet Atkins, by this time a legendary guitarist, took the concept to its ultimate end – a solidbody 'acoustic' guitar. As a Gretsch endorser in the 1960s, he had pushed Baldwin unsuccessfully to further develop the piezo pickup. After terminating his Gretsch endorsement in 1978, he took matters into his own hands and began working with luthier Hascal Haille to develop a solidbody guitar with a piezo pickup. Gibson brought the new model to market in 1982 as the Chet Atkins CE. It had nylon strings – CE stood for Classic Electric – which Chet had come to prefer. He never envisioned it as anything but a classical guitar, but its solidbody design made it almost free of feedback problems, which made it ideal for rock'n'roll. The only thing it needed was steel strings, which Gibson added in 1987. The Chet Atkins SST, as the steel-stringed version of this revolutionary instrument was called, found a home in the music of such rockers as Mark Knopfler and Sting.

Unplugged

Just as the acoustic guitar was finally catching up to the electric in performance capability, just when the acoustic was becoming truly assimilated into rock'n'roll music, MTV pulled the plug, so to speak, drawing a line once again between acoustic and electric guitars. MTV, the music-video TV channel, arranged for a series of *Unplugged* concerts by rock'n'roll acts, all on acoustic instruments. (*Unplugged* was of course a figurative term; the instruments were acoustic, but many of them had piezo pickups and were indeed plugged in.) A pilot, featuring Squeeze (Glenn Tilbrook and Chris Difford) with Elliott Easton of the Cars helping on guitar and vocalist Syd Straw, aired on November 11, 1989. The subsequent series was an unqualified success for MTV, attracting not only acoustic veterans such as Crosby, Stills and Nash, Bob Dylan and Paul Simon, but a diverse group of previously all-electric artists highlighted by Stevie Ray Vaughan, Hall and Oates, Elton John, Aerosmith and Nirvana. (A notable holdout to the concept, but not the show, was Bruce Springsteen, who played most of his show "plugged.") *Unplugged* didn't represent a new direction in rock'n'roll as much as it offered interesting new arrangements of old songs. Rock or not, these were shining hours for acoustic guitars.

The biggest *Unplugged* success was Eric Clapton's segment, first aired on March 11, 1992. The man who pioneered the concept of 'power trio' in the late 1960s with Cream, the man whose electric guitar prowess inspired devotees to write "Clapton is God" all over public places, was suddenly one of the world's leading acoustic guitarists. Clapton's show yielded not only a hit album and two hit singles – 'Tears in Heaven' and a laid-back version of 'Layla' – but a hit guitar as well. One of the guitars Clapton played was a vintage Martin 00-42 (smaller than the dreadnought, with abalone pearl trim). The Martin company took notice and struck a deal to reissue it as the Eric Clapton signature model. Unveiled at a 1995 trade show, it sold out its limited run of 461 before the show was over. *Unplugged* helped put the acoustic guitar in the rock'n'roll spotlight, which prompted amplifier designers to develop new amps that accommodated the wider range of tonalities of an acoustic guitar. New versions of the old contact microphone reappeared – not replacing but complementing the piezo. By the mid-1990s, with special amps for acoustic guitars and 'hybrid' onboard amplification, acoustic guitarists onstage could come closer than ever to the true, natural sound of their instruments.

Fly Times

At the same time *Unplugged* was separating acoustic guitars from electrics, a former guitar repairman in Boston was joining them at the hip. Ken Parker's creation, called the Parker Fly because of its ultra light weight, sported a conventional magnetic pickup and a piezo pickup together on one solidbody guitar. The melding of modern and traditional ideas was one of Parker's original concepts: "I was inspired by a combination of Renaissance lute making and modern high strength-to-weight ratios in racing toys – particularly sailboats," he said. A futurist would predict that the influence of the Fly, the Godin LG, the Burns Nu-Sonic and others would mean that the new sound in rock'n'roll would be a hybrid of acoustic and electric sounds. And early evidence points in that direction. Dave Navarro of the Red Hot Chili Peppers and David Bowie's bandleader Reeves Gabrels are among the first converts to the Parker Fly, and the sound has appeared uncredited on records by artists who endorse other brands. Furthermore, Larry Fishman has uncovered a strong after-market demand for the Parker-style piezo unit. However, history sometimes takes left turns, and new technology doesn't always continue in the direction it started. Some piezo pickup

Gibson Chet Atkins CE

Introduced: 1982

Chet Atkins designed this radical solid body classical guitar after his endorsement deal with the Gretsch company expired. Its steel string version has been used by Sting and Atkins fan Mark Knopfler.

systems are actually six individual systems, one for each string. These 'hex' systems break down the guitar sound into components that digital sound tinkerers can handle. In other words, the potential of the guitar synthesizer may finally be fully explored. "The Roland Virtual Guitar, the VG-8, is very at home with a piezo under the saddle with hex outputs," Larry Fishman pointed out. "They do all kinds of interesting morphing of sounds. It flips the whole thing back. What begat what? The electric or the acoustic or the synth?" Technology has blurred the lines between acoustic and electric guitars today. What looks like an electric can sound like an acoustic, and vice versa. But if you get lost, all you have to do is go back to the beginning of rock'n'roll. And at the beginning was one rockin' acoustic guitar.

Eric Clapton's 1992 appearance on MTV's Unplugged *generated a hit program, a hit CD, and a hit guitar. Martin launched the 000-42EC Limited Edition Signature model (inset) based on Clapton's 00-42. All 461 examples – the number derived from Clapton's 1974 album* 461 Ocean Boulevard *– were sold at the launch show.*

Synthesizers & Hi-Tech

"A case could be made that MIDI, together with the new generation of synthesizers, has been the single most significant musical instrument development since the electric guitar."

DAVE SMITH, FOUNDER OF SEQUENTIAL CIRCUITS

Popular music is an electronic medium: recorded by electronic means, distributed by electronic means and, from the 1960s, played using electronic means. It has taken the advent of the microprocessor for synthesizers and electronic instruments to assume a significant role within popular music, but in reality electronics have played a crucial part in the development of musical theory and style ever since the invention of the telephone demonstrated to the public and musicians that sound could be created and manipulated electronically.

In the post-WWII era, when popular music was evolving rapidly, electronically produced music was a strictly classically orientated phenomenon. Early 20th century composers like Scriabin, Richard Strauss, Satie and the Italian Futurists had consistently searched for new modes of expression, many of them embracing musique concrète - sounds taken from non-musical sources. Others were inspired by experimenters such as William Duddell, who in 1899 demonstrated a 'singing' electrical arc; and Thaddeus Cahill, whose amazing 200-ton Telharmonium used giant inductor alternators linked to rotating cogged wheels to produce music over the telephone network. In the 1920s and 1930s, more practical electronic musical instruments were developed by Friedrich Trautwein (the Trautonium), Maurice Martenot (the Ondes Martenot); and most crucially Lev Termen (the Theremin). The Theremin used an oscillator, the frequency and volume of which varied according to the proximity of the player's hands to the Theremin's two aerials; the vertical rod aerial controlled pitch, the horizontal looped aerial controlled pitch. The Theremin's expressive 'hands off' playing technique added to the novelty of its eerie sound, and it was played in regular recitals throughout America in the 1930s. Later it was much used in soundtracks for horror and science fiction films such as Bernard Herrmann's for *The Day The Earth Stood Still*, before gradually finding its way into popular music, most famously in the Beach Boys' 1966 single 'Good Vibrations.'

Composers such as John Cage, Karlheinz Stockhausen, Anton Webern, Edgard Varese and Vladimir Ussachevsky of the Columbia-Princeton Electronic Music Centre experimented with avant-garde forms of composition and novel methods of processing, from the 1930s to the 1960s. However, this remained a strictly highbrow taste, and if the average listener heard 'electronic' music, it was probably a movie soundtrack such as Louis and Bebe Barron's for *Forbidden Planet*, or television theme music such as that of the celebrated U.K. science-fiction serial, *Doctor Who*, from the BBC's Radiophonic Workshop under Delia Derbyshire. By the early 1960s, and the blossoming of rock music, the time was ripe for the development of an electronic instrument which would be both practical to use, and available to a wider market. Hence the real story of the synthesizer starts in 1964 with the work of Robert Moog.

Lev 'Leon' Termen, pictured in 1927, demonstrates the forerunner of today's synthesizers, the Theremin. The player's left hand controls volume, the right hand pitch.

The Advent of The Moog

In 1964 Robert A. Moog (it rhymes with 'rogue') published the paper *Voltage-Controlled Electronic Music Modules* for the Audio Engineering Society of America. Several other experimenters, including Don Buchla and the German Harold Bode, were working along the same lines, but Moog is generally credited as the inventor of the definitive synthesizer. An electrical engineer who has never claimed to be a musician himself, Moog became fascinated with the Theremin, built one for himself in 1949, and went on to construct and sell over 1000. This success led to experiments with voltage control of audio modules, which resulted in Moog selling his first modular synthesizer system in 1964. Moog's modular systems were complex beasts: vast cabinets containing many separate modules studded with knobs, sliders and sockets, connected together with

The Moog modular system, which appeared in 1964, was bulky and expensive, but versatile. Although later systems were easier to use, their pre-programmed routing restricted sonic options compared to this complex pioneer.

Robert Moog, pictured circa 1971 with a MiniMoog, defined the architecture of the analog synthesizer.

The U.K.'s Electronic Music Systems was an early rival to Robert Moog: the company's VCS-3, or 'Putney' was patched by means of a pinboard, and was used extensively by Pink Floyd.

jungles of patch cords (hence the term 'patch' for a programmed synth sound). These early synthesizers were generally monophonic: capable of playing one note at a time.

Both electronically and conceptually, Moog broke down the elements of a synthesizer into oscillators, filters, and amplifiers. Moog's concept allowed for each of these parameters to be voltage controlled, and thus continuously variable. Moog patented designs for voltage controlled oscillators, filters and amplifiers which, although frequently imitated by other manufacturers, were rarely matched.

Other companies such as E-mu and ARP competed to sell modular systems, but Moog's association with Walter (now Wendy) Carlos proved a turning point. Carlos realized that the sonic flexibility of the synthesizer combined with multi-track recording techniques could suggest a new approach to classical music, and recorded what was at one time the biggest-selling classical LP, *Switched-On Bach*, using a Moog modular system. The album fanfared the advent of the synthesizer.

In the U.K., Peter Zinovieff's E.M.S. (Electronic Music Systems) produced a more manageable system with 1969's VCS-3 (Voltage Controlled Studio), or 'Putney'. This wooden-cased oddity was also available in a black ABS briefcase with a $2^{1}/_{2}$-octave capacitance-triggered non-mechanical 'touch' keyboard featuring a monophonic digital sequencer, the Synthi-A KS. EMS's instruments replaced the patch cables of typical modular systems with a pinboard matrix, and a joystick was provided for weird performance effects.

53

54

 In 1972 many performers regarded modular monophonic synthesizers as unsuitable for live performance: Keith Emerson set out to prove this was untrue...

Analog Synthesis

The basic electronic components of analog synthesis are the oscillator, noise generator, modulator, filter, amplifier and mixer.

The high frequency **Voltage-Controlled Oscillator** (VCO) produces an audible pitch which can be controlled by a voltage from, say, a keyboard. The harmonic content of the signal is determined by the waveshape of the oscillator. A sine wave gives a pure, flute-like tone; a sawtooth or triangle

■ *Stevie Wonder was a pioneering user of the ARP2600 monophonic. His customized example features Braille panel labels.*

■ **MiniMoog**
Introduced: 1971
The definitive monophonic synthesizer.

analog sequences, washes of Mellotron sound and strange VCS3 tonalities, *Phaedra* developed a whole new musical style, as well as using a new sound palette. Variously described as 'ambient,' 'trance,' 'New Age,' or 'EM,' the classic Tangerine Dream sound is still enormously influential. Crucially, Tangerine Dream was always as much a live as a studio act, using an arsenal of instruments including Moog modular systems, Mellotrons, early EMS and ARP synths, later Roland and Korg polysynths, and custom-built digital sequencers. The best-remembered line-up of Edgar Froese, Christoph Franke and Peter Baumann began to fragment in 1977, and after several personnel changes the band now survives in the form of Froese and his son Jerome.

Working along parallel lines, Klaus Schulze started his musical career as a drummer for Psy Free before joining an early incarnation of Tangerine Dream in 1969. He later played with Ash Ra Tempel and the Cosmic Jokers before going solo to concentrate on experiments with keyboards, first with organs and oscillators, then with synths. His style developed into what has been called 'classic EM' (Electronic Music), and is still enormously influential. Though he has dabbled with classical, operatic and dance forms, Schulze admits, "My style of music is always the same, but the expression is different... it's like Fellini said; 'I made so many films, but in the end I did only one film.'"

Keith Emerson's keyboard antics with Emerson Lake and Palmer became legendary, and his use of the bulky Moog modular system and later the Yamaha GS-1 pioneered electronic stage performance.

The MiniMoog

Despite the heroic efforts of the likes of Tangerine Dream and Keith Emerson, for most players modular synths were expensive and impractical – particularly for live performance.

Robert Moog tackled the problem in 1971 with the launch of the MiniMoog, of which over 13,000 were eventually sold. This legendary synth, now enormously sought after and much imitated, had three advantages. Its oscillators, mixers, filter and envelopes were pre-patched in a logical, performance-oriented

The Synthesizer In Performance

Early modular synthesizers had several major drawbacks. They were huge; expensive; complex to use; could not memorize sound patches; and were usually monophonic. Though normally confined to recording studios, they were also used on stage, notably by German synthesizer pioneers Tangerine Dream and Klaus Schulze, and by Keith Emerson of The Nice and ELP.

Tangerine Dream evolved from its roots in 1967 as a free-form psychedelic jazz ensemble into the definitive synthesizer band. After several experimental releases, the commercial breakthrough was the 1974 album *Phaedra*, championed by John Peel and released on the Virgin label. Combining burbling

---

wave a harsher, buzzing note; a squarewave, a reedy tone.
Oscillator pitch can also be affected by a **Low Frequency Oscillator** *(LFO, or modulator). The LFO's sub-audio frequency signals, used to modulate the VCO, create a vibrato effect. Noise generators create an apparently random hissing which can be filtered into different types such as white, red or pink. Noise sources can then be combined with the output from VCOs of different waveforms and footages (pitch*

ranges) in the mixer stage.
The Voltage-Controlled Filter *(VCF) removes, or subtracts, certain components from the frequency spectrum of the audio signal - analog synthesis is sometimes referred to as subtractive synthesis, for this reason. Different types of filter - High Band, Low Band, Band-Pass and so on - will emphasize or de-emphasize different elements of the sound, and at its peak setting the filter can often resonate to act as a form of VCO itself. The*

performance of the filter is the dominant factor in defining the sonic signature of a particular synthesizer.
Levels of each of these preceding components can be controlled by a **Voltage Controlled Amplifier** *(VCA). The VCA is usually equipped with an envelope controller which defines the 'shape' of the effect; commonly, it will have stages for Attack, Decay, Sustain and Release (ADSR), which respectively set the speed with which the envelope builds up (quickly for a piano, more*

slowly for a violin, say); the speed at which it drops to a constant volume; the level of this constant volume; and the speed at which it fades after the sustain portion, when the key is released.
The VCF can also have an ADSR section, which allows the tonality to change over the length of a note. Pre-patched syntns such as the MiniMoog have a fixed signal path (VCO-LFO-Mixer-VCF-VCA), but modular systems or more flexible synths allow free cross-connection.

layout; it was portable, with the front panel folding down into the case for transport; and it was relatively affordable, initially costing around $1,495. Most importantly, it was truly playable, with pitchbend and modulation wheels, and a distinctive, powerful sound which was ideal for strong lead lines and thumping basses. The MiniMoog was used by Rick Wakeman and Patrick Moraz (on solo albums and with Yes), Jan Hammer (who developed a powerful electric guitar patch using a MiniMoog and Oberheim modules), Tim Blake (with Gong and solo) and Keith Emerson, who sometimes abandoned the keyboard in favor of ribbon and drum controllers. For live work the synthesizer would typically be used as a lead instrument, with chordal parts left to organs, electric pianos and string ensembles.

Oberheim DS-2
Introduced: 1972

Pioneering sequencer – with just 72 notes.

The main competition for Moog came from E-Mu's modular systems and from another American company, ARP, named after founder Alan R. Pearlman. ARP offered the 2500 modular system, and from 1970 the 2600, a large semi-modular synth with a pin-board patchbay, used by Joe Zawinul, Edgar Winter (on *Frankenstein*) and Stevie Wonder. Later came the compact ARP Odyssey, a monophonic performance synth favored by Chick Corea, and generally judged to be more flexible if less powerful than the MiniMoog. Development of the monophonic synthesizer continued as Tom Oberheim, who at one stage designed modifications for ARP synths, introduced the OB-1, the first monophonic synth with programmable patch memories, while Moog Music went on to produce other monophonic synths like the Multimoog and Micromoog, the cheap and cheerful Rogue and Prodigy, and the programmable Source.

Sequencing Events

The development of electronic music can be divided into two areas: sound sources, and controllers. Analog synths were developed in tandem with sequential voltage controllers - 'sequencers'. Analog sequencers featured rows of potentiometers which were adjusted to set pitch, filter setting, transposition and trigger information. The number of notes in a sequence was limited by the number of 'pots'; thus early users relied on repetitive 8- or 16-note sequences. Hence, the technology was defining the compositional style of the music. Later analog sequencers from ARP, Roland and Korg refined the triggering capabilities of the machines, but did not add to their note capacity. What was needed was a system which could turn

control voltage information into digital data and back again, offering larger note storage capacity.

In 1972 Oberheim introduced the DS-2, a 72-note monophonic digital sequencer, but it wasn't until 1977 that Roland's MC-8 Micro-Composer, appeared. Used by Japanese classical stylist Isao Tomita, American keyboard player Suzanne Ciani, and Toto's Steve Porcaro, the MC-8 featured a 5000-note memory, and eight voltage-controlled monophonic channels. Data was entered numerically using a keypad, and could be saved to cassette tape. MC-8 sequences could be synchronized with previous takes by 'striping' one track on the tape – recording a synchronization signal which, fed back from the tape to the sequencer, would synchronize new sequences with already recorded ones. The less expensive MC-4 appeared later, and, with the development of MIDI, machines like the Roland MSQ-700 and Yamaha QX1 became popular. Roland's MC-500, launched in 1986, is typical of advanced digital sequencers; it featured MIDI IN, OUT and THRU, an LCD panel, a 3½" disk drive, five mergeable tracks, step-time and real-time recording, extensive quantisation and editing features, and a 25,000-note memory. One of the most quirky 'sequencers' was the Roland TB-303 Bassline, designed to produce bass accompaniments for the TR-606 drum machine. The Bassline was hopeless at synthesizing bass sounds, and impossibly complex to program, but would later be picked up by Detroit and Chicago techno pioneers for its ability to produce psychedelic resonant 'acid' sequences. Once practically impossible to give away, the Bassline is now sought after and much imitated. Apart from some stage applications, and pocket composers like Yamaha's QY20, hardware sequencers have now largely been replaced by computer-based software sequencer programs.

Musician and programmer Larry Fast helped pioneer computer control of synthesizers, but it wasn't until the advent of MIDI that this became practical for the average musician.

Synths On Record

1951: *Bernard Herrmann's score for Robert Wise's The Day The Earth Stood Still uses Theremins and electronic oscillators.*

1952: *Otto Luenin and Vladimir Ussachevsky give the first concert of 'electronic' music on tape in the U.S.A. John Cage's experimental piece Imaginary Landscapes uses feedback and tape manipulation of natural sounds via contact mikes.*

1968: *Walter Carlos's Switched On Bach becomes a best-seller, introducing the sound of the Moog synthesizer to the mass market.*

1974: *Tangerine Dream's Phaedra introduces a new style of electronic music, combining Moog synthesizer, Mellotron sounds and VCS3 tonalities. Kraftwerk's 'Autobahn' kick-starts electro-pop. Later releases greatly influence U.K. electro-pop and U.S. house, acid and techno scenes.*

■ Although Rick Wakeman (left) was an enthusiastic user of synthesizers, probably the most significant group to explore the possibilities of purely electronic music in the long term was Tangerine Dream (Chris Franke, right) whose album Phaedra introduced 'EM' to the masses.

1975: Brian Eno invents ambient music with the album Discreet Music.

1976: Jean-Michel Jarre's 'Oxygene' is a huge world-wide hit. Using ARP synthesizers, RMI keyboards, Mellotron, Farfisa and Eminent organs and custom-designed sequencers, Jarre adds melody and rhythm to the electronic tonalities of Tangerine Dream.

1979: Georgio Moroder (producer of Donna Summer's 'I Feel Love') releases

$E=MC^2$, a live digital recording using 25 synthesizers controlled by Roland's Micro-Composer. Gary Numan's Replicas and hit single 'Are Friends Electric?' launch a wave of U.K. synthpop artists. Major albums include the The Human League's Reproduction (1979) and 1980's Travelogue, and Orchestral Manoeuvres In The Dark's self-titled debut, released in 1980.

1981: Electro-pop breaks into the mainstream with the Human League's

Dare, produced by Martin Rushent using the Roland Micro-Composer system, Roland synths and LinnDrum.

1983: New Order's definitive techno track 'Blue Monday' is driven by Oberheim DMX drum machine, Emulator 1 and Simmons electronic drums. New Order will later work with techno producer Arthur Baker.

1988: Pet Shop Boys release seminal synth-pop album Please.

1990: New York hip-hop and electro, and the Detroit techno and acid sounds of Juan Atkins, Eddie Fowlkes and Kevin Saunderson will influence UK bands such as 808 State, The Grid and Orbital.

1996: Electronics dominate the music scene, from European dance hits to the synth pop of Erasure and The Pet Shop Boys, the ambient house sounds of The Orb, Aphex Twin, and Moby, the doomy electronic rock of Nine Inch Nails, and inDustrial sound of Front Line Assembly.

Phase two: Polyphony and Programmability

Early synths were usually monophonic - capable of producing only one note at a time. They were also not programmable - once a sound had been set up, it couldn't be saved; in some cases the only solution for live performance was to have several synths set to different sounds. With the advent of cheaper microprocessors, polyphony and programmability became a far more practical proposition.

■ *Sequential Circuit's Prophet 5 (below) was a huge step forward in synthesizer technology: sonically versatile and – most crucially – programmable. Roland's Jupiter 8 (bottom), was probably its most significant long-term rival.*

Moog was one of the first companies to produce a fully polyphonic synth. The Polymoog of 1978 in effect put a complete synth-on-a-chip under each key. Unfortunately its programmability was limited and its sounds were more akin to those of an organ with a synth filter bolted on, and despite its use by artists such as Gary Numan it was not a big success. The later MemoryMoog, very much more like several MiniMoogs in one box, was a powerful and versatile instrument, later versions featuring MIDI, but it came too late to save Moog Music from Japanese competition. Bob Moog quit the company he founded in 1977, and now runs Big Briar, a small company specialising in designing exotic performance controllers and, ironically, Theremins.

The real breakthrough in polyphony and programmability came in 1978 with Sequential Circuits' Prophet 5. Realising that a fully polyphonic instrument was not practical, designer Dave Smith took elements of the ARP Odyssey's voice architecture, and basically shoved five of them in a box with a digitally-scanned keyboard and microprocessor-

■ *Oberheim pioneered the concept of polyphony, but its SEM-based systems were crushingly expensive; this is an 8-note synth which offers separate controls for each oscillator.*

controlled program memories. The Prophet 5's polyphony, programmability, lush cross-modulated sounds and powerful unison-key mode made it an instant success, and there were many revisions incorporating more program memories, better editing facilities and finally MIDI. Practically every keyboard player in the late 1970s to early 1980s played the Prophet 5; Japan's *The Tin Drum* and The Thompson Twins' *Quick Step And Side Kick* are awash with it. There was also a two-manual version, the 10, and a velocity-sensitive weighted-keyboard version, the T8. After dabbling in multi-timbral instruments like the Multi-Trak and Max, drum machines and the VS digital synth, Sequential was bought out by Yamaha in 1988. Despite the efforts of American companies – and Italian organ makers Elka who produced the excellent Synthex, as used by Keith Emerson, Jean-Michel Jarre, and later Stevie Wonder – the Japanese companies were the final winners in the polyphony war.

Poly Synthesizers

1976: Oberheim produces the massive 2-, 4- and 8-Voice synths, incorporating multiple monophonic SEMs (Synthesizer Expander Modules) and a programmer/controller keyboard. Bulky and difficult to program, the Oberheims nonetheless offer lush polyphonic sounds.

1978: Moog launches the Polymoog. Although fully polyphonic, the Polymoog's sound range and programmability are limited, and despite wide use by artists such as Gary Numan it is not a great commercial success.

1978: Sequential Circuits launches the Prophet 5. Dave Smith's design cracks the problem of polyphony by using five individual synth voice circuit boards and a keyboard with a digitally-scanned voice assignment system. The Prophet 5 is also fully programmable - original examples are popular to this day. Later versions include the dual-manual 10 and the velocity-sensitive T8.

1978: Yamaha launches the CS80, still one of the most powerful synths ever. Eight-voice polyphonic, velocity and aftertouch sensitive with a weighted keyboard, ring modulator and ribbon controller, despite its bulk and limited programmability it becomes one of the favourite instruments of players such as Vangelis and Klaus Schulze.

1978: Roland's Jupiter 4 introduces the idea of programmable, polyphonic synths at an affordable price

1981: Roland launches the Juno 6, and Korg the Polysix, both attempts to bring polyphony to the mass market, priced at about a third the cost of a Prophet 5 or Oberheim OBX. Later versions add extended programmability and MIDI.

1983: Yamaha DX7 introduces FM synthesis. Its realistic digital sounds, MIDI, velocity and aftertouch sensitivity make it a best seller, despite its lack of conventional knobs and sliders and its complex synthesis system.

The NED Synclavier II was for many years the world's most expensive musical instrument, the 32-voice version with floppy and hard disk drives, computer terminal, printer and pedals coming in at $40,000 (1983 price). So advanced that it was banned from export to the Soviet Bloc, the Synclavier was extensively used by Trevor Horn (for Frankie Goes to Hollywood, Propaganda and Grace Jones), Nile Rogers (for Grace Jones' 'Slave to the Rhythm') and Frank Zappa, who called it his 'Barking Pumpkin Digital Gratification Consort.' The Synclavier system was based on 24-harmonic synthesis, but later evolved into a multi-track direct-to-hard-disk sampler for audio/video post-production, before, inevitably, NED went bust in 1992 in the face of competition from manufacturers of increasingly affordable samplers. Nonetheless, the Synclavier is still widely used in movie and TV soundtrack productions, including Patrick Gleeson's score for *Apocalypse Now*, and Mark Snow's well-known score for *The X-Files*.

German design pioneers PPG produced early programmable monophonic synths and custom sequencers and lighting controllers for Tangerine Dream, Rolf Trostel and Thomas Dolby, and in 1982 came up with the Wave 2 synth. An 8-voice polyphonic instrument with a five-octave keyboard and built-in sequencer and arpeggiator, the Wave used 'tables' of digitally-generated waveforms, processed through analog envelopes and filters. Korg experimented with digital waveforms in the DW8000 keyboard and its derivatives, expanding on the idea with the later M1 series. Larry Fast, later programmer and live keyboard player for Peter Gabriel, experimented with the Alpha Syntauri system, based on an Apple 2 computer, but the real breakthrough for digital synthesis was Yamaha's DX7.

Rod Argent pictured here around 1980 models the typical set up for the well-heeled synthesizer user, including SCI Prophet 5,

Mellotron, the tiny Wasp synth, Yamaha's bulky but powerful CS80 polysynth, and a huge Moog modular system.

The Roland Corporation was founded in 1972 by seven designers including Ikutaro Kakehashi, designer of AceTone's early Rhythm Ace drum machine. Roland soon moved from research-and-development into manufacturing, producing programmable drum machines such as the CR-78, and later modular, monophonic and polysynths. Roland's 1978 4-voice Jupiter-4 gave way to the enormously powerful and flexible Jupiter-8 in 1981, and the more affordable Jupiter-6 in 1983.

Korg started up in 1968, producing organs and drum machines, and by 1973 had progressed to the MiniKorg monosynth, then polyphonic ensembles, the PS-3100 polyphonic modular system, and in 1978 the popular MS-10 and MS-20 monosynths and VC-10 Vocoder.

Going Digital

In conventional subtractive analog synthesis, the musician starts with a harmonically rich source, filtering out unwanted harmonics to define the sound. As computer systems became cheaper, exciting alternatives were opened up. One approach was additive synthesis, in which the programmer starts with nothing, and adds harmonics at different amplitudes to define the sound.

1987: Roland's D50 introduces LA (Linear Arithmetic) synthesis. Sampled 'partials' combined with conventional filters and envelopes make it, and its derivative keyboards and modules, immensely popular.

1988: Korg's M1 introduces the concept of the workstation. Combining a keyboard, sampled synth sounds, drum bank, effects unit and sequencer in one box, the M1 sets the standard for modern professional instruments, and

establishes Korg, now owned by Yamaha, as a market leader. The M1 will evolve over the next few years into the T, 01 and X series.

1991: Korg's Wavestation introduces the concept of wave sequencing, by which sampled partials can be chained to produce complex rhythmic sounds or slowly-evolving tonalities.

1996: With older analog synthesizers highly collectable, several maufacturers

including Novation, Doepfer and Clavia produce retro-sounding keyboards. Other units offer sampled classic synths. The Korg Trinity represents a quantum leap in the workstation concept; it features the first truly digital effects unit, a touch-responsive programming screen, 24Mb of sample data, and the options of digital interfacing, on-board hard-disk recording, and a slot-in Prophecy virtual synthesis board.

Previously a member of Tangerine Dream, Klaus Schulze went on to explore classic electronic music as a solo artist. Like Rod Argent, Schulze was a fan of Yamaha's velocity-sensitive CS80, here teamed with two MiniMoogs and a battery of other equipment.

The Beatbox and Beyond

With synths and sequencers providing the melodies and basslines, electronic musicians soon found they could replace the drummer with a rhythm machine. The first rhythm machines were preset organ-top boxes from Hammond and others, but generally credited as the first programmable drum machine is the PAIA Programmable Drum Set. This used a simple step-time programming system and resonant oscillators to synthesize eight drum sounds. Roland's CR78, launched in 1978, also used synthesized sounds, together with preset and programmable patterns and some clever variation functions, and was used by Gary Numan, John Foxx, Peter Gabriel and Phil Collins. The first drum machine to have any street cred, however, was Roland's TR-808. It still didn't sound like real drums, but its metronomic timing, expressive sounds (especially the snare, cowbell and clap), easy programming and useful clock/trigger interfacing made it popular, particularly with hip-hop artists. Its definitive appearance is on Marvin Gaye's 'Sexual Healing.' In 1980, Roger Linn introduced the LinnDrum, which set new standards with sampled drum sounds and flexible programming (check out the Human League's *Dare*).

Ignoring the success of sample-based drum machines such as the LinnDrum and E-Mu's sampled Drumulator, in 1983 Roland came out with the TR-909, which had synthesised drums but sampled cymbals. Now much treasured by dance musicians for its inimitable kick and snare sounds, the TR-909 was the last classic drum machine - subsequent products like the TR-505 and TR-626 used sampled sounds which lacked character. While Roland's R-series and Yamaha's RX-series rolled on, sampling, the workstation concept and MIDI sound modules really killed the idea of the standalone drum machine, though Alesis's 16-bit sampled HR16 and SR16 provided a last

■ *Roger Linn pioneered the development of sampled digital drum machines with 1980's LinnDrum, and its successor, the LM-1. Whereas rival company Roland persevered with analog sounds, Oberheim and E-Mu systems weighed in with similar sample-based products.*

gasp of excitement. Ironically, the trend in the late 1990s is to imitate classic drum machines, with the sounds of Roland's TR-808 and TR-909 offered by Novation's DrumStation and Roland's own MC-303 workstation.

Synth-Pop

Synthesizer pop was kick-started by Dusseldorf combo Kraftwerk ('power station'). Founder members Ralf Hutter and Florian Schneider, together with percussionists Wolfgang Flur and Karl Bartos, defined a style which enormously influenced the Euro-disco of Georgio Moroder ('I Feel Love,' 'E=MC^2'), David Bowie's 1977 *Heroes*, and a whole generation of electro-poppers; among them The Human League, Gary Numan, Yellow Magic Orchestra, Depeche Mode, Soft Cell, Daniel Miller, Japan, Cabaret Voltaire, New Order and The Eurythmics. While Kraftwerk built or modified much of its own gear, its electropop acolytes were able to exploit the 1970s and 1980s explosion in affordable mono- and polysynths, as competition and the advent of the microprocessor enabled more powerful instruments to be made at an ever-lower price.

In 1981 Roland came out with the SH-101, a portable monosynth with built-in sequencer and strap-buttons for over-the shoulder playing, while Sequential bucked the trend for cheap polysynths by cutting down the specification of the Prophet 5 to produce the powerful Pro 1 monosynth. Roland opened up the market for basic but affordable polysynths with the Juno 6 and its successors the Juno 60 and 106, while Korg fought back with the value-for-money Polysix. One of the most innovative synths of all time was the Wasp, developed in 1978 by Chris Huggett and Adrian Wagner of U.K. company EDP (Electronic Dream Plant). A tiny plastic-cased unit with a two-octave black-and-yellow non-mechanical touch keyboard and built-in speaker, the Wasp nonetheless featured powerful

■ *Vince Clarke was a pioneer of U.K. electro-pop with Depeche Mode, then went on to form Yazoo in 1981. Clarke formed Erasure with vocalist Andy Bell in 1985; here he shows how one of his favorite synths, Roland's SH-101, may be played on a strap, guitar-style.*

■ Roland SH-101

Introduced: 1981

With only one true oscillator, this Roland monosynth was less versatile than Sequential Circuits or Moog rivals, but was reliable, featured an on-board sequencer - and was available in red, blue or grey. It became one of the most popular monosynths ever produced.

digitally-controlled oscillators and analog filters. A digital connection port, a precursor of MIDI, allowed the Wasp to link up with the Caterpillar (a conventional mechanical keyboard), Spider digital sequencer, other Wasps, and the even smaller Gnat synth. Users included Dave Greenfield of The Stranglers, who used four on stage for many years, and Dave Stewart of The Eurythmics, who used to mike up the internal speaker to capture its tinny sound.

The Sheffield-based Human League, one of the few bands which was completely electronic from its beginnings, produced the ground-breaking electro-pop epics *Being Boiled / Circus of Death* in 1978. After some personnel changes, Martin Rushent produced the huge-selling *Dare* in 1981, making heavy use of the LinnDrum and Roland MC-4 sequencer, and, after later disastrous experiments with the Synclavier, The Human League still uses a great deal of classic gear such as the Roland System 100 modular set-up, Jupiter 4, 6 and 8 polysynths, Oberheim 4-Voice and Xpander, ARP 2600 and MiniMoog, in conjunction with more modern instruments such as the Novation BassStation and Roland JD-800.

Electro-pop pioneers like Kraftwerk inspired a whole new generation of musicians when their sound reached out from Europe to America. After Kraftwerk's appearance in Detroit in

1982, hip-hop artist Afrika Bambaataa sampled *Trans-Europe Express* for 'Planet Rock.' Juan Atkins, as part of Cybotron and later Model 500, is generally credited as having invented techno, which combined the Teutonic rhythms of Kraftwerk with the soul of James Brown. Other artists such as Derrick May, Kevin Saunderson and Lenny Larking created what came to be known as house and acid music, picking up cheap instruments such as the Korg MS-10, Roland TB-303 Bassline, Roland TR-909 drum machine and later the Yamaha DX100 FM synth.

■ EDP Wasp

Introduced: 1980

Although its printed keyboard alienated some users, EDP's Wasp represented a terrific package at a U.K. price of £199; as the most affordable synth on the market,

it was one element in the 1980s U.K. synth-pop boom. ESP founder Chris Huggett later went on to found the Oxford Synthesiser Company, manufacturer of the OSCar, a pioneering programmable analog synthesizer with digital oscillators.

WASP SYNTHESISER   ELECTRONIC DREAM PLANT

MIDI and The Computer Age

Once affordable, programmable, polyphonic synths were available, there remained one major problem: compatibility.

All the major manufacturers understood the value of being able to interface one piece of equipment - a synthesizer, sequencer or drum machine - with another. The problem was that they all had their own proprietary systems, which were mutually incompatible. It is Dave Smith of Sequential Circuits who is credited with proposing a universal synthesizer interface, after having problems designing a polyphonic sequencer for the Prophet 5 synthesizer. The Japanese manufacturers suggested a serial system with digital 'flags' to identify different functions, and it was decided that the system would run at a clock speed of 31.25KBaud and be isolated optically to prevent ground-loops and possible damage from high or inverse voltages.

Though not as flexible as a parallel-processing system, which would effectively send several signals at once, but require multi-connector cables, the proposal had the advantage of being cheap to implement, with inexpensive DIN connecting cables. Named MIDI - Musical Instrument Digital Interface - the specification was published by Sequential Circuits, and first appeared in 1983 on the Prophet 600 poly synth, shortly followed by the Yamaha DX7. The rest is history.

The launch of instruments featuring MIDI hugely expanded the possibilities for tone generation, and sequencing. The possibility of using affordable home computers as MIDI-based sequencers brought electronic music to new heights of sophistication. Third party designers came up with MIDI interface boxes for Apple II, Kaypro, Commodore 64 and even Sinclair Spectrum computers. The launch of the Atari ST was the real turning point for sequencing software. Designed as an inexpensive competitor for the Apple Macintosh, the ST came with MIDI IN and OUT/THRU sockets built in. With the Atari ST, musicians were being offered what looked like a tailor-made music workstation – "the difference between a computer that makes music, and one that makes trouble" in the words of the Atari ad campaign.

The subsequent flood of MIDI software from C-Lab, Steinberg, Digidesign, Dr. T, Passport, Hybrid Arts and others established the ST, and indeed the idea of computing, as central to the work of the electronic musician. Now sequencing packages from E-Magic and Steinberg have become industry standards, while synth patch and sample editing programs have eased the job of creating new sounds.

MIDI also opened up live performance possibilities never before available. Firstly it allowed the controller keyboard and the sound-producing module to be separated. It became common for MIDI instruments to be offered in two forms; the keyboard version (Korg M1, Roland D50, Kawai K1 for instance); and a space-saving keyboardless desktop or 19″ rack-mounting version (Korg M1R, Roland D550, Kawai K1R/M).

Modules saved money, but also left the musician free to invest in a superior controller ('master,' or 'mother') keyboard. Extended, weighted keyboards with advanced touch response, program splitting and layering became available, such as Oberheim's XK, Yamaha's KX88, Roland's MKB-1000, Kurzweil's MIDIBoard and a huge line from the now sadly defunct U.K. company Cheetah. Also available were strap-on performance controllers like Yamaha's KX5, Roland's Axis and Casio's beautifully-designed AZ1, which (with a long enough MIDI lead) finally liberated the keyboard player from behind the rack.

Now MIDI is standard on practically all serious keyboard-based instruments, and has also found its way onto alternative controllers such as guitars, violins, drum pads, digital effects units, mixers, and even lighting controllers.

There are perennial proposals for a faster, more powerful standard, and it's certainly true that there are things which can be done easily with CV/Gate systems which can be troublesome when using MIDI. Still, it seems that this laudable example of industry-wide co-operation will continue to benefit electronic musicians for decades to come.

The DX7 and FM Synthesis

Yamaha's groundbreaking synthesizer came from research conducted by Stanford University's John Chowning, who developed the theory that all sounds could be produced from a combination of simple sine waves, modulating each other to produce overtones. Yamaha experimented with the idea in the giant GS1, as used by Keith Emerson, and refined it into FM (Frequency Modulation) for the launch of the DX7 in 1983. FM synthesis used a system of six sine-wave oscillators for each voice which could be configured as 'operators' or 'modulators' depending on the 'algorithm' or arrangement in which they were combined - even more possibilities were offered by the fact that each sine wave source had its own envelope generator. As Phil Oakey of The Human League commented, "The modulator and the oscillator on the DX7 are the same, and the Japanese thought this would make it easier. In fact it made it harder." The

MIDI Methodology

The basic function of MIDI is to allow one instrument to be played from another, in order to layer sounds together, but it's commonly used to connect a master controller to an arsenal of instruments. MIDI defines the pitch of the note and performance parameters such as pitch bend and modulation. This information is sent out at 31.25KBaud (31,250 bits per second, divided into 8-bit 'words'). As a serial system,

MIDI transmits only one event at a time, so even when it appears to be playing a chord, there are in fact small delays between notes. It takes a large amount of MIDI data to cause a perceptible delay, however.

The presence of the MIDI system is normally indicated by three 5-pin 180-degree DIN sockets on the back of an instrument. MIDI IN carries information from another keyboard or sequencer to the instrument; MIDI OUT transmits data from the

instrument to another; and MIDI THRU passes information unaltered through the instrument to another.

MIDI THRU is necessary to connect, for example, several sound modules to one sequencer. MIDI supports 16 discrete channels, so theoretically one MIDI source such as a sequencer can drive up to 16 instruments, each playing a separate track of music. In practice, instruments are often multi-timbral (responding to more than one MIDI

channel, with each channel allocated a different sound patch).

Most instruments respond to MIDI data in a number of different modes. In Omni mode, the instrument responds to all MIDI data on all 16 channels. In Omni Off/Poly mode, the instrument responds to just one selected MIDI channel. In Mono mode (now rarely used), each synthesizer voice is controlled by a separate MIDI channel. The MIDI system can also transmit performance data such as

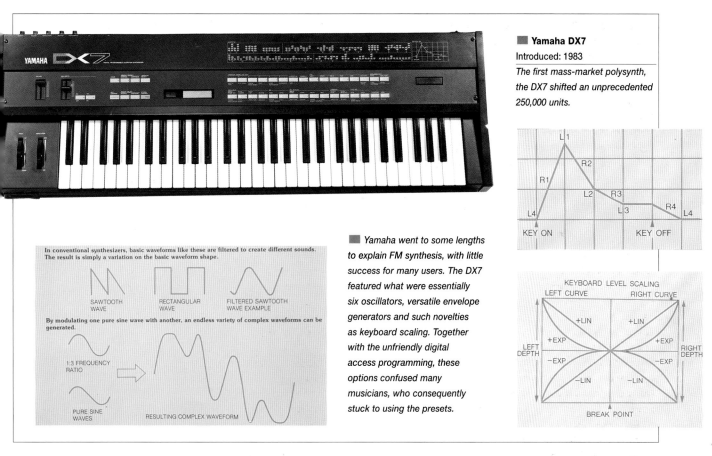

In conventional synthesizers, basic waveforms like these are filtered to create different sounds. The result is simply a variation on the basic waveform shape.

SAWTOOTH WAVE   RECTANGULAR WAVE   FILTERED SAWTOOTH WAVE EXAMPLE

By modulating one pure sine wave with another, an endless variety of complex waveforms can be generated.

1:3 FREQUENCY RATIO

PURE SINE WAVES   RESULTING COMPLEX WAVEFORM

■ *Yamaha went to some lengths to explain FM synthesis, with little success for many users. The DX7 featured what were essentially six oscillators, versatile envelope generators and such novelties as keyboard scaling. Together with the unfriendly digital access programming, these options confused many musicians, who consequently stuck to using the presets.*

KEYBOARD LEVEL SCALING
LEFT CURVE   RIGHT CURVE
+LIN   +LIN
+EXP   +EXP
LEFT DEPTH   RIGHT DEPTH
−EXP   −EXP
−LIN   −LIN
BREAK POINT

63

difficulty was compounded by the digital access programming system and relatively small LCD panel.

Digital access programming replaced the synth's familiar (and expensive) knobs and sliders with a numerical parameter display and increment/decrement buttons, so sound parameters could only be edited one at a time. This became a standard cost-saving exercise, which unfortunately led many musicians to give up on programming their own sounds. The advent of patch-editing software programs did give back some element of control, but few DX7 players went further than choosing a preset sound or buying additional sound cartridges. Nonetheless, the impact of the launch of the DX7 in 1983 was enormous. Apart from FM synthesis, the DX7 featured MIDI, a velocity-responsive keyboard, a breath control port and 16-voice polyphony. Its sounds blew away every keyboard player who heard it; it was

particularly good at percussive tones such as marimbas, harpsichords and electric pianos, and single-handedly killed the Fender Rhodes electric piano. Yamaha enjoyed remarkable success with the DX7, which sold an unprecedented quarter of a million units, and with its cut-down relative the DX9, and derivatives such as the TX7 module, DX21, 27 and 100 keyboards, FB01 and TX81Z multi-timbral modules, and the DX7MkII. FM technology was licensed to other manufacturers such as Korg, who attempted to make it more accessible by introducing programming short-cuts on the DS8.

Finally, though, digital synthesis largely fell out of fashion; too complex for the average musician to program, it was overtaken by the advent of sampling and sample-plus-synthesis instruments, which offered the musician a full array of complex tones without any significant programming effort.

the velocity with which the key is hit, pitchbend and modulation; program changes; and non-channel-specific 'system' data such as clock information for drum machines and sequencers, MIDI Time Code and System Exclusive information.

System Exclusive is MIDI's way of making up for the fact that most modern synths have too many programming parameters for each to be assigned an individual MIDI code. Using system exclusive messages, a

synthesizer can transmit its patch data to another synth, or to a software-based librarian/editor package. The MIDI Sample Dump standard allows the same to be done for digital sound sample data.

To iron out one last area of incompatibility, General MIDI (GM) was developed in 1992. General MIDI introduced the concept of a standardized Tone Map, roughly matching generic patches such as piano, string, bass or percussion

voices, so that a song written for one GM synth will make sense when played on another; piano patches, say, and drum voices will match up. This is a boon for cocktail-bar entertainers and consumers of pre-recorded song sequence files, although it's been suggested that GM (and its Roland and Yamaha versions, GS and XG) simply cater for the lowest common musical denominator, operating as a kind of karaoke for keyboards.

The Sample Option

Strictly speaking, sound synthesis and sampling are completely different areas. A sampler is in effect a digital audio recorder, incapable of generating its own sounds. However, with synthesizers now based largely on sampled sound-bites, and samplers incorporating many synth-type processing features, the lines between the two are increasingly blurred.

The first commercial attempt to reproduce real sounds on a keyboard instrument was the Bradley Brothers' Mellotron, an unwieldy instrument which used banks of ten-second tape recordings, one for each note; its distinctive sounds had a striking impact on classics such as the Moody Blues' 'Nights in White Satin,' Led Zeppelin's 'Stairway to Heaven,' and much of the early output of Yes, King Crimson and Genesis. Genuine sound sampling relies on an analog-to-digital conversion process by which the waveforms of acoustic signals are stored in computer memory as numeric data. Reversing the process through a digital-to-analog converter recreates the sound. In between, various processing tricks such as editing, looping and filtering can alter the sound. Crucially, altering the 'clock speed' of playback alters the sound's pitch, making it possible to play any sample as a melodic tone. For most musicians, the first exposure to sampling came with the Fairlight CMI (Computer Musical Instrument) in 1979. Named after the ferry which crossed Sydney harbour, Fairlight developed the CMI as an additive synthesis engine - you could, for instance,

draw a waveshape on its computer terminal and mutate it through time into another waveshape. Designer Kim Ryrie threw in sampling almost as an afterthought, but it was this ability to digitally record, edit and play back sounds under keyboard control which really captivated musicians.

For many years in competition with the N.E.D. Synclavier as the world's most expensive musical instrument, the Fairlight (as it was usually known) was initially used as something of a novelty. In imaginative hands, however, it created amazing soundscapes. David Vorhaus, electronic music pioneer with The White Noise,

■ *U.K. synthpop band Depeche Mode used found sounds for percussion, reportedly hitting motor* cars with hammers and sampling the result with its Emulator for a heavy metal rhythm track.

was the first in the UK to get his hands on a Fairlight, and years later lauded its abilities to produce in hours what conventional recording techniques would have required days to create.

The Fairlight was extensively used by the Pet Shop Boys, The Art of Noise, Yello and Jean-Michel Jarre (notably on *Magnetic Fields*), but as seems to be the way with all companies relying on one expensive product, despite continual updates Fairlight ran

■ *Heavyweight sampling keyboards of the 1980s included clockwise from left, the NED Synclavier II, Fairlight, PPG Wave, and Emulator.*

THE SAMPLE STORY

1979: Fairlight CMI launched. A digital production system for studios, with resynthesis, sequencing, and audio-visual functions, sampling is just one of its features. Costing from $39-175,000 it includes a 73-note keyboard, up to 28Mb of memory and 8″ floppy disk storage system. NED's Synclavier digital synthesizer launched. Initial versions offer monophonic sampling.

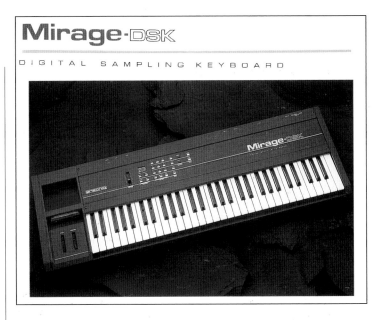

Mirage-DSK
DIGITAL SAMPLING KEYBOARD

into trouble as sampling became cheaper. Although the company still survives producing post-production equipment for the broadcast and movie industries, the last version of the CMI was the Series III, which cost up to $175,000 in 1988.

The first affordable sampler was the E-Mu Emulator. Dave Rossum and Scott Wedge of E-Mu (nothing to do with big birds – Mu is the Greek letter m) started off building analog modular systems, and were commissioned to build a computer-controlled analog synth for Peter Baumann (ex-Tangerine Dream). E-Mu subsequently changed direction and designed the Emulator as an affordable alternative to the Fairlight's sampling capabilities. Stevie Wonder bought the first Emulator in 1980, Michael Jackson used one extensively for *Thriller*, and the sampling stampede was on its way. Eight-note polyphonic and using 5 1/4" floppy disks, the Emulator 1 was replaced in 1984 by the Emulator 2, which increased the memory, disk and sequencer capacity, and then came the E III, Emax, E IV and so on. Emulators were used by producer Arthur Baker on Freeez's seminal Brit-funk opus 'IOU,' by Paul Hardcastle on '19' and by New Order on 'Blue Monday.' The latter group boasted of a unique method for dealing with their early Emulator's occasional crashes; they kept a rubber mallet with the instrument; bashing the Emulator's leg at a certain point would, reportedly, unfreeze the keyboard...

Sampling quality is usually expressed in terms of 'bit-rate'; in other words, the length of the binary number which defines each fragment of the sample. The Emulator 1 was 8-bit, as was the Ensoniq Mirage, and the comparatively grainy quality of these early samplers has its own appeal. The Akai S900 was 12-bit, the Akai S1000 and most subsequent samplers are 16-bit; higher sampling resolution is deemed unnecessary, as the human ear wouldn't be able to detect any further improvement. Other factors such as bandwidth, filtering, data compression and clock speed can influence overall sampling quality, but modern samplers now offer quality equal to that of CD. Hence manufacturers are concentrating more on improving sample editing and processing facilities. Of course, sampling is in effect nothing more than digital recording, and the practice of lifting samples from the recordings of other artists has given rise to a number of interesting copyright actions. After a slow start, music publishers are now fully aware of the implications of sampling, and rub their hands together at the thought of royalty payments when they hear their clients' work being sampled without copyright clearance. An expensive court case suffered by De La Soul has made many performers aware of the pitfalls.

Ensoniq introduced sampling to the masses, breaking the $2000 barrier with the Mirage and DSK.

Custom-designed chips made the company's products less expensive than the competition.

Ready-To-Wear Sampling

In 1987 Roland launched the D50, an immediate hit which became the 'next big thing' after the Yamaha DX7, and which certainly offered more accessible programming. The D50's Linear Arithmetic (LA) synthesis system uses tiny sampled 'partials' as its basic waveforms. These partials can be processed through a fairly conventional modulator-filter-envelope system, and a series of digital effects, giving rich, dynamic and striking tones.

D50 factory sounds soon became over-used to the point of cliché (check out Prince's *Lovesexy*). Inexpensive imitators like Kawai's K1 and K4 continued the progress of sample-plus-synthesis instruments, and Yamaha finally bowed to the inevitable and merged the technology with a version of FM for the SY99 synth. Practically all modern instruments now use a form of sample-plus-synthesis, whether it's called AI2 (Korg), AWM (Yamaha), VAST (Kurzweil), QS (Alesis) or whatever else, while Korg's Wavestation keyboard (and A/D and SR modules) use a form of wave-sequencing first seen on Sequential's innovative VS synth. By allowing one sound-sample to modulate or warp into another, the Wavestation can produce gradually evolving or sharply rhythmic sounds. It's arguable that the sample-plus-synthesis instrument has killed the true synthesizer, but there is hope for the future.

65

1980: *E-mu's Emulator keyboard, at under $10,000, is a more affordable alternative to Fairlight. Two second, 8-bit samples are stored on 5" disks.*

1985: *Ensoniq's Mirage 8-bit sampling keyboard breaks the $2000 barrier by combining most functions onto a custom chip. Later models such as the DSK and ASR series compete strongly with Akai. Akai launches the SE612 rack-mounting MIDI sampler module.*

Cheap at $1000, and easy to use, it offers eight seconds of six-note polyphonic 12-bit sampling, although editing is limited and its 2.8" Quick Disks impractical.

1986: *Akai's rack-mounting S900 offers 63 seconds of 12-bit sampling, advanced editing functions, a large LCD panel and a 3.5" disk drive. It rapidly becomes the industry standard. Its successor the S950 adds enhanced*

editing functions, expandable memory, and improved interfacing. Korg's DSS1 combines samples and synthesis, while Roland's S50 keyboard offers 12-bit sampling, 16-voice polyphony, and an optional monitor interface.

1987: *Casio enters the pro sampler market with the 16-bit FZ1.*

1988: *Yamaha's TX81W 12-bit stereo sampler module makes little impact but*

Akai's S1000, the first affordable stereo 16-bit sampler, soon becomes the industry standard.

1992. *Akai's S01 offers 16-bit mono sampling at under $900.*

1996: *The ultimate sampler? E-mu's £3500 E4K keyboard offers up to 128 voices, a 76-note weighted keyboard, built in 150Mb hard drive, onboard sequencer and digital effects processor.*

Clavia Nord

Introduced: 1994

A 'virtual analog' synth, the Clavia Nord produces its sounds in the digital domain, but is intended to replicate the sound of traditional 1970s analog equipment such as the MiniMoog.

The Future Of Synthesis

Once MIDI became established, the demand for instruments with more polyphony and flexibility led inevitably to the development of multi-timbral instruments - capable of playing more than one sound at a time.

Sequential Circuits' early experiments, the SixTrak and Max, didn't make much impression, but Roland's tiny MT32 module certainly did. Launched in 1987, it featured lush LA sounds, eight-part multi-timbral operation, plus an additional track of multi-sampled drum sounds. The ultimate integration of electronic technology came in 1988 with Korg's M1: synthesizer, sampled drum sounds, keyboard controller, digital effects unit and sequencer in one package. The 'workstation' was born, and for the first time a keyboard player could produce a finished composition from just one instrument.

Using AI, a easy-to-program sample-plus-synthesis technique similar to Roland's LA, the M1 boasted 4Mb of PCM-sampled and synthesizer waveforms, making it capable of producing particularly convincing sounds including an impressive piano. The M1 lacked a resonant filter, its effects routing options were basic, and its 8-track sequencer was limited, but it (and its modular version, the M1R) are still justifiably popular. Later derivatives added increased waveform memory, built-in disk drives for patch and sequence storage, and larger keyboards. Most manufacturers now offer workstation keyboards, as well as powerful, inexpensive entry-level synths like Roland's X10, Korg's X5 and Yamaha's CS1X.

Another trend is cutting down synths into the form of sound cards for desktop composition, although this approach probably appeals more to games-players than to real musicians. At the other end of the scale there's heavy demand for the well-proven sound qualities and intuitive editing facilities of classic knobs-and-sliders analog synths.

External control problems can be overcome by retro-fitting MIDI to CV/Gate instruments, and even tuning instabilities can often be ironed out (although some musicians swear by them...). Artists like Aphex Twin, Moby, Autechre, Black Dog, Alex Reece, Erasure, The Shamen, Orbital, The Human League and Mu-Ziq could not survive without an

This photo of Orbital's Phil (right) and Paul Hartnoll illustrates a typically eclectic 1990s mix of hardware. Modern units including the Korg Prophecy and Emulator EIIISX sampler are complemented by vintage drum machines such as the Roland R8, TR-808, and TR-909, which although regarded as sonically dull on its launch is now regarded as one of the most collectable drum machines ever made. The Orb (right) plump for more tradition still, using a real drummer for live performance.

arsenal of lovingly-restored vintage synths. The result is that analog gear (which would today be impractically expensive for the manufacturers to reproduce) now commands outrageous second-hand prices.

Manufacturers like Novation, with the BassStation keyboard and rack mount, Doepfer with the MS-404 synth module and A100 Modular System, and Clavia with the Nord Lead, offer good reproductions of classic analog sounds, while modules like Peavey's Spectrum, E-Mu's Vintage and Classic Keys, Roland's M-VS1 and Akai's SG01V duck the issue by offering digital samples of analog synths. As for the future, the current buzz-word is Acoustic Modelling, a sophisticated process which recreates the expressiveness of real instruments through complex algorithms.

First launched on Yamaha's VL-1 and VL-7, and more recently the keenly-priced VL-70M module, Acoustic Modelling is also used on the Technics WSA1, Korg Wavedrum percussion instrument and Korg Prophecy, a 37-key monosynth. Also available as an add-on board for the Trinity workstation, the Prophecy might turn the clock back in terms of polyphony, but in other ways it's at the cutting edge of technology. It features an advanced arpeggiator and performance controls, and five types of synthesis; Standard Oscillator, using a resonant filter; Noise and Comb Filtering, which extracts harmonic elements from white noise; Variable Phase Modulation, which controls the waveform shapes in a sound's harmonic content; Cross/Ring modulation for bell-like sounds; and Physical Modelling for brass, reed and guitar-type sounds. Whether acoustic modelling is the key to the future of synthesis, only time will tell. However, the radically different approaches and applications used in the various instruments designed in the synthesizer's relatively short history mean that today's players enjoy a uniquely wide palette from which to draw. Without doubt, as they continue to embrace new instruments, they will also continue to use machines which hark back sonically or conceptually to that first mass-market synthesizer, the MiniMoog.

67

Brass & Woodwind

"You can reach places with a saxophone that you'll never reach with any other instrument. With The Stooges we wanted to combine the sound of Coltrane or James Brown with heavy guitars, and I think it worked. The only problem was when our album came out and a Billboard review said the sax player was the leader of the band. I knew my days were numbered."

STEVE MACKAY, THE STOOGES

The story of brass and woodwind in contemporary popular music is as American as apple pie. The 1920s saw the emergence of jazz as the predominant influence on popular music, and that has not changed to this day. From the swingy rhythms of hip-hop to the lush voicings of trance, from 'Careless Whisper' to 'Cardiac Arrest,' from the key change in the latest dancefloor confection to metal riffs, elements of jazz abound. But music certainly hit a speed bump fast enough to shake, rattle, and roll its progress at the end of the 1940s.

Throughout the 1920s, popular music followed a fairly straight line: it was melodic, acoustic, romantic, and song-based. The big bands ruled, led by Count Basie, Glenn Miller, Duke Ellington, Benny Goodman and many others. This was sophisticated ensemble music using highly skilled musicians, which fully exploited the expressive power of the clarinet and the newly invented saxophone. The 'big band' line-up usually consisted of five saxophones, four trumpets, four trombones, plus a four-piece rhythm section. Saxophones would usually be called upon to 'double' on flutes and clarinets, offering the arranger a wide palette of tonal colors.

However, after World War II the methodology of music changed seemingly beyond recognition. Suddenly there was rock'n'roll. This musical revolution derived from a wide range of causes: changes in the radio industry which opened up the airwaves to blues, R&B, gospel and country, population shifts from rural South to urban North, and the advent of amplification. Leading a big

band had always been a precarious financial prospect; now, as smaller bands with electric guitars and stripped-down horn sections competed for the same jobs, the financial outlook was grimmer still. In the 1930s, huge numbers of big bands who had perhaps not enjoyed national success – 'Territory Bands' – enjoyed their own regional empires, employing thousands of musicians. By 1950, the hundreds of territory bands ranged across the USA had effectively disappeared.

Let The Hard Times Roll

Although rock'n'roll might have supplanted the big band, the music's originators evolved from the big band sound. Louis Jordan, perhaps the most crucial early innovator, was a profound influence on Bill Haley (who worked with Jordan's producer Milt Gabler in an effort to echo Jordan's sound), Chuck Berry, B.B. King, and many others. Jordan's big band credentials

were impeccable: he had served his time playing saxophone in the bands of Louis Armstrong, Clarence Williams, and Ella Fitzgerald. Yet ironically, Jordan's Tympany Five showed that small combos could make popular music which was less staid than its big band rivals. Jordan helped make his fellow saxophonists redundant.

Yet although brass sections diminished in size in the early days of rock'n'roll, they were still a vital part of the music. Admittedly, in Chicago or Mississippi, where electric blues was almost entirely guitar-based, brass sections were rare. But elsewhere brass sections remained, perhaps in cut-down form, with performers such as B.B. King. King's first records featured a two or three-piece brass section, but as soon as the budget allowed, King used up to eight or nine pieces, touring with alto and tenor saxophones, trumpet and trombone. King's sidemen

■ *King Curtis was one of New York's most in-demand sessionmen, playing with artists as diverse as*

Andy Williams and Buddy Holly. Curtis later racked up hits including the R&B No. 1 'Soul Twist.'

■ *Tenor saxman Lee Allen established his reputation in Dave Bartholomew's legendary New*

Orleans studio band; Allen later recorded hits under his own name including 'Walkin' With Mr Lee.'

Louis Jordan, playing alto fourth from left in an augmented version of The Tympany Five, helped map out the sound of rock'n'roll. Jordan's imitators would help the guitar to gain ascendance over the sax, but Jordan persevered, turning to jazz-influenced music late in his career.

probably grew up playing big band music, or pure jazz in its remaining strongholds. The same applied to huge numbers of other pioneering rock'n'roll records, for the sound of early hits by Little Richard, Fats Domino, or Big Joe Turner was suffused with saxophones. All three of these musicians recorded their greatest hits in New Orleans thanks to the pool of talent available in the city

Adolphe Sax's first instruments were taken up by the French military; this 1914 Conn illustrates how the instrument was soon widely copied.

regarded as the birthplace of jazz; and the brass sections, while adept at depping on rock'n'roll sessions, spent the rest of their time in the city's still-burgeoning jazz scene. As Robert Catfrey, a New Orleans sax player who fronted his own R&B combo and also toured with the likes of Guitar Slim and Little Richard puts it, "record companies sent their people down to record here, 'cos they knew New Orleans had the musicians. The same guys would be playing jazz on Bourbon Street, jamming in the Dewdrop Inn after hours, and playing sessions in the studio." The key players in the New Orleans session scene included members of Dave Bartholomew's band, notably Lee Allen on tenor and Alvin 'Red' Tyler on baritone; Allen himself went on to enjoy solo hits such as 'Walkin' With Mr. Lee' and 'Tic Toc.'

Although many of the saxophones present on early rock'n'roll records were recorded by session musicians, there was no

■ *Big Jay McNeely's raucous R&B sax playing provoked reactions similar to those later inspired by rock'n'roll, as shown by this 1951 photo taken in a Los Angeles theater. Established jazzmen were unconvinced. A disapproving story in this January 1953 Down Beat reports that McNeely "tortures something out of a tenor sax that sends audiences of susceptible teenagers into semi-hysterical stomping and even shouting outbursts that outdo any Sinatra or Goodman demonstrations."*

Chicago, January 14, 1953 — Rhythm And Blues — DOWN

Big Jay McNeely Big Noise In R&B

BIG JAY MCNEELY, who is blowing up a storm of publicity on the west coast, heads eastward soon, is hardly a static tenor man, as is shown by these photos—he gets around a little. Some of his various maneuvers are the thrust, the leap, and the sprawl. The latter appears to be giving Johnnie Ray moments of sheer ecstasy at right. Pics were taken at a recent concert in Los Angeles.

McNeely, McSqueally—Either Way You Pronounce It, Means Box Office

Hollywood—California, which has contributed more than its share of strange and even weird performers in all fields from evangelism to politics, seems about to unloose some...

duced excitement sets off a chain reaction and before long headline hunters among newspaper and magazine reporters come up with such things as:

"Big Jay McNeely, 'Mr. Honk' in Person—the 'Go-Go-Go Boy' (terms picked up easily from the...

came into his own with the big boom in the rhythm and blues business, when he started doing concerts in outlying communities where he caught the high school and junior college set (both white and colored). Then things started to happen.

70

shortage of distinguished names: Curtis Ousley, better known as King Curtis, began as a New York session man and came to fame with performances like The Coasters' 'Yakety-Yak.' He later made many records under his own name. His powerful, rhythmic, instantly recognizable style has continued to influence any reed-biter who takes a funky solo. West coast bandleader and tenor saxman Big Jay McNeely's flamboyant performances earned him hits with 'All Night Long' and 'There Is Something On Your Mind.' Danny Flores, better known as tenor saxman Chuck Rio, had an enormous instrumental hit with his group of L.A. session men The Champs when rock'n'roll went Latin in 'Tequila.' The down-home funky tenor sax of Junior Walker was more influenced by the earlier R&B honkers like Sil Austin and Red Prysock than the more sophisticated soul of his Motown stablemates. Hits like 'Shotgun,' and 'Road Runner' established

him as a star. Sax virtuoso Earl Bostic began as a featured soloist with Lionel Hampton's band, but soon formed his own R&B band (which included a young John Coltrane as one of his sidemen). Bostic is probably best known for his hit 'Flamingo.'

Even in the rockabilly-oriented field, the saxophone was an integral part of the band: Duane Eddy, that prototype guitar hero, relied on tenor saxman Steve Douglas as a key part of his sound, which to some extent was derived from the popular sax instrumentals of Bill Justis. Yet Eddy's records marked a

The Selmer Story

1890: *Celebrated French clarinettist Frederick Selmer's two sons, Alexandre and Henri, take up business careers. Henri Selmer makes reeds, and later clarinets and mouthpieces. Alexandre plays and promotes Henri's instruments, and sets up a New York retail outlet, which will become Selmer U.S.A.*

1894: *Adolphe Sax, inventor of the saxophone, dies, leaving the Sax company to his son Charles.*

1910: *Alexandre returns to France, appointing George Bundy as manager of the New York distribution enterprise; Bundy later becomes president of H&A Selmer (USA) Inc.*

1920: *Both French and USA Selmer sell 'stencil' saxophones – instruments made by another company and engraved with the Selmer name. U.S. Selmers are made by Conn, Buescher and Martin, the French versions by Couesnon and Sax. Selmer (Paris) buys the Sax*

company after it hits financial difficulties.

1922: *Selmer (Paris) introduces the 'Modèle 22', initially derived from an Adolphe Sax design.*

1927: *Selmer USA moves to Elkhart, Indiana. It distributes the popular new Modèle 26, and goes on to sell more stencil instruments, later buying the Buescher company and selling U.S.-made instruments under the Buescher and Bundy names.*

1930: *The 'Super Sax' model, also known as the 'Cigar Cutter' appears. The latter term – not used officially by Selmer – refers to the distinctive octave mechanism.*

1934: *The 'Radio Improved' model is the last to concentrate on a rich lower register. Soon the emphasis will shift to a brighter upper end.*

1936: *Selmer radically alters keywork in the Balanced Action, making the*

Selmer Mark VI Alto

Introduced 1954

The Selmer Mark VI has now become legendary, the most sought-after vintage saxophone. Design input for the Mark VI came from classical player Marcel Mule, who had played a Selmer saxophone in the early 1920s but switched to rival French company Couesnon before returning to the Selmer fold to help develop the new instrument. The Mark VI reflected a policy of continued improvement by the Selmer (Paris) company, and is now regarded by many as the summit of saxophone development. This reputation was augmented by the poor performance of the model's successor, the Mark VII. Although perhaps not as bad as its reputation suggests, the Mark VII was inferior in some respects, notably the heavy keywork for the left hand little finger, and in the tonal balance, which is exceptionally bright in the upper register. Whereas the Mark VI remained in production for 20 years, the Mark VII was replaced five years after its launch by the Super Action 80.

Catalogue français de 1935.

Alexandre Selmer (1864-1953) présentant l[e] modèle 22, tout premier saxophone Selmer

71

■ Boots Randolph endorses the popular Selmer Mark VI in this 1966 Beat Instrumental. Randolph was a popular Nashville session musician, playing with Elvis Presley and Roy Orbison among many others. Randolph's 1963 hit 'Yakety Sax' is now best known as the closing theme for TV shows by the U.K. comedian Benny Hill.

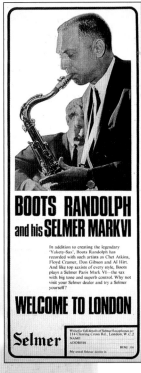

BOOTS RANDOLPH and his SELMER MARK VI

In addition to creating the legendary 'Yakety-Sax', Boots Randolph has recorded with such artists as Chet Atkins, Floyd Cramer, Don Gibson and Al Hirt. And like top saxists of every style, Boots plays a Selmer Paris Mark VI—the sax with big tone and superb control. Why not visit your Selmer dealer and try a Selmer yourself?

WELCOME TO LONDON

Selmer

Write for full details of Selmer Saxophones to: 114 Charing Cross Rd., London, W.C.2
NAME
ADDRESS
My usual Selmer dealer is

work of the left hand little finger far easier. Bell keys are moved away from the player's body, further improving the instrument's ergonomics.

1948: The 'Super Action' is a flexible blowing saxophone, particularly with Selmer's Soloist "D" chambered mouthpieces – as always, Selmer improves mouthpiece design in tandem with 'tube' design.

1954: The Mark VI is introduced. The model name derives from its final, sixth, prototype. The Mark VI, developed in conjunction with classical virtuoso Marcel Mule, has a direct blowing feel which helps keep it in production for 20 years. It will later become a cult classic. Over its 20 year production span there are numerous keywork alterations and also new tooling for cup shapes.

1974: The much anticipated Mark VII fails to win the popularity of its predecessor. The tube taper is altered to produce an even brighter upper register, while many players find the keywork uncomfortably heavy.

1981: The Super Action 80 is a much more refined instrument and more flexible for player nuance. As with other Selmers, this instrument is made of a harder alloy than most other makes, contributing to the 'weightiness' of the instrument's sound.

1986: An easier response is available from the Super Action 80 Series II, particularly in the low register, possibly as a result of Yamaha's success in this area with its YAS and YTS range.

significant point in the history of rock'n'roll. By now the legacy of the big bands had dwindled, and the guitar had reached a natural ascendancy. Duane Eddy's followers dispensed with the sax, before the surf boom and the English invasion contributed to wiping the horn section off the airwaves.

As rock'n'roll and English beat music changed at a dizzying pace, jazz was evolving too; the influence of many of the movement's heroes – Miles Davis, John Coltrane, Archie Shepp, Ornette Coleman – was not confined to jazz; Byrds guitarist Roger McGuinn was one of many rock musicians of the mid-1960s who claimed to have absorbed Coltrane's unique melodic approach. Profound musical changes were also taking place in the R&B scene. One Nat King Cole-style crooner and occasional arranger on the New Orleans music scene of the early 1950s was Ray Charles, who spotted the commercial potential of fusing blues with gospel to create a recipe for soul. Charles found a ready-made horn section led by David 'Fathead' Newman in Lowell Fulson's blues outfit; Newman found little difficulty in making the musical leap from blues to soul. Charles had his own influence on another nascent soul musician, James Brown, who won an important early break in 1957 when rock'n'roller Little

Brass and Woodwind

Wind instruments are divided into two categories: brass and woodwind. Brass instruments are played by vibrating the lips against a cup-shaped mouthpiece; woodwind instruments may in fact be made of wood or metal, but the sound is generated by vibration of air (in a flute, for instance) or a reed (in a clarinet or oboe). For any wind instrument, skilled players can change pitch harmonically, by say an octave, merely by breath control. Playing a scale, however, requires changing the sounding length of the instrument. On a brass instrument this is achieved by depressing valves or moving a slider; on woodwind instruments by opening or closing openings in the tube with fingers or keys. Major instruments in the brass family used in popular music include trumpet, cornet, trombone, French horn and tuba. Major woodwind instruments include the flute, clarinet, oboe, bassoon and the saxophone family: sopranino, soprano, alto, tenor, baritone and bass.

The word embouchure refers to the the application of mouth to instrument, and hence interaction of player and mouthpiece or reed. Embouchure differs greatly between brass instruments, single and double reed instruments and flutes, and it is an admirable feat to achieve mastery of more than one group.

■ *James Brown's horn section was the most influential such unit of the 1960s, ushering in a new golden age for brass and woodwind players. Brown toured with up to nine pieces, but of the many players who passed through his band, the best-known were the late 1960s triumvirate of tenor saxman Pee Wee Ellis, alto player Maceo Parker, and trombonist Fred Wesley (above). Wesley and Parker would both leave Brown's band in the early 1970s to join George Clinton's Funkadelic.*

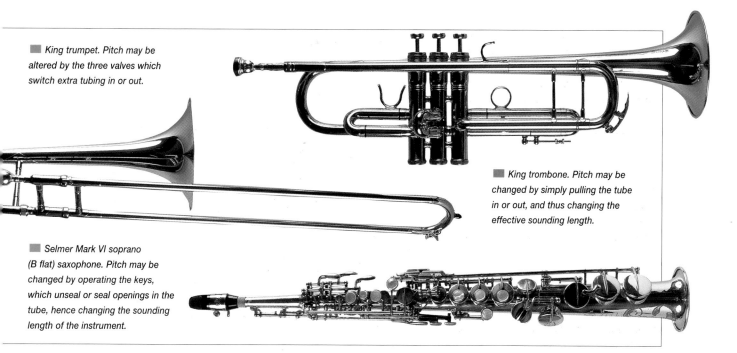

■ *King trumpet. Pitch may be altered by the three valves which switch extra tubing in or out.*

■ *King trombone. Pitch may be changed by simply pulling the tube in or out, and thus changing the effective sounding length.*

■ *Selmer Mark VI soprano (B flat) saxophone. Pitch may be changed by operating the keys, which unseal or seal openings in the tube, hence changing the sounding length of the instrument.*

Richard discovered religion, renounced rock'n'roll, and refused to complete the southern leg of a US tour. Brown toured in Richard's place and recruited some of his backing group, The Upsetters, to augment his own Flames. As soul music gained a new audience, both black and white, horn sections were about to make a comeback, albeit in stripped-down form compared with the glory days of the big band.

Sound Your Funky Horn

One of the most influential early horn sections as soul music evolved was the Memphis Horns, featuring Wayne Jackson and Andrew Love, who were part of the house band for Stax Records, alongside Booker T And The MGs – Steve Cropper, Duck Dunn and Al Jackson. The essence of their sound is rhythm, and in the use of brass on the records of Wilson Pickett, Otis Redding and Al Green you're hearing stabbing, relentless attacks whose raison d'etre is to physically strike the listener.

The most distinguished and influential horn section of the 1960s soul music was doubtless that of James Brown, who effectively created a whole new context for brass and woodwind. Although Brown's sound owed an undoubted debt to Ray Charles and Little Richard in the early days, it constantly evolved as Brown worked his way through a succession of talented bandleaders. Tenor player J.C. Davis led a three piece section from 1959, which by 1961 included St. Clair Pinckney on tenor and Al Clark on baritone sax. Maceo Parker joined, initially on baritone, in 1964, shortly before the recording of the epochal 'Papa's Got A Brand New Bag.' The definitive 1965 recording of this song used a nine-piece horn section, but was devastatingly concise, Parker's

■ *Maceo Parker (left) joined the Brown outfit in 1964, initially on baritone before switching to tenor.*

Pee Wee Ellis (right), arranger of hits such as 1967's 'Cold Sweat,' joined Van Morrison's band in 1996.

73

Sly Stone's funk was destined for crossover, aided by the playing of tenor saxman Jerry Martini.

baritone solos dedicated specifically to accentuating the rhythm. When tenor saxman Alfred 'Pee Wee' Ellis, a skilled jazz musician, joined Brown's outfit in 1966, he had to stand at the side of the stage and watch the horn section at work for a week to gain a sufficient understanding of how the minimal but still intricate arrangements operated. While Brown was a demanding boss, he allowed his musicians considerable latitude; the musicians would turn Brown's grunts or yelps – basic 'head arrangements' – into music. It was Pee Wee Ellis's horn arrangements, reportedly invented while wandering around a music store in Cincinnati, together with Brown's injunction to "Go for The One" – hit the first beat of each alternate bar in unison, then fly off into dazzling rhythmic territory for the next seven beats – which effectively created the funk genre in the form of 'Cold Sweat.' This was complex, sophisticated music, despite its minimal feel, and it was so changed from its big band legacy as to be almost unrecognizable. Trombonist Fred Wesley joined in time for 1968's 'Say It Loud – I'm Black And I'm Proud,' confirming the band's reputation as the tightest in the business.

Brown's ascendance heralded a new resurgence for brass and woodwind players, aided by the growing sophistication of late 1960s rock music. Sly & The Family Stone built on the funk foundation Brown had created and came up with one of the most commercial crossover sounds of the era: Jerry Martini's tenor saxophone was an integral part of Sly's crossover-friendly sound. George Clinton's Funkadelic was another outfit influenced by James Brown – Clinton recruited Maceo Parker and Fred Wesley, along with bassist Bootsy Collins, from Brown's JBs. Even hard rock bands were turned on to the sonic appeal of the saxophone. Perhaps the most surprising example of this move was pioneering punk outfit The Stooges, led by singer Iggy Pop, who recruited sax player Steve Mackay into the band in 1970 with the bizarre notion of blending James Brown's stripped down funk with their own gonzoid punk attack. The resulting album, *Fun House*, showed how the saxophone could cohabit with heavy metal guitar, and the album's metallic grooves have gone on to influence modern rock-funk stylists such as The Red Hot Chili Peppers. Other white rockers incorporated R&B horn styles into their music with more commercial success, in particular Blood, Sweat And Tears. Formed by Al Kooper, the

The Harmonica

Perhaps the world's best-value and most portable instrument, the harmonica was produced by several manufacturers, most famously the German Hohner company, from the 1850s, and was favored by those on the move: sailors, soldiers and even American cowpokes. The harmonica's popularity in the Blues field was almost exclusively due to John Lee Williamson, better known as Sonny Boy. Along with Sonny Terry, who was in a popular musical partnership with Brownie McGhee, Williamson put the harmonica on the map from the late 1930s via a number of blues hits including 1938's 'Good Morning Little Schoolgirl.' Williamson's expressive use of the harmonica influenced many early blues players including Big Walter Horton, Little Walter Jacobs and Rice Miller, who assumed the Sonny Boy Williamson name when he started broadcasting on the influential King Biscuit Time radio show in 1941. Practically all these players used either the Hohner American Ace harmonica, or the 10-hole diatonic Marine Band which would become the definitive blues harmonica. As Billy Boy Arnold, who followed John Lee Williamson in his youth, puts it: "Sonny Boy was the first guy I ever saw using one – the Marine Band was the best harmonica for the price, and the best for blues. It was just a regular 10-hole harmonica, but it had a better sound and overall tone – it was made better, and held up better than any of the competition."

A major turning point in the instrument's history was the advent of amplification: John Lee Williamson started playing amplified harmonica for club dates around 1946, as did namesake Sonny Boy Williamson II.

Within a couple of years players including Snooky Pryor and, most significantly, Marion Jacobs, later known as Little Walter, perfected a swooping powerful sound which he named the 'Mississippi Saxophone.' Little Walter's work with Muddy Waters, and solo efforts such as his 1951 single 'Juke,' established the simple $2.50 instrument as one of the staple sounds of the blues. Since then, although the harmonica has been primarily associated with blues, other players including Toots Thielemans, John Lennon and Stevie Wonder have used the harmonica in jazz, rock and soul formats.

renowned organist who had worked with Bob Dylan and Paul Butterfield, Blood, Sweat and Tears featured a highly prominent horn section which included Randy Brecker. Kooper left the group after its first album *Child Is The Father To The Man* and the group, with new singer David Clayton Thomas, went on to even greater success with hits including 'Spinning Wheel' and 'You've Made Me So Very Happy.'

By the late 1960s, the very groups who had helped put brass players out of work were hiring them, and just as in the New Orleans scene of the 1950s, most of the sessionmen were skilled jazz musicians. The Beatles had, of course, started augmenting their basic sound with 1964's 'Yesterday'; by 1966's *Revolver*, the Beatles were using French horn and full brass sections. One of the major spurs for The Beatles' development came from The Beach Boys' Brian Wilson, who in turn was influenced by both Phil Spector and The Beatles to use ever more lavish arrangements. Spector used practically symphonic instrumentation on songs such as Ike & Tina Turner's 'River Deep, Mountain High.' Spector's arrangements were generally penned by Jack Nitzsche, but Brian Wilson, perhaps even more obsessed with minute detail, took on this task himself, working closely with his session musicians to obtain exactly the right texture for his epic work, *Pet Sounds*. Steve Douglas, of

Duane Eddy fame, was the musician who generally translated Wilson's hummed head arrangements into charts which could feature up to nine players, some of whom doubled on other instruments. Plas Johnson, whose tenor sax can be heard on Henry Mancini's *Pink Panther* theme, Larry Williams' 'Bony Maronie,' and the Coasters' 'Youngblood,' was just one distinguished name in the talent-packed section. All of a sudden, it became obvious that rock arrangements could use just about any instrument the composer could imagine. In some cases this might mean state of the art synthesizers, or 1930s Theremins; but more often this meant a living, breathing horn player, who could generate real emotion within the first couple of notes.

■ *Little Walter (left) was the master of the 'Mississippi saxophone,' although other players including Sonny Boy Williamson II (main shot) had amplified the harmonica even earlier. The instrument's image soon changed from the staid one portrayed by the Hohner brochure, below, which was printed in the 1950s, just as Walter was making his name.*

Three in harmony with

HOHNER

■ *Blood, Sweat And Tears showed the commercial potential of the horn section with many tightly-arranged* hits including 'You've Made Me So Very Happy,' 'And When I Die' and 'Spinning Wheel.'

Blowing In the Seventies

As the 1960s ended, the prospects for horn players were considerably brighter than they had been at the beginning of the decade. Aside from smaller bands augmenting their sound with brass section on record, there were many bands using brass as an integral part of their sound. Chicago, formed in 1970, was a very slick outfit featuring superb jazzy brass arrangements which blended surprisingly well with rock guitar. The band had many hits including '25 Or 6 To 4,' and 'If You Leave Me Now.' Like BS&T, it is still going strong. Tower of Power made its debut in 1970, encouraged by Fillmore Auditorium boss Bill Graham. Including Steve 'the funky doctor' Kupka (baritone sax), Greg Adams (trumpet), Mic Gillette (trumpet and trombone), Emilio Castillo and Lenny Pickett (tenor saxes), these guys burned – and still do. Serious use of the baritone sax, jazzy voicings and stuttering rhythms make the fat Tower of Power sound instantly recognizable. On the commercial end of the market there was some pretty hip stuff happening in the 1970s. Trumpeter Jerry Hey, originally with a Christian jazz-funk group called Seawind, became the supremo L.A. studio cat. You can hear his work on the brilliant Al Jarreau and Michael Jackson records of the 1970s and 1980s. It's interesting to note that Hey was responsible for the brass arranging on arranger Quincy Jones' smooth groove productions.

As James Brown's successors packed the charts, several major bands popularized the sound of the funky horn. The Ohio Players, who evolved from Wilson Pickett's backing band, were a huge commercial success; Earth Wind and Fire's stratospheric groove created one of the most influential brass section sounds of all time, characterized by repetitive semiquaver (16th note) riffs. Their album *I Am* is essential listening. It is interesting to note that although the band had a brass section of its own, The Phenix Horns, the section on its records was augmented with other players, including the phenomenal British trumpeter Derek Watkins, who played lead on some of their classic tracks. The extremely popular jazz-funksters The Crusaders had many hits, led by pianist Joe Sample, featuring saxman Wilton Felder and trombonist Wayne Henderson.

As the 1970s progressed, even punk saxophone became popular, perhaps in the guise of David Bowie (whose playing has been compared by namesake Lester Bowie to that of Bill Clinton), or else with the U.K.'s 'Two Tone' movement, which revisited the Jamaican ska of Prince Buster. Andy Mackay of Roxy Music demonstrated that saxophone could be a vital accompaniment to the hippest art-rock. In the U.S.A. playing reached new heights of sophistication when Dave Grusin, originally Andy Williams' musical director, started a label with his engineer Larry Rosen and GRP records was formed. One of the world's foremost film composers (*On Golden Pond, Tootsie*), Grusin could create a sophisticated funk when he wanted to, notably in his score for the Robert Redford thriller *Three Days of The Condor*. Grusin also made numerous fine solo albums featuring trumpeter Chuck Findley and sax man Grover Washington Jr. (*One Of A Kind*), as well as production and arrangements in the 1970s and 1980s for artists such as Earl Klugh, flautist Dave Valentin and Lee Ritenour.

No discussion of brass can be complete without mentioning The Brecker Brothers Band. Trumpeter Randy Brecker and brother Michael were known as great jazz players on the New York scene before they ripped their way into our musical consciousness with their first album in 1975. Joined by Dave Sanborn, the Brecker Brothers' sound was innovative, exciting and musically hip. Randy Brecker's techniques of bebop over funk, counterpoint and polytonality including liberal use of upper structure triads (polyharmony) had never been used in this way before, as demonstrated by the explosion of creativity and power on 'Some Skunk Funk.'

Winds Of Change

In the last decade the popularity of funky, commercial jazz has encouraged many players to sound alike. The best players such as Tom Scott, Grover Washington Jr. and Ernie Watts have retained their individuality and made fine albums. But the most popular and most imitated of them all must be David Sanborn. After leaving the Paul Butterfield Blues Band, he joined The

The Grafton saxophone was a short-lived 1950s attempt to explore alternative materials. The instrument was used by Roxy Music's Andy Mackay (above) and briefly by Charlie Parker, whose own Grafton (below) was sold for $140,000 in 1994.

Brecker Brothers Band in 1975. Soon becoming the most in-demand studio soloist, his alto sax was featured on records by the likes of Stevie Wonder, Steely Dan, and David Bowie. His many solo albums are melodic, soulful and compositionally excellent featuring his gutsy yet lyrical style. In a world of Sanborn sound-alikes, he's the real thing. Michael Brecker is considered by many to be the finest tenor sax player on the planet. His prodigious technique and fluid mastery of many styles, as displayed with The Brecker Brothers Band and Steps Ahead, in addition to his many brilliant solo albums, gives him an unassailable place in sax history. He also pioneered the use of the EWI (Electronic Wind Instrument) which looks something like a chair leg – and occasionally sounds like it in less gifted hands. Though he plays tenor and alto sax masterfully, Branford Marsalis is probably best known for his soprano work with Sting on such hits as 'Englishman in New York.' His three year stint as musical director of *The Tonight Show* made him one of the highest profile jazz musicians of our time (his trumpet-playing brother Wynton, while rather more circumspect about crossing over to the rock field, has also been a crucial jazz evangelist). Add to that a number of critically and financially

successful solo jazz, blues and classical albums, acting roles, film scores, tours, and a wicked sense of humor, and it's obvious why he has been so influential. With 1990s projects such as *Buckshot LeFonque*, Marsalis takes elements from hip-hop, rap, and hard bop.

Today we are in a world where there seems to be very little innovative music being marketed. As a result, what we get that has value is 'retro,' looking back to classic music of the past for inspiration. We see an example of this in the brass of the excellent group Incognito whose 1990s version of 1970s smooth funk is beautifully executed. Elsewhere, a new generation of rap bands is sampling classic horn riffs by the likes of James Brown and George Clinton's Funkadelic, as well as classic sax-driven records on soul labels such as Kent and Stax. As in the 1960s, wind instruments remain expensive to purchase, difficult to master, and problematic to record compared to a D.I.'d sampler, but still capable of supremely moving music in the right hands.

■ *While the saxophone remains popular thanks to players such as Branford Marsalis (below), the flute is less ubiquitous, with Jethro Tull's Ian Anderson (top) its main champion. Gil Scott-Heron collaborator Brian Jackson has helped popularize the flute in the soul field, influencing records such as Prince's 1992 hit 'Gett Off.'*

77

■ *Although Japanese companies have been less dominant in the brass and woodwind field than in other areas of musical instrument manufacture, both Yanigasawa and Yamaha have gained respectable reputations. Yamaha's easy blowing 61 and 62 series saxes such as the YAS 62 (left) are thought to have had some influence on Selmer's successful Super 80 Mark II (above).*

Live Sound

"I think that at the beginning of the 1960s the standard of live sound was terrible. But then it went on to develop in tandem with the music. The bands that were playing then, The Who, Fleetwood Mac, The Move, all cared about how they sounded on stage, so as a PA manufacturer you'd work hand in hand with them. Those first festivals were a special time, and I was happy to be part of it."

CHARLIE WATKINS, WEM

The parts that make up the PA system have arrived through distinct evolutionary paths. The mikes, mixers and processors – or 'front end' parts – owe much to recording studio techniques. But the 'back-end' parts – crossovers, amplifiers and speakers – are unique to bringing music in the flesh to crowds the size of cities, while their technological development has been largely driven and funded by the music.

When rock'n'roll music was evolving in 1948, the transistor had just been invented, but was scarcely known to the public, and wasn't ready to amplify music. The key to electronic amplification had been unlocked 40 or so years earlier. Primitive microphones and speakers had been developed for telephone, but the advent of electronic amplification vastly increased their potential. Electronic engineering was born in the U.K., with Fleming's patent for a two element 'diode' tube, or valve, inspired after a meeting with Edison. The diode couldn't amplify but with only small further steps it was turned into a three electrode tube, or triode, which could. Lee de Forest patented the triode in the U.S.A. in 1906, and by 1907 he had used it to broadcast music by wireless for the first time.

The subsequent development of entertainment technology advanced more quickly in the U.S.A. than it did in the U.K. and Europe, hindered by an uncertain political climate and World War II. In 1915, tubes were used in the U.S.A. to amplify speeches at mass gatherings. By 1921, crowds of 125,000 were being covered with what would have sounded like a very loud telephone. The first music to be amplified by a PA system was the kind that would have accompanied political speeches and state occasions.

In 1925, the first electric record player was launched in America and the everyday cone loudspeaker was developed in the U.S.A. from the telephone earpiece, by replacing the vibrating steel plate with a paper cone. In the same year, talking movies began, hugely increasing the impetus for the development of amplification, and in subsequent years Western Electric, the manufacturing arm of Bell Labs, and later Altec and RCA made rapid progress with developing sound equipment. Towards the end of the 1930s big band boom, singers, or crooners, would generally carry their own small combo amplifiers and microphones; in the U.K. the singer in a well-equipped dance-band could be using a Coles or STC microphone, fed into a large and heavy three tube 'power' amplifier which delivered typically 15 watts to a 10" cone speaker. Of course, swing bands, with their loud horn section needed little amplification: merely a few watts of power for the singer. Even so, the advent of amplification helped foster a new generation of singers who understood the basics of what we'd now call microphone technique – Frank Sinatra was perhaps the best-known crooner who utilized the full dynamic range enabled by amplification. As rock'n'roll developed, PA systems remained cinema-oriented, and early performers invariably used in-house PA systems. Performers would use small onstage amplifiers, 40 watts maximum, while the drummer would rely on the acoustic volume of the kit to cut through. A maximum of two microphones would generally be used for one band, with a PA system of around 40 watts to amplify the vocalist.

Into The Sixties

If late 1950s rock'n'roll PAs were primitive, those in Europe as the skiffle boom prepared the ground for the beatboom were more basic still. Vocalists would typically utilize a domestic Grundig tape recorder, switching to 'record' and pressing the 'pause' button to create a makeshift four watt amplifier. Other equipment pressed into use included Leak hi-fi amplifiers with a separate preamp; Vortexion 'Wireless' and Grampian public address amps; and even Philips domestic radio sets. As the Merseybeat boom got underway, bands progressed to using equipment which was at least part intended for the rigors of the road. Mikes, often square Reslos, would be limited to vocals,

■ *Rigging a P.A. in Liverpool, England, in the early 1960s rarely involved a soundcheck, according to veteran live sound engineer Baz Ward. The gear was simply thrown on stage and everyone helped everyone else to set up. Most clubs, cinemas and theaters had a house PA, which should have saved bands from carting their own around. But the house PAs were hopeless, often with facility for only one mike and barely audible speakers. The pivotal Cavern Club in Liverpool had one of the better PAs with two 12" speakers either side of the stage – U.K. beatgroup Gerry And The Pacemakers use Selmer all-purpose cabinets in this early 1960s shot. A favorite PA cab of the era was a thin, Vox column speaker with four 10" Goodmans 10 watt drive units inside, and tall, spindly legs to raise the cab to project over and into the audience. The roadies of the era did one better; they drove big nails into the plaster and hung the unstable contraptions upside-down, like bats.*

MEAZZI FACTOTUM
STEREO ECHOMATIC

Here's the last word in combined echo-reverb-amplifiers, the amazing Meazzi Factotum, specially designed with emphasis on group or orchestra use. Five separate inputs enable a number of instruments to be amplified through two independent 18 watt amplifiers—with a variety of echo and reverberation effects controlled by simple push buttons. Two speaker columns complete with floor stands and wall supports, each carrying 6 highly efficient speakers provide high fidelity stereophonic sound reproduction. The Factotum is undoubtedly the finest value in its class to-day.

No. 133. Including waterproof cover for amplifier section .. **175 gns.**

SPECIFICATION

2—18 watt independent amplifiers feeding each tone column. Total 36 watts.

6 Speakers in each tone column.

5 Inputs. Built-in mixer.

Separate volume control for each tone column.

Separate Bass, treble and echo-volume controls.

Push-pull on/off echo switches on input controls.

Remote on/off control.

Remote wander lead.

Fan cooling in metal cabinet.

8 combinations of Reverb and Echo effects.

Varying degrees of echo.

Illuminated on/off indicator.

Valves : 6—type 12AX7, 1—type 6AT6, 5—type EL84, 2—type EZ81.
Mains supply : 110, 125, 140, 160, 220, 245 volts. 50 cycles A.C.

and possibly sax. Purpose built PA amplifiers of the era included Linear Concorde and models by Vortexion, which had simple, integral mixers. Giant Bakelite knobs provided gain control for four mikes, and overall tone control. Failing this, WEM's Dominator tube guitar amplifier, rated at 25 watts with 2x10" speakers, would be pressed into use, together with the WEM Copicat or Binson Echorec tape echo machines, which could be used as a primitive mixer.

Five years later, when The Beatles played the giant Shea Stadium as the opening date of their third U.S. tour, the PA was limited to public address trumpet horns. The terrible sound quality was, perhaps fortunately, masked by the audience's screams.

■ *Early PA systems were regarded as distinctly unglamorous, and in the early 1960s were sometimes combined with early tape echo units in order to present a more attractive package to aspiring vocalists. The Meazzi Factotum was typical of many Italian-built PA systems distributed throughout Europe. Most of these tape delay-based units evolved from amplification systems designed for accordions. The Factotum offered five inputs, a variety of tape delay effects, 36 watts of tube power, and two speaker columns, each with six speakers.*

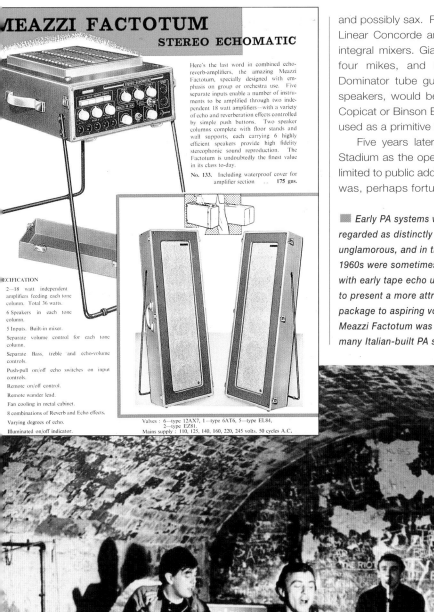

By this time several companies, including the U.K. Selmer and Vox companies, had started producing portable 100 watt PA amplifiers. But as the vogue for 100 watt Marshall stacks evolved within the next year, PA technology struggled to keep up. Using more than one tube PA amplifier did not help, because their 'peaky' frequency response in combination with the early PA mikes and primitive speakers soon caused feedback. This frustrated the attainment of higher sound levels for the vocals.

Solid State Logic

At the onset of this period, solid state electronics took over musical PA. Transistor amplifiers had been around since the late 1950s, but it wasn't until 1965 that relatively high powers, above 10 watts and up to 200 watts, were being achieved.

Perhaps the chief architect of the modern PA system was Charlie Watkins, trading as Watkins Electric Music. Watkins was a visionary who knew the future would be electric music when he set up in 1953. In WEM's first decade, he'd established the Dominator guitar amps and the ubiquitous Copicat tape-echo. But 1965 was a bad year for WEM, and 1966 worse, as he supplied U.S. band The Byrds with equipment for their U.K. tour.

The concept of the rock festival – and the festival PA – evolved from the U.K. Windsor Jazz and Blues festival, which started in 1966 and grew into the popular Reading festival. This 1967 photo shows the debut of both Fleetwood Mac, and the WEM 1000 watt Festival PA.

This attempt to keep up with the powerful Marshall instrument amps failed. Therefore Watkins resolved to build a hugely powerful PA, using the new, transformerless transistor amplifiers. Without the transformer required by output tubes, the frequency response was far smoother; thus the anticipated gain in sound level could be practically developed without acoustic feedback. The 1000 watt WEM PA comprised ten 100 watt amplifiers, using the new RCA silicon transistors and circuitry, driving 4x12" column speakers with smoother response than earlier kinds. There was no High Frequency (HF) horn yet; the Goodmans

Axiom cone drive-units had a secondary 'drone-cone' to help the high frequencies. The combination of new technologies worked, and premiered with great success at the 1967 Windsor Jazz and Blues festival, precursor of the long-lived U.K. Reading Rock Festival. It was the world's first, high clarity, high power, touring PA system.

The more image-conscious groups, like The Move and The Pink Floyd, were soon vying to own the most power. Before long, British bands were touring the world with PA systems of 4000 watts – previously undreamt of power. Musicians suddenly developed an interest in PA, and WEM's factory became an important meeting place where they could exchange ideas. Between 1966 and 1971, the arrangement of touring PA systems as they are known today was largely developed and established by WEM, driven by Charlie Watkins, his determination and his receptiveness to his clients' ideas. The link between musicians and the PA equipment creator had never been closer.

Early in 1968, after three years of development, WEM made their first Audiomaster mixer available – the first 'outboard' mixer to be accepted for music PA. The Audiomaster was not only much quieter and more sophisticated than the earlier tube mixers; several could also be linked to provide as many input channels as were needed. Meanwhile, better mikes began to appear as the ones brought over by touring U.S. bands were studied. Shure's Unidyne III and 545 rapidly found favor, as did the Unisphere. It would later became famous as the SM58.

While American rock had been taken by surprise by the British invasion, by 1967 entrepreneurs such as the Fillmore's Bill Graham had hired researchers from Berkeley University to help develop lighting and electrical systems. The Fillmore East sound system was based on a 1940s design, the Altec Voice Of The Theatre system, which was compact yet loud,

ωεм

AUDIOMASTER MIXER

▇ WEM founder Charlie
Watkins with Festival
speaker stack.

and by 1969 venues such as the Fillmore were starting to use microphones on every instrument. As in the U.K., the 'roadie' doing the mixing had to periodically race out into the audience to check the sound. But there were also soundchecks – the musicians would play a few numbers before the gig to allow the roadie to set-up the sound on the mixer.

Influenced by American techniques, U.K. roadies began to 'mike-up' all the instruments, and Audiomaster mixers were soon joined together to handle as many as 20 microphones. Miking-up allowed each instrument's contribution to be controlled – at least in theory – and also gave a new set of sounds. Miked-up drums were particularly dramatic.

Stage monitoring was invented in a day in 1968 at the Kempton Park 'pop' festival, in south-west London. Singers had already complained that they couldn't hear themselves sing on stage, even though their vocals were loud on the PA out front. Coincidentally, Charlie Watkins, who was providing the WEM PA, had rigged up a long signal cable, an amp and a spare speaker so he wouldn't miss the Savoy Blues band playing in the adjacent marquee. Nearby him, British R&B star Chris Farlowe was trying to sing, unable to hear himself. Hearing music coming from the listening-in speaker, he gestured wildly: "Turn it round on me." Charlie did this, gave him an earful of the Savoy Blues' set, then quickly realized he could re-plug the amp into the stage's Audiomaster, to relay the vocals. That done, Farlowe's face took on an ecstatic expression, the quality of his singing improved dramatically and the sidefill monitor had been invented. The news reached the other bands before the set finished and when Roger Chapman came on with Family, he grabbed the 1x12" 'monitor,'

Woodstock 1969 was amplified with a state of the art system designed by Bill Hanley. The three-way speakers used Altec and JBL units. MacIntosh M1200 and 3150 amps, plus the brand new Crown DC300, provided the 10kW of power, which in hindsight was inadequate for the 700 acre site. The 20-input desk was also custom-made.

and put it on the floor, using a sweater to prop it up at 45 degrees, creating the first wedge monitor. By 1969, Bobby Pridden, The Who's sound engineer, had persuaded Watkins to modify their Audiomasters, adding an output especially for driving stage monitors. In the same year, Bill Hanley equipped the Woodstock festival with early 'sidefill' monitors.

Remote Control

In 1970, 'Dinky' Dorson, engineer with Fleetwood Mac, brought back Belden multicore cable from the U.S.A., where it was used

for factory intercoms, and using the Audiomaster mixers, he mixed 'out front' in the middle of the audience at London's Lyceum, for the first time. By 1970, Charlie Watkins had pioneered touring and festival PA systems consistent with the U.K.'s reputation as a world center of progressive rock. But after the second Isle of Wight festival and the death of Jimi Hendrix, the magical atmosphere soured, and other innovators took over to complete the development of music PA.

The more widely traveled bands wanted to use the 'bin and horn' cinema speakers they had seen and used in the U.S.A. It was, ironically, because U.S. venues were well equipped that the lead in developing touring PA was taken by British bands. The old horn-loaded speakers were attractive because when fitted with adequately rated speakers they could produce far more sound level than conventional cabinets. In 1970, Iron Butterfly toured the U.K., bringing with them a 1937 RCA cinema speaker system with a giant eight foot high 'W' bass-bin. The size and loud bass developed by these speakers caused something of a sensation and at the tour's end, they sold the PA to their support group, Yes. PA soon began to suffer from a 'power at all costs' syndrome.

Before long Bill Kelsey and Jim Morris (as Kelsey-Morris) were manufacturing modified versions of cinema horns in London. King Crimson, T.Rex and Alvin Lee's Ten Years After were among the users. British bands also turned to Vitavox, who had long been the native maker of horn technology. At this time, bands began to experiment with some of the high power amplifiers built in the U.S.A., most of them designed for industrial use. These included Crown's DC300, and models by SAE, one rated at up to 1000 watts into 1 ohm. By now, PA systems had caught up with the instrument amplifiers, already called 'backline'. But the early horn

■ Stage monitoring debuted at Woodstock with sidefill monitors. There was no intercom from the stage to the outfront mixer – consequently the mix engineer had to guess which fader was which.

speakers could sound harsh and painful: creating high sound levels without destroying the music's nuances required skill.

The horn speakers' sound was readily improved by going from 2-way to 3-way operation, where a separate, dedicated speaker handled the midrange. This required an extra section in the crossover, which directed the bass frequencies to the bass-bin. The crossovers of the time were 'passive,' designed for a few watts in cinemas, yet were being pushed into handling hundreds of watts. In 1971, Kelsey-Morris experimented with low level crossovers ahead of the amplifiers. One early example was built for Pink Floyd in an Old Holborn tobacco tin. A typical system of this time comprised Electrovoice 1829 or Vitavox S2 HF drivers, a JBL D120 paper-edged cone speaker on midrange, and 15″ JBL drivers on bass. Then in 1972, the new Midas PA, designed by Jeff Byers and Chas Brooke with advice from Scott Thompson of Colac, advanced clarity at high levels with the first active system. Here, the 'frequency division' was accomplished at low signal levels, using ICs, and the music could be readily split into three, four or more bands, to suit the speakers, without power loss. Supertramp was the first user.

Around this time, British and American speaker practice flipped. The large numbers of horns used in the huge, impressive-looking PA systems of this period created a painful sound, described as 'ear ripping,' even when they were stacked and angled with great care

so the sound sources did not fight and create 'comb filter' or 'phasey' effects. This caused U.S. PA operators to largely abandon horn-loading. Instead, they reverted to basic direct-radiator speaker boxes (like huge domestic hi-fi speakers) which were 10 times less efficient at turning amplifier watts into useful sound pressure. It took 15 years for users scared off horns to realize that this made the problems of interacting sound sources far worse, as even more cabs were needed to achieve the same sound levels. More typically, fewer cabinets were used, and even fitted with very high power

■ By the mid 1970s monitor levels increased, partly thanks to the likes of Keith Moon who had these Martin monitors designed for increased volume.
■ On the far left, Ralph McTell plays at the 1970 Isle Of Wight Festival; the WEM Festival system was on this occasion augmented with The Who's touring PA.

rated drive-units (from 100W in 1971 up to 1000W each by 1989), these had to be driven hard into distortion to 'kick.' Meanwhile, some designers stuck with horn speaker technology.

One was Dave Martin, an Australian living in London who had previously built powerful horn speaker systems for fun back home, and had helped Kelsey-Morris design a bass bin that was smaller and yet more effective than the RCA W-bin.

In 1974, he set up Martin Acoustics and teamed up with Midas, whose co-founder Jeff Byers had moved on from making transistor guitar amps in London to professional PA mixers. Midas had also produced, in 1973, a dedicated 'block' of four amplifiers totaling 1000 watts, to simplify PA rigging. The Martin-Midas PA was the first mass-marketed, expandable, modern format package PA, with 4-way

■ *By the late 1970s 'Flying' systems, hung above the stage to improve sightlines, were becoming popular. This Martin Audio System dates from 1982.*

■ *Martin PA package includes the company's trademark 'Philishave' cabinet, top left.*

cabinets – bass, low and hi-mid and treble. By 1975, it incorporated the visually memorable M212 'Philishave' midrange cabinet – looking like a huge electric razor. For nearly a decade afterwards 'Martin-Midas' (or a look-a-like) was synonymous with PA.

Another key player was Tony Andrews, also residing in London, who had begun building PA speakers in 1969. In 1970, he designed and supplied the PA for the anarchic Hawkwind and Pink Fairies' free festival – staged outside the second Isle of Wight festival compound. Even then he had outdone WEM's column, with a 4x15″ cabinet with two Midax (HF) horns on top. He wondered why it wasn't possible, even with efficient horn speakers, to get sound as good as that of hi-fi headphones. By 1973, working with Tim Isaac, he was hiring out a PA with purple speaker cabs, working as Sonic Trucking (later Turbosound Rentals) and the two had hit upon a radical improvement over the painful midrange compression drivers used with horn and bin PA speakers of the time. Their curious invention, a round midrange horn that looked like a jet engine, was soon dubbed 'the Turbo' by avant-garde musician Tim Blake. The new horn, and a similarly well tuned bass bin that developed out of competition with Dave Martin, formed a system that captured the imagination of those musicians who appreciated the unusually clean sound – far superior to the commercial PA sound of the day. Steve Hillage was an early user of what would be later known as the Turbosound festival system. But it would take ten years of continuous experimentation, listening, testing on the road, and supplying the sound for the Glastonbury Festival before musicians the world over would benefit.

Hire Ground

By 1975, the equipment needed to stage a professional show was such that only a few major bands continued to own their PA systems. The notable exceptions at the time were The Grateful Dead in the U.S., with a huge system developed from that designed by electronic guru and acid king Stan Owsley; and in Britain, The Pink Floyd, Jethro Tull, and The Enid. In September 1974 Crosby, Stills, Nash and Young's rented system, weighing

---

The Modern PA System

The equipment in a modern show begins with the sound sources, which may be microphones (mikes) chosen for their diverse sonic qualities, and rejection of other sounds on stage; or DI boxes, where the signal from an 'electric' or electronic instrument (typically keyboards and bass guitar) is directly injected. Or they may be 'bugs' – contact mikes that are clipped to a soundboard. Neither bugs nor DI boxes cause howlround – the bugbear of all PA systems. But all three types are needed at different times to do justice to different kinds of music in differing conditions.

The individual signal cables converge at stage boxes, at the rear wings of the stage, where they enter the multicore cable(s). To enable stage monitor consoles and also broadcasting and recording trucks to connect to the signal sources, without problems with noise, safety and sound quality, active mike splitters are increasingly used, which boost the low-level signals. Up to 4″ thick, the main multicore cable conveys from 16 up to 128 signals to the F.O.H. (front of hall) mixer. In the future, digital or even better, optical transmission will be used. Using techniques established in data communications, they can carry hundreds of signals on a single wire – as long as they are digital. Microphones, bugs and DI boxes, all, at present, produce analog signals.

The PA mixing console (or 'desk') has much in common with its recording studio counterpart. Each signal source is allocated its own channel. The signal emerging from each of the channels is grouped with logical relatives. For example, all the mikes on a drum kit will usually be combined in a secondary channel, called a subgroup. Here, one fader can be used to change the level of the entire drum sound. The subgroups are then 'mixed down' in turn to the stereo outputs. There are now just two signals – left and right. The desk's stereo output signals pass on to an FX (sound effects) rack, containing equipment used to give overall control over the signal, usually a third octave EQ (equalizer), and sometimes a delay line (which may be tapped, so there are outputs with different delays sent to different PA speaker locations). A recent possible addition is an electronic howlround eliminator, which uses a computer to track and 'tune out' the

■ *Carver PT series amplifiers use 'Class G' operation, delivering high power with high efficiency.*

72,000 pounds, was flown in a Boeing airliner across the Atlantic along with a technical crew of 36, for a concert at Wembley Stadium along with The Band and Joni Mitchell. This was an early measure of the increasing size, complexity and logistics that soon led to the development of PA hire companies. The original big hire company was IES Entertainments in 1970, which supplied Led Zeppelin and Rod Stewart with impressively loud but mediocre sound until 1973, when its owner sold up. Other early large touring U.K. PA hire outfits included Electrosound, owned by Rikki Farr, who had staged the Isle of Wight festivals. ENTEC was short for Entertainment Technicians, and run by Harold Pendleton, owner of The Marquee venue and studio, and promoter of the Reading Festival. TASCO, The American Sound Co (which was in fact British), evolved from Marshall Equipment Hire, founded in 1970 with £200 from Jim Marshall, and supplied The Rolling Stones. The British dominance of touring PA was illustrated by the fact that Clair Brothers and TFA were the only comparable U.S. rental companies in the early 1970s, later to be joined by MSI (Maryland Sound Inc), Showco and Eurotech.

Between 1980 and 1996, as sound equipment technology matured, and with increased competition in the worldwide hire market and the chaotic fluctuations in the amount of major tour work, many of the established, large rental companies merged with their competitors. For example, Britannia Row Productions of London, Europe's largest hire company, is the result of the merging of at least five companies including the descendants of Pink Floyd's own PA company, TFA and Turbosound Rentals. Others disappeared.

Monitoring The Situation

Stage monitoring was slow to develop in comparison to the out-front PA. The musicians' attitude generally split into two

precise frequencies which are causing acoustic feedback. Every rack concludes with an active crossover which sends the appropriate frequencies to the different loudspeaker drive-units.

The left and right channel high, mid and low frequency signals then travel back to the stage (and also down the field, in big outdoor events) on the returns multicore cable, where they are connected to the racks of power amps. Each frequency band feeds a number of amplifiers in tandem. At the amplifiers' outputs, heavyweight multicore speaker cables provide independent connection to the bass, mid and high-frequency drive-units in each (speaker) box, which may be stacked under the stage (sub-bass and fill-ins); stacked in the wings; or flown above on a truss, as shown in the system used by U.K. band Take That, above right.

■ *Clair monitors: The Clair Brothers company is now one of the longest established PA companies.*

■ *Soundcraft Delta desk: one of several popular U.K. lines.*

Modern festivals routinely feature PA systems boasting 1000 times the power of their 1960s equivalents. Woodstock 1994 and the Masters Of Music Hyde Park concert of 1996, with The Who and Eric Clapton, each used PA systems of around one million watts.

camps. Disciplined and well-seasoned musicians got on with their job, regardless of whether the monitors were good, bad or absent; other players found the adrenalin that came from having ultra-loud sound on the stage improved their playing and stamina. Martin Audio satisfied the latter camp with the first modern, seriously loud wedge monitor speaker, LE-200, in 1973. The related LE-400 is still made 20 years later. But it wasn't until 1975 that Midas introduced purpose-built monitor mixers which had six or more outputs, so each musician could have an individual mix of instruments – choosing whatever they needed to play well. Before this, most musicians had to make do without dedicated monitoring mixing, and rely instead on one of the four monitor sends from the 'out front' engineer – who was mostly too busy to give proper attention. Members of highly equipped bands such as ELP had individual mixes – even if this meant each musician having a complete monitor system including a separate Audiomaster mixer. But this was cumbersome to set up and operate. It was also in 1975 that Midas introduced the first large out front mixer for PA – called a desk – with a control layout (almost horizontal), features (such

as subgroups), and controls (such as 4 band EQ) that have remained standard. About the same time, third-octave graphic equalizers were introduced, at first by Stephen Court on the Roxy Music tour. With 27 bands of tonal adjustment, these were initially used to help control bad acoustics out front. But before long, they were also in use on monitors where they could be tuned to get louder levels before howlround. In 1979, Brooke-Siren Systems (later BSS), founded by ex-Midas co-founder Chas Brooke, produced a new active crossover, MCS-100, which soon became established as standard PA equipment.

The Modern PA

By 1980, digital effects and processors had started to appear in PA equipment racks. Other than supplying the sound effects ('FX') used in the studio, these included delays which enabled PA speakers at widely spaced locations in big venues, and also outdoors, to be synchronized. Without delays, spaced speaker stacks (other than the usual two stacks either side of the stage) would create horrible echoes and distortion. Also in 1980, Muscle Music, a London hire company, developed 3-way, active wedge monitors specially for The Jam and Iron Maiden. These achieved a stunningly loud 125dB SPL at the mike position (just four feet from the speaker) before howlround, without being painful. Clair Brothers in the U.S. had produced their first full-range 'integrated' PA cabinet in 1970. By 1977, British designers had gone further: Red Acoustics produced 3-way 'active' PA speakers (4 x 8″ plus 4 x HF) with amplifiers on-board, but the U.K. safety regulations forbade their use at major gigs, effectively killing powered cabinet technology world-wide. In the Clair Brothers and also Court's Black Box system of 1975, one box – as compact as possible – contained the appropriate number of bass, mid and high frequency speakers for tonal balance and sound coverage. Any number of these boxes could be stacked like bricks by relatively unskilled crew – at least in theory. Others copied. By 1981, this kind of cab was becoming increasingly common on U.S. tours, where the simplified wiring and set-up saved expensive, unionized labor costs, particularly with the new emphasis on 'flying', with most speakers hung above the stage. This cleared sightlines, allowing more seats to be sold, but could also improve sound quality for a variety of reasons.

Round The Horn

In 1982, Turbosound launched their TMS3, an all-horn-loaded, all-in-one box cab which challenged the Clair Brothers' S3 enclosure. Turbosound followed up with a range of efficient, compact and clean sounding horn speaker enclosures, and pioneered easy ways to fly the cabinets in hemispherical arrays. Subsequently in the U.S., Klipsch and Community, who had maintained the development of niche horn technology, were rediscovered, while other U.S. makers followed. In 1990 and again in 1994, Turbosound set the technological pace, by launching Flashlight and then Floodlight horn speaker systems, which were finely attuned to the modern needs of no-waste, focused sound in stadiums and large festival PA rigs. More improvements arrived as the previous bipolar transistors used in the output stages of most amplifiers were replaced by MOS

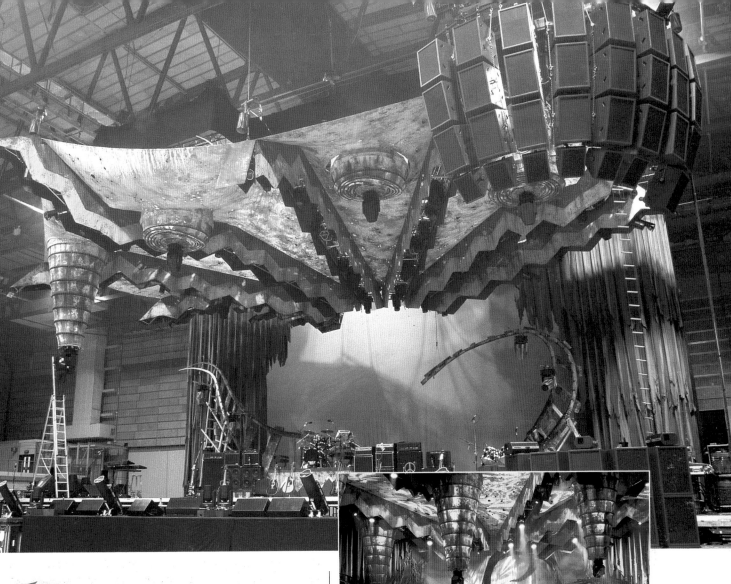

■ Oasis at Manchester's Maine Road stadium in 1995. The band's 1996 appearance in front of a 250,000-strong crowd at Knebworth required a Britannia Row system which used 13 delay towers.

■ U.K. alternative band The Cure used a Britannia Row BRP Arena system, with flying cabinets, for their 1996 'The Swing Tour.'

power transistors (or MOS-FETs) which combined great ruggedness with speed, and were responsible for much of the subsequently enhanced treble at concerts.

Between 1980 and 1996, PA systems have shrunk in size and quality has greatly improved in the better systems, without being any less powerful. They have become quicker and easier to set-up. The sound quality has increased immensely. But the sound on the night is as ever down to the skill and wits of the mixing engineer and the limitations and vagaries of the venue's acoustics. In the meantime, live performance technology is increasingly bogged down by social, 'noise' and safety legislation, as well as tight, competitive budgets.

Drums

"People say rock'n'roll is about pianos or guitars, but that ain't a fact. Rock'n'roll is about rhythm. When all the record companies came to New Orleans to make rock'n'roll records, it wasn't for the horn players, or the pianists. They all said, We've come here for the rhythm. The drums are the heartbeat of rock'n'roll – it wouldn't even be alive without them."

EARL KING, NEW ORLEANS SONGWRITER

Instruments of percussion are among the oldest artefacts known to mankind. But the modern drum kit is barely 60 years old. It started its evolution around 1900, when the diverse percussion of music theater combined with the marching drums of the military, sparking the new music of jazz. By the mid 1930s Gene Krupa – the charismatic young star with Benny Goodman's swing orchestra – was playing a drum kit essentially similar to that used by rock groups today. So the modern drum kit was around before rock'n'roll was invented. Still, we only have to go back a few decades to see how it came about.

The drum kit came out of the theater, where money and space were both tight, and multiple percussion was regularly handled by one or two individuals; hence the idea that by sitting and using their feet, one player could cover more instruments.

■ *Despite being known for playing a rhythm part on his thighs on Buddy Holly's 'Peggy Sue,' Crickets drummer Jerry Allison normally opted for the more conventional white Ludwig four-piece shown here.*

This imaginative leap was sealed in 1909 when the Chicago percussionist William F. Ludwig – overworked by fast ragtime tempos – fashioned for himself the first modern foot-operated bass drum pedal, and with his brother Theobald was pressed into making them for other drummers. Playing the bass drum with the foot became less tiring, and the hands were free to play anything that could be mounted within reach. The drum kit's evolution had taken a crucial step; it was now inevitable the adventurous drummer would gradually develop the four way co-ordination which has led to the amazing virtuosity of some of today's players.

Early 'traps' kits often featured a 'console' device (the precursor of today's rack systems) with a 28″ or bigger bass drum (now termed a kick drum because of its foot-operated status), multiple sound effects, Chinese toms with single tacked-on heads, and small Chinese and Turkish cymbals. One of the most extraordinary set-ups – an accumulation that wouldn't shame a symphony orchestra – belonged to Duke Ellington's Sonny Greer. But such colorful collections of oddities were doomed when the advent of talkies reduced the need for sound effects in the cinema. Then suddenly the swing era ushered in the fashion for large and loud touring jazz orchestras with a wicked, driving dance beat. The success of the Benny Goodman Orchestra, which epitomized the swing era, was comparable to the later commercial impact of rock'n'roll; and the handsome, flamboyant Gene Krupa became a household name. Krupa persuaded the Slingerland drum company to make him a kit with the first double-headed tunable toms; the consequent Radio King set is the model from which the modern kit would develop.

Putting The Beat In Rock'n'Roll

Since, as we've seen, jazz predates rock, it was inevitable that the earliest American rock drummers started out playing jazz. Fred Below, who played with Chuck Berry and Muddy Waters, and Earl Palmer – a New Orleans session legend who recorded with Fats Domino and Little Richard – soon adapted their jazz triplets feel to the straight eighths of rock'n'roll, and developed a strong back beat.

The American drum industry, despite the cutbacks of World War II, was well established by the advent of rock'n'roll in the 1950s. Krupa-style kits were everywhere and although most companies suffered ups and downs (Ludwig, for instance, has had a checkered history) the rock drummer had an excellent choice of equipment from the great names such as Ludwig, Leedy, Gretsch, Slingerland and Rogers, along with

Zildjian cymbals. For a decade or more after W.W.II, Japanese and many European companies were ravaged, but the Premier Drum Company of the U.K., which had benefited from the war by being transplanted from London to Leicester and fulfiling military contracts, was in relatively good shape. Premier's engineering expertise improved through the war experience, and its drums became the choice of many American jazz legends during the 1950s and 1960s – from be-bop pioneer Kenny Clarke to brushes master Ed Thigpen.

■ *Benny Goodman's various bands had a substantial influence on rock'n'roll thanks to guitarist Charlie Christian, and flamboyant drummer Gene Krupa, shown here with Goodman circa 1935. Krupa's Slingerland Radio King set, with its double-tensioned toms as seen below, became the basis of the modern drum kit.*

■ **Trixon Telstar Kit**

Introduced: circa 1964

German-made Trixon kits, badged as Vox in the U.S., were used by many drummers including Clem Cattini of The Tornados, whose 1962 hit 'Telstar' inspired the name of this Trixon kit. The Trixon Telstar, which

Cattini would ironically never play, used a distinctive conical shape designed more for looks than sound. This 1964 Trixon catalog lists finish options as 'Croco' or crocodile skin only, in red, blue, silver or gold: Bill Haley's drummer Dick Richards models the red version below.

Drums on Record

1935: *Gene Krupa drums on 'Sing Sing Sing' with the Benny Goodman orchestra, contributing a drum solo to the record. For perhaps the first time, the drummer is the star.*

1949: *Chris Columbus, drummer with Louis Jordan's Tympany Five, records proto-rock'n'roll songs such as 'Let The Good Times Roll' and 'Caldonia.'*

1955: *New Orleans session king Earl Palmer plays drums on Little Richard's*

'Tutti Frutti' and 'Kansas City.' Next year's hits include 'Long Tall Sally.'

1957: *Chicago jazzman Fred Below plays with Chuck Berry for influential rock'n'roll singles such as 'School Day' and 'Sweet Little Sixteen.'*

1959: *Sandy Nelson, inspired to take up drums by Gene Krupa, drums on Phil Spector sessions including 'To Know Him Is To Love Him.' His self-financed recording of the drum-based instrumental, 'Teen Beat,' goes on to*

sell a million copies. Nelson plays drums on Gene Vincent's 'Wild Cat' and The Hollywood Argyles' 'Alley Oop' before scoring another million seller with the instrumental 'Let There Be Drums.'

1962: *Ringo Starr makes his live debut with The Beatles on 23 August. His no-frills drumming provides the rhythmic impetus for 1963 hits such as 'I Wanna Hold Your Hand.'*

1963: *Charlie Watts, drummer with Blues Incorporated, is persuaded to join*

The Rolling Stones. His idiosyncratic drumming, together with Keith Richard's rhythm guitar, is a vital element in the band's sound. Future Watts innovations included the distinctive use of the cowbell on 'Honky Tonk Women,' perhaps influenced by Chicago drummer Odie Payne.

1964: *The Detours are playing in Acton Town Hall, London, when an inebriated drummer sits in and meshes perfectly with the group's sound; his name is Keith Moon. He is asked to join the*

As post-war Britain struggled to rebuild its industries imports were restricted, and American gear was largely unobtainable. British drum companies had a monopoly and as in the U.S.A. there was a fair choice, with names like Ajax, Carlton, Beverley and Autocrat as familiar as the market leading Premier. Yet British drummers had long dreamed of American gear – unsurprisingly, since America was where it was all happening, and American drum gear, as with everything else American, had a quality and charisma lacking in 1950s Britain. Britain's early images of rock glamor revealed Elvis's D.J. Fontana on a Gretsch kit and Buddy Holly's Jerry Allison on his white pearl Ludwig (although early pictures show him with a minimal Premier kit). British rock drummers of the late 1950s and early 1960s, from Ringo Starr to Ian Paice, learning their craft in Hamburg, Germany, mixed with the touring American stars and hankered after American kits. They also discovered Trixon drums, which were made in Hamburg by the imaginative Karlheinz Weimer. Trixon (some badged as Vox in the U.S.) were imported into Britain by Ivor Arbiter. Pioneering British pop/rock drummers like Clem Cattini (Billy Fury, The Tornados) and Bobby Elliott (The Hollies) played Trixon for a while. Then in 1962

Arbiter opened Drum City in Shaftesbury Avenue London, and began importing Ludwig drums. Although they were literally twice as expensive as Premier, once Ringo Starr had been to Arbiter and traded in his rather staid brown mahogany Premiers for the famous oyster black Ludwigs, there was no stopping them. For the next decade or more American kits were the height of British fashion. Ludwig was undoubtedly the most popular company, but Rogers, Gretsch and Slingerland also enjoyed success in Britain.

■ *Cliff Richard and The Shadows were a virtual shop window for professional equipment in pre-beatboom Britain. In this 1962 still from the film* Summer Holiday, *Tony Meehan's champagne sparkle Gretsch four-piece complements guitarist Hank Marvin and bassist Jet Harris's top-line Fenders, all bought directly from the U.S.A.*

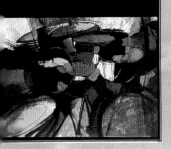

band, which changes its name to The High Numbers, and subsequently The Who. 1965's 'My Generation' boasts arguably the most electrifying drumming ever captured on a single.

1966: U.K. rock drumming becomes even more competitive as Cream's Ginger Baker and Mitch Mitchell, drummer with Jimi Hendrix's group, The Experience, burst on to the scene. Both drummers soon start using extended kits to expand their tonal range.

1969: Led Zeppelin's self-titled debut album hits the Top 10 in the U.S. and U.K. The album opens with John Bonham's triplet bass drum figures, amazing rock drummers worldwide. Bonham's carefully engineered sound, reportedly recorded in a stairwell for extra ambience, will become widely copied and sampled.

Billy Cobham comes to public attention the same year with The Mahavishnu Orchestra, demonstrating the potential of ambidextrous drumming, leading with both left and

right hand. Similar ambidextrous techniques are today used by Simon Phillips and other fusion masters.

1970: A new generation of skillful, tasteful U.S. drummers includes Bernard 'Pretty' Purdie, who has played on many Atlantic sessions, Jim Keltner who drums with John Lennon and Ry Cooder, Little Feat's Richie Hayward, and Jeff Porcaro, who makes his name at 19 with Steely Dan, plays sessions with Boz Scaggs and Jackson Browne and goes on to form Toto in 1978.

LOUIE BELLSON

deep and warm. They can have quite a wide tuning range from flappy to hard as a board. Double thickness heads are stronger and darker in sound. Others have reinforced patches of double thickness. Each manufacturer has different variations on these basic types. Over the years materials other than Mylar – such as woven Kevlar – have been tried for special applications.

The Remo Story

The first Mylar drum head was probably made by Jim Irwin for Sonny Greer as early as 1953. By the mid 1950s several people were pursuing the idea, but there were technical problems concerning the method of clinching the head into the hoop. An early pioneer was Marion 'Chick' Evans (of Evans Heads fame), closely followed by Ludwig and Premier. Remo Belli, the name most associated with the plastic drum head, and Marion Evans were both experimenting with hoops and sheets of Mylar by late 1956. But Belli's commercial flair contributed to his success. Belli developed the famous Remo Weather King drum head in conjunction with chemist Sam Muchnick, introducing the heads at the Chicago NAMM trade show in June 1957 and going into full production later that year. However, it took several years of experiment to produce exactly the right formulation of Mylar for reliable drum heads.

Remo introduced further heads over subsequent years. The first head was similar to the Ambassador, today's standard head. A thinner head, the Diplomat, followed, as did the thicker

■ Louie Bellson rose to fame filling Gene Krupa's old seat with Benny Goodman shortly after winning a Gene Krupa talent contest in 1940, and subsequently worked with the celebrated likes of Tommy Dorsey, Harry James and Duke Ellington. As this 1950s photo demonstrates, Bellson was one of the first to use a double kick drum kit.

Drum Heads

The earliest rock recordings were made on drums fitted with calf skin heads; 1960s session giant Hal Blaine kept the calf skin head on his kick drum throughout most of his career. The special warm tone was part of his sound. But calf skins could never have fueled the rock explosion, with its dramatic increases in playing intensity. And with the Remo Weather King plastic drum head of 1957 – made from a polyester film called Mylar – the livestock of the Midwest could finally breathe a sigh of relief... Not only are plastic heads stronger than animal skin, they are weather proof, uniform and consistent, and less expensive. Although Remo is the market leader worldwide, there have been several other important independent companies, including Evans, Aquarian, Compo and Cana-sonic (unusual for their colored fiberglass coating on a Mylar base). Some drum companies – particularly Ludwig, Premier and Sonor – make their own heads; some others fit Remo heads overprinted with their own logo.

Most drum heads are mounted on hoops of aluminum, and there are different ways of clinching the plastic so that it doesn't pull out. Premier, Ludwig, Aquarian and Sonor all use an aluminum channel with a squared inner ring which the plastic wraps around before clinching. They all claim to be unique, but look suspiciously alike – using a similar 'headlock' principle. Remo and Evans use a slightly deeper hoop with the head stuck fast in resin. Heads vary from thin, bright and resonant to thick,

■ U.K. drum company Premier boasted its Everplay heads were exported to 'Czeckoslovakia and Russia' in an early 1960s edition of its Talking Drums news-sheet, with its snare heads' see-through qualities demonstrated by the model on the right.

Emperor, for marching bands. The Controlled Sound (CS) Black Dot came as a response to Buddy Rich stamping his way through kick drum heads. The black dot, a center-reinforcing double thickness, makes the head stronger without sacrificing too much resonance. Consequently these heads have been popular ever since with rock drummers. Then came the Pinstripe, a double thickness of Mylar sealed around the outer perimeter; this gives a darker, more damped, punchy sound initially associated with the distinctive warm studio sound of Steve Gadd. The Pinstripe later became popular with rock and funk drummers too, because of its durability, ease of tuning, and suitability for close-miking. As more open, resonant sounds have returned to fashion the Ambassador has regained popularity.

Remo has continued to come up with innovative designs, including Fiberskyn heads, aimed at approximating the warm sound of real calf skins. Falams heads use woven Kevlar laminated between thin layers of Mylar, designed for the extremely high tensions preferred by marching band drummers.

Perhaps the most unusual recent Remo innovation was the company's PTS – Pre-Tuned – heads, originally designed to slip on to Remo's Innovator and Liberator drums. This line of heads required no further tensioning.

The Classic Sixties Rock Kit

Most rock drummers of the late 1950s and early 1960s used generally similar four piece drum kits. Sizes had standardized at a 22″ (occasionally 24″) kick drum, 12x8 or 13x9 mounted tom, 16x16 floor tom, and 14x5 or 5½″ snare drum. Cymbals would

■ *Buddy Rich rose to fame with the Harry James, Artie Shaw and Tommy Dorsey big bands in the late 1930s and early 1940s, going on to record many jazz classics with Art Tatum, Lionel Hampton and Oscar Peterson. Rich was one of Ludwig's most important endorsers in the 1950s, as this advertisement from Down Beat stresses.*

■ *Ludwig's Supra-phonic is reputedly the best-selling metal shell snare drum of all time, and is still produced in essentially similar format to the original.*

...for sheer beauty and Rich tone LUDWIG...most famous name on drums!

LUDWIG
SUPRA-PHONIC 400
with Acousti-Perfect shell design

Ludwig's SUPRA-PHONIC 400 all-metal snare drums have long been the world's most popular drum, outselling all other makes and models.
Drummers get the six features they want most: Instant response over the entire drum head. Vivid tonal definition, each beat crisp and clear. Brilliant sound, choke-free at full volume. Full power without distortion. Full projection at all dynamics. Increased stick rebound for faster action with less effort.
The SUPRA-PHONIC all-metal snare drums are constructed with a one-piece ACOUSTI-PERFECT seamless shell, beaded in the center and flanged at the edges for triple strength.
Ten self-aligning tension casings provide extra fine head adjustment. The new P-85 snare strainer gives complete and instant snare control with full drop of snares. Triple-flanged hoops assure a solid rim shot every time.
You hear the difference, feel the difference in this superior drum. Try it! Offered in two popular sizes: 5″ x 14″ and 6½″ x 14″ and as standard equipment with all popular Ludwig outfits. Supplied with Ludwig WEATHER MASTER plastic heads and with 18 strand, wire snares.

No. 400—5″ x 14″ SUPRA-PHONIC SNARE DRUM, chrome.
No. 402—6½″ x 14″ SUPRA-PHONIC SNARE DRUM, chrome.

This outfit especially designed for Buddy Rich by Ludwig Drum Co., chicago, illinois

The drumming Ludwigs – Bill Jr. & Sr., present their greatest catalog!

50 GOLDEN YEARS OF DRUM PROGRESS

Surviving various financial problems over the years, the Ludwig company celebrated its 50th anniversary in 1959, with press advertisements featuring Bill Ludwig Jr. (left) and Sr.

comprise a ride, one or two crash cymbals, and a pair of hi-hats. A 'modern jazz' set might have a 20" or perhaps 18" kick drum and 14x14 floor tom. Additionally, Premier manufactured a deep 16x20 floor tom (Ringo's can be seen in the photos of the Beatles' first Abbey Road sessions). Shallower snare drums were also common; Premier and Ajax made popular models, while the American companies made piccolo snares, generally 13x3.

The Ludwig kit which became the goal of many players was the Ludwig Super Classic, featuring the famous Supra-phonic 400 metal shell snare drum. This kit more than any other is the rhythmic standard of the 1960s – countless American and British bands used them. Charlie Watts played a blue oyster pearl Ludwig in his early Rolling Stones days. Interestingly, Ringo's first Ludwig kit was a Downbeat, with the smaller 20" kick drum, and 14" floor tom. These kits had the reputation for being louder than Premier's – though there's no easy answer as to why. Premier and Ludwig both made thin-walled shells with reinforcing hoops. Were Ludwig's better? Or was it simply – as some say – the Ludwig heads were better?

During the latter third of the 1960s the five piece kit with 12" and 13" mounted toms became standard. Premier, however, declined for a long time to make a 13" tom, instead perversely insisting on the easier option of producing a 14x8. One of the earliest and certainly the highest profile British drummers to feature two toms mounted on the kick drum was Dave Clark – who sat out front of his band on a red glitter Rogers kit. The Dave Clark Five was hugely successful in Britain and in the States during the mid 1960s.

The Ludwig Black Oyster Pearl kit used by Ringo Starr has become iconic along with The Beatles' drummer. The renewed interest in vintage kits has resulted in the recent reissue of this distinctive kit (front and back view shown). Although the new version duplicates the general cosmetics of the original, several details, including the inlaid kick drum hoops and original style Ludwig keystone badge, have not been accurately reproduced. Other changes, including substantial new hardware which is considerably improved over Ringo's rickety original, have been more warmly received by Ludwig fans.

94

■ *Keith Moon's drumming was arguably the most distinctive aspect of The Who's radical sound. Moon's drums dictated the dynamics of The Who's performances, in some instances taking over the lead role from Pete Townshend's guitar. By 1967, Moon was already using a nine-piece kit with two bass drums.*

■ *Ginger Baker, previously a member of The Graham Bond Organisation, popularized extended kits after forming the modestly-titled supergroup Cream with Eric Clapton and Jack Bruce in 1966. The comprehensive cymbal setup was a Baker trademark; here he is using four double-tiered pairs, plus hi-hats.*

Stretching Out: The Extended Kit

Although the British beat boom had conquered America, in some ways it wasn't as wild as the earlier naive days of rock'n'roll. Jerry Allison with Buddy Holly used four toms with his Ludwig, and L.A. session legend Hal Blaine introduced multiple toms to studio playing. In the 1960s and 1970s Blaine drummed on more West Coast pop hits than anyone – The Byrds, The Beach Boys and Sonny and Cher were just some of the hits featuring his drumming. But it was Keith Moon and Ginger Baker who caught the public's imagination, taking rock drumming to a new energy level. The Who's definitive hit 'My Generation' features the most exuberant, heart-stopping piece of rock drumming ever recorded; Moon explodes out of the arrangement like a circus cannon. Close on The Who's heels, in 1966, erstwhile jazz drummer Ginger Baker joined up with fellow Graham Bond Organisation bassist Jack Bruce, enticed guitarist Eric Clapton from John Mayall's Bluesbreakers, and formed the first British virtuoso rock group, Cream (nothing modest about the title...). As they were a trio bent on pursuing ever longer improvisations, Baker found room to explore the possibilities of extending his kit – an imposing silver sparkle Ludwig with two kick drums, four tom toms and double stacked cymbals.

Baker used every bit of his kit. With his background in jazz, and his keen interest in African music, he envisaged more sound colors than the average rocker of the time.

Z. ZILDJIAN CYMBALS

Zildjian History

The most famous cymbal company – Zildjian – dates back to 1623 when a Constantinople (Istanbul) alchemist named Avedis hit on a special process for producing cymbals. His reputation became such that he was given the name Zil-djian – Turkish for cymbalsmith. Surviving all the ups and downs, the secret of the Zildjian process has been handed down within the family to the present day. K. Zildjian cymbals, imported from Turkey, were

the number one cymbals during the early part of the century. But the special standing of the modern Zildjian company is due primarily to the efforts of Avedis Zildjian III, who emigrated to the United States early this century. When in 1927 his uncle Aram bade him return to Turkey to take up the family business, Avedis wisely prevailed on his uncle to transplant to the States instead. They set up in Boston – near to the salt water supply used in manufacturing – and began producing cymbals in 1929 –

just in time for the great Depression, and the start of the 'talkies,' both of which put paid to many a percussionist's career. However, Avedis soon made contact with the great contemporary jazz drummers, and by the time of the swing era in the mid 1930s Avedis Zildjian was established as the number one cymbal company.

During this period, back in Turkey, the Turkish branch of the family (Zilcan) had been producing K. Zildjian cymbals. (These Ks are the cymbal fan's

equivalent of the Slingerland Radio King snare drums. Hand-made, some were fabulous while others were dreadful.) However, as a result of political troubles, the family, aided by Avedis, moved to Canada, where Zildjian had set up a second plant, during the 1970s. After Avedis Zildjian III died in 1979, differences surfaced between his two sons, Armand and Robert (who'd grown up with the company). In 1982 they split up and Robert took over the Canadian factory at Meductic to form a new

cymbal company named Sabian. Sabian sales are now second only to Zildjian, on a par with Paiste. More competition arrived in the mid 1980s, when two former employees of the K. Zildjian plant set up the Istanbul company, making fine cymbals in the K. Zildjian tradition.

Zildjian cymbals, as the archetypal 'Turkish' cymbals, are traditionally made from a 'B20' bronze alloy: 80 per cent copper to 20 per cent tin. Many other manufacturers, both American and European, use a similar blend.

Baker also initiated the start of larger cymbal set ups. Keith Moon, on the other hand, perhaps only wanted the extra armory to make as much racket as possible and look flash. This is probably half the truth, but Moon was also an original musician of great flair, who showed that rock didn't have to be the controlled and prissy 'beat' music of the sub-Beatles clones; and the impetus for extending his kit was at least partly musical – especially when Pete Townshend came up with the rock 'opera' *Tommy*. By the late 1960s Moon had assembled a monster kit with double kick drums and as many tom toms as feasible (or not), including three of Premier's unlikely 14x8 toms. Moon stayed with Premier throughout his career, and they responded in style by customizing some of the first and most distinctive kits in rock for him, the 'Pictures of Lily' kit being the most famous; Premier later undertook other custom finishes, including a tartan kit for Kenney Jones of Rod Stewart and The Faces. Hence Moon was a surprising part of that trend which was the result of the optimism and adventurous spirit of the times – with rock musicians extending their music to include elements of classical, jazz and folk. This was the start of the general move to larger set-ups. Soon dozens of

drummers were at it – even Jimi Hendrix's inspired drummer Mitch Mitchell played a black double kick drum Gretsch kit at the 1970 Isle of Wight Festival.

The drum and cymbal companies were obvious beneficaries of this move, as the drum kit expanded to include elements of percussion not seen since the early days of the console kits. Drummers like Carl Palmer played orchestrated parts on the kit, often incorporating massive gongs and timpani. Palmer's band ELP, as good Europeans, were bravely attempting what was probably impossible: to fuse rock and classical music, leading the much maligned progressive rock movement. The safer, or perhaps more realistic, path had been suggested by Cream and Jimi Hendrix – a mixture of the earthiness of the blues with the improvisational scope of jazz. During the late 1960s the bluesier side was extended to see the birth of heavy metal, while the jazzier side saw the emergence of jazz-rock fusion – Jack Bruce went on to play with the great jazz drummer Tony Williams, who'd begun the jazz rock fusion movement as a protégé of Miles Davis. The early heavy metal bands had imagination and humor – from the H.M. blueprint of Black Sabbath and Bill Ward (who played a double kick Slingerland) to Deep Purple with the brilliant Ian Paice. ELP was followed by bands like Yes (with Bill Bruford) and Genesis (with Phil Collins). Although critically detested in the U.K., progressive rock is still big business in the 1990s with bands like Canada's Rush (with the perennial poll-winning Neil Peart) and more recently Dream Theater (with Mike Portnoy). Jazz rock, meanwhile, attracted some of the greatest talent around and by the end of the 1960s drumming took a giant leap forward with Billy Cobham and The Mahavishnu Orchestra. Cobham, like Baker a jazz player able to express himself subtly on a relatively small kit, now went for the big one. Cobham brought home to a larger audience what Tony Williams had begun – the awesome potential of what a world class powerhouse virtuoso drummer could do to little old rock'n'roll, given the scope of every jazz and fusion trick in the book: labyrinthine riffs and compound time signatures, million note solos and all the rest.

Before heavy metal – like progressive rock – became stultified and ponderous, it was illuminated by a remarkable talent. Considering the vast world-wide appeal of heavy rock, Led Zeppelin's John Bonham is undoubtedly the most influential British drummer of all time. Bonham used a four or

16" x 16" x 14" x 14"

Mounted Tom Toms (2)
13" x 9" & 12" x 8"

Snare Drum 14" x 5½"

Single T.T. Holders (2)
Spurs (2) – T.T. Legs (2 set

Cymbal Arms (1) included

2236 Hi Hat
2238 Bass Drum Pedals (2)
2237 Snare Drum Stand
2240 Drum Stool
2239 Cymbal Stands (2)

Finishes: Solid Silver; Go
Midnight Blue.
NEW: MATT BLACK
RED; ICEBER(
through); NAT'
PINE (Laminat

HAYMAN
Jon Hiseman
(Colosseum)

■ *Hayman kits, as modeled here by Jon Hiseman, were an early U.K. attempt to make a U.S.-style kit. Hayman kits were similar to the Camco and later Drum Workshop design, but after short-lived success fell prey to the 1970s recession. The Hayman snare's painted 'Vibrasonic' interior again echoes the Camco look.*

The Cymbal Story

1851: Zildjian first appears as a brand name on the Istanbul firm's cymbals.

1929: Avedis Zildjian III establishes the Zildjian company in Boston, Mass. American-made Zildjians are sold as A. Zildjians; the Turkish made cymbal retains the K. Zildjian name. Both are termed 'Turkish' cymbals, to distinguish them from Chinese cymbals, which feature a gong-like, less refined sound. In future years KZ cymbals will be regarded as having a darker, jazzier

sound while the AZ cymbals are more consistently made, with a brighter, more cutting tone.

1932: The Paiste company, at this time based in Estonia, commences exports to the U.S.A. Around this period, cymbals in general use are small, 12" or less. It will be the bebop era before cymbal sizes increase, as players such as Kenny Clarke start 'riding' on cymbals as large as 28". While fashions change, typical ride cymbal size will standardize at around 20" by the 1960s.

1957: Paiste is established in Switzerland, and two years later introduces its Formula 602 range; Paiste's first professional B20 cymbal.

1965: Paiste introduces the B8 formula Giant Beat cymbal. B8 cymbals will be termed 'European,' even though other makers such as Ufip of Italy use the high-quality B20 blend.

1967: Paiste launches its Sound Edge hi-hats, with a distinctive wavy-edged bottom cymbal.

Plastic, fiberglass and steel shells became popular in the 1970s in a quest for more attack and volume. John Bonham (right) used Ludwig Vista-lites, which were available in clear, tinted and multi colored stripes. Iron Butterfly's Ron Bushy used transparent perspex Zickos; Billy Cobham tried the flared fiberglass North drums and the clear acrylic Fibes set. Non-wood drums are rarer today, but several Canadian companies including Stingray, Impact and Milestone persist with fiberglass, while U.S. company Monolith makes both drums and a rack system from carbon fiber. By far the most commercially successful synthetic shell is Remo's Acousticon, used by Terry Bozzio and many others.

five piece kit – though of generally largish sizes. This stripped-down approach is consistent with the fact Bonham was a groove player as well as a soloist. Although Bonham took in blues and rock styles, he was also much influenced by the master groover Al Jackson whose playing on the Stax soul hits of Otis Redding and the others had shown British drummers the way. Bonham's influence has echoed through every musical style in rock over the past two decades. In America, Bonham's counterpart, Carmine Appice, went on to use a much bigger kit through the 1970s. And this showman/virtuoso branch has dominated American and world heavy metal, with spectacular players like Lars Ulrich, Alex Van Halen and Tommy Aldridge developing massive set-ups and forests of heavy cymbals. With the impact of all these players, by

the 1970s rock music was into its most diverse period of experimentation. Drumming was getting louder than anyone could have foreseen, and the venerable traditional drum kit was literally bursting at the seams. Skins broke, sticks broke and cymbals cracked. Drum kits slipped and slid, fell over, tom mounts groaned and cymbals stands collapsed, kick drum pedal straps snapped, stools toppled. Every element of the kit was found wanting – the music had progressed beyond the gear. In particular the hardware was not up to the job, and needed profound redesigning. The problem was the enormous re-tooling and design costs. For a variety of business reasons the Americans were slow to address this problem, and so it ultimately fell to the Japanese to modernize.

1968: The U.S. Zildjian company buys the K. Zildjian trademark from the Istanbul family, and opens the Azco factory in Meductic, Canada.

1970: The first 'new' K. Zildjian cymbals are produced at Azco in Canada..

1971: The Paiste 2002 series is introduced. The B8 successor to the Giant Beat range, it becomes hugely successful with European rock drummers including John Bonham, Stewart Copeland and Bill Bruford.

1979: As heavy rock and metal drummers demand more volume, the Zildjian Earth Ride appears; the first unlathed cymbal. Paiste responds with its own unlathed range in 1980, named the Rude Series. In the same year Robert Zildjian takes over the Canadian plant following a family split, to form what will become the Sabian Company.

1981: Zildjian introduces the first all-American made K series cymbals. Within the next two years Sabian, located in the factory which previously

produced the K series, starts to make inroads into the U.S. and Europe.

1982: Zildjian responds to Paiste's popularity by introducing its 'European' style B8 series, termed Amir.

1984: Paiste introduces colored cymbals: the Color Sound 5 series. This is at least partly an attempt to counter the popularity of electronic drums and drum machines by adding a new visual spin to the drum kit. In the same year, German company Meinl introduces its

Profile series – the first computer-controlled machine-hammered cymbals.

1986: Zildjian introduced its own machine-hammered range, the Z series. The company introduces the top line K Custom range, influenced by Steve Gadd and Dave Weckl, the next year.

1989: Paiste introduces its Paiste LIne, which the company claims is the most radical new cymbal alloy since Avedis's formula of 1623.

Snare drums

The snare drum is the heart of the drum kit. Whereas most drum shells are wood, snare drum shells are as likely to be metal: brass, steel, aluminium or bronze. As on all drums, the playing head is termed the batter head; the bottom head, which is much thinner in order to heighten snare response, is called the snare head. Snares are made from coiled strands of steel, or occasionally brass. Historically, snares were made from gut, which gives a much drier sound. Some players prefer to use gut today, while others use custom made snares – perhaps aircraft wire or shark cable. Standard snares have around 20 strands, but occasionally double that; many recording drummers prefer fewer strands – perhaps six or eight – for a more concise response.

The snares are tensioned by the snare strainer, sometimes called a throw-off. The simplest and most common type of strainer works via a straightforward side action tension-and-release lever. When the lever is moved to the side the snare falls away from the bottom head. Snare tension is adjusted by a knurled knob which screws down to increase the pull on the strings or tape attaching the snare to the strainer (and, at the other side of the drum, to the butt plate). A less common version of strainer features a large die cast plate which pulls away from the drum, rather than a side lever. A third, more complicated, and more rarely-used type of strainer uses a parallel action to keep the snares under tension even when the strainer is released. Famous classics using parallel action strainers include the Rogers Dyna-sonic,

LUDWIG SUPER-SENSITIVE
with Acousti-Perfect shell design

■ *The Ludwig Supra-phonic's classic simplicity has aided its enduring success. The drum is made in two sizes, the 5″ deep 400 and the 6¹/2″ 402. The aluminum*

shell version of these drums, whilst probably the most popular, is notorious for flaking its chrome plating. Note the middle drum has the earlier P83 snarestrainer.

■ *Ludwig's 1970s Super-Sensitive snare (above) featured a parallel action snare mechanism, designed to extend response right to the edge of the drum.*

■ *The reissue of Ludwig's wood shell snare, as used by Ringo, is fitted with Ludwig's Classic lugs, as opposed to the Supra-Phonic's Art Deco-styled Imperials.*

with its undercarriage frame, the Ludwig Super-sensitive, with individual snare strand adjustment, and the Premier Royal Ace, with its inner 'floating' mechanism.

The depth of a snare drum affects not only the depth of tone, but also the speed of snare response. The standard depth, for nearly 70 years, has centered on 5″. But occasionally a shallower 3″ or 4″ drum is effective, for a fast bebop or snappy funk sound, as may be a deeper 8″ drum for a slow tempo ballad. A 6.5″ drum is popular as a compromise between power and speed of response for rock playing.

For many years artists who used the new super-reliable Japanese drum kits still preferred to use old American snare drums. The most famous example was Steve Gadd, always seen with his black Yamaha kit and a Ludwig 400 snare. Many other players retain vintage Slingerland Radio Kings or Ludwig Black Beauty snares for recording only.

Snare drums, being the most crucial part of the kit, were the last area the Japanese managed to crack. But over the past decade several Japanese companies have taken the 'artist signature' approach, producing a host of different snares featuring different materials, sizes and novel features – from the brass piccolo of David Garibaldi or the dual snare design of Dave Weckl, to the steel shell drum of Chad Smith and the mahogany shell drum of Omar Hakim. American companies have in response turned to classic values and a small scale, high quality approach, evoking the days of Gene Krupa and his Slingerland Radio Kings. Radio King snare drums were made from a single steam-bent plank of maple, with no plies, and good examples have become the Stradivarius of the drum world. Unfortunately many of these old drums featured poor bearing edges and out-of-round shells. Enter Noble and Cooley, America's largest toy drum manufacturer, who created a modern version of the solid shell snare drum featuring original brass tubular pipe lugs – the Classic SS of 1984. Since Noble and Cooley, the major manufacturers have all brought out lines with 1920s-style tubular lugs, and opened the way for a host of smaller specialist companies. N&C stressed the importance of fixing lugs at what they term 'nodal points' on the shell – which minimizes interference with resonance. Again, all the other companies have copied this concept with their top-line snares.

SUPER SOUND KING
CHROME SHELL
SNARE DRUM

WITH DUAL SUPER SNARE STRAINER

The Super Sound King Snare Drum is the most sensitive and responsive snare drum ever designed. Its extra sturdy solid brass shell, triple chrome plated, needs no sound disturbing center bead. Supplied with tone control, rim shot counter hoops, twenty wire snappy snares, and plastic heads.

The Dual Super Snare Strainer releases the snares on both sides simultaneously with the one strainer handle. Either side can be adjusted separately up or down. One knob adjusts tension on the snares. Note strainer protector guard.

BUTT SIDE	THROW OFF SIDE	
(Shown without guards)		
120	5″ x 14″ Ten Lugs	$150.00
121	6½″ x 14″ Ten Lugs	155.00

Slingerland THE FOREMOST IN DRUMS

PAGE 18

■ As close miking of individual drums took hold in the 1970s, every overtone, rattle and hum became noticeable. Hence engineers and drummers started to remove the bottom heads from toms, giving a deader, rather one dimensional sound, which was, however, easier to control. Drum companies responded to this trend by re-inventing single headed tom toms (previously synonymous with cheap). This time they were called concert toms, often marketed in sets of four on a pair of stands. Phil Collins became a convert and is one of the few major players who still advocates single head toms in the 1990s, featuring regularly in Gretsch adverts.

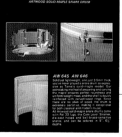

SOLID MAPLE
ARTWOOD SOLID-MAPLE SNARE DRUM

■ The Slingerland company's solid maple Radio King snare drum is now highly sought after, but by the 1970s, when the catalog above was produced, the company had lost its lead. Slingerland has recently been revitalized, while modern rivals including Tama (left) introduce solid wood drums which hark back to the Radio King.

The Japanese Kit

Although, ironically, it was during the early 1970s that rock stars like Led Zeppelin and Pink Floyd started touring and making money on the grand scale, it was at this time that the economies of the U.S. and the U.K. took a nose dive. It was the opportunity that the recovering and re-structured Japanese (and West German) economies had been waiting for. During the first half of the 1970s 'Made in Japan' was a phrase greeted with suspicion – indicative of junk. By the end of the decade it was clear 'Made in Japan' meant something quite different. Although the American and European drum makers held on through the 1970s – indeed Premier moved to its larger new factory in 1977 – the writing was on the wall. This period gradually saw off all the other historic U.K. lines – Ajax, Edgware, Carlton, John Grey, Autocrat, Broadway, Shaftesbury, Beverley, Olympic, Gigster, even the relatively new Hayman. And in the U.S.A. the magical names of Ludwig, Slingerland, Gretsch and Rogers changed hands at a bewildering rate. By the 1980s they were mostly struggling, if not consigned to history. Three major Japanese companies established themselves by the turn of the decade –

Stewart Copeland's drumming was integral to The Police's minimal but intelligently-arranged sound. Copeland was one of Tama's first important endorsers, via his use of the blue Imperial Star kit shown here. Note the use of Tama Octobans, each tuned to a specific note, as used by Billy Cobham and, more recently, Simon Phillips.

Pearl, Tama and Yamaha. Because the Japanese were dealing with the alien Western culture of jazz and rock, they cleverly secured top endorsers and worked closely with them to address weaknesses and make improvements.

Tama first impressed with their hardware. Although Ludwig had begun beefing up hardware with their Atlas range around 1970, there was still plenty of room for improvement all round. Tama's Titan line was a great success. Tama signed Billy Cobham – who greatly influenced the Superstar drum line – and Stewart Copeland of the Police, who played a blue Imperial Star. Yamaha broke through with the Recording Custom kit in revolutionary black piano lacquer, endorsed by Steve Gadd. And Pearl – who'd earlier secured impressive endorsements from the likes of Art Blakey – climbed back with top endorsers from Jeff

Porcaro through to Dennis Chambers. With the unequaled success of their Export budget kit, Pearl became the most widely used drums on the planet.

In 1975 Yamaha introduced the (9000 series) Recording Custom drums. This kit became synonymous with Steve Gadd, the most widely revered drummer since Buddy Rich. Borrowing from their many years experience of lacquering pianos, Yamaha applied a deep lustrous finish to the RC kit. The six ply birch shells, together with Remo's double ply Pinstripe heads, gave Gadd the controlled, dark and warm sound which became his trademark and spawned a generation of copyists. This sound, although having superficial similarities with the single headed concert tom sound of the 1970s, was warmer with a richer timbre: a stepping stone to the much brighter, open sound around the corner in the 1980s and 1990s. Following Yamaha, all the major drum companies were soon offering similar lacquered finishes. Having revolutionized hardware, the Japanese companies now upped the standard of drum shells and finishes. As the companies used better quality timbers and – using the latest technology – vied to produce the best shells, so they reverted to natural stains to show off the beautiful hardwood veneers. Although the better vintage drums had been made from prime maple and other excellent timbers, shell quality had been variable through much of the rock explosion. Heavy

plastic covers on the outside and painted interiors disguised the realities of shell workmanship and indifferent timber. The new move to perfectly finished natural wood – inside and out – went hand in hand with the increase in quality of recorded sounds, and the ability of engineers to cope with long, resonant and deep sounds without panicking and plastering heads in gaffa tape.

Typifying the Japanese companies' concentration on improved hardware, Pearl, in conjunction with the late great studio drummer Jeff Porcaro, introduced the first rack system, reminiscent of the console racks of the 1920s. Pearl's rack has a squared section of lightweight aluminium, while Tama's Power Tower and Yamaha's Super Rack use tubular sections. The independent company Gibraltar introduced budget rack systems which can be adapted to work with different makes of drum, as can the up-market Voelker stainless steel rack which suspends everything including the kick drum. Although at first racks looked likely to offer extra flexibility and convenience, in practice they've proved to be at least as much work as ordinary stands – great if you've got a roadie.

The Japanese trio of Tama, Pearl and Yamaha have stayed on top since the 1970s. They've been joined in the 1990s by a fourth, Mapex, advised by (surprise, surprise) Billy Cobham. The German scene has been dominated by Sonor, a long-established company which since the 1970s has built a reputation second to none for producing expensive drums of superb quality – the Mercedes of the drum world. Premier remains the only major U.K. company, and after a period of modernisation under the ownership of Yamaha, is again independent and stronger today than ever, making the best drums in its three-quarter-century history. Meanwhile the U.S. industry has diversified, with smaller high quality companies from Noble and Cooley to Drum Workshop. Ludwig, after a long period of indifferent form, bounced back in the mid 1980s when the influential Neil Peart decided they were the drums for him. Acoustic drums survived the electronics and computer revolution of the 1980s and are more popular than ever.

103

Raw Power

The second half of the 1980s saw the wholesale move to so-called 'Power sizes': adding a couple of inches of extra depth to standard size drums. Thus 12x8 became 12x10, 22x14 became 22x16 and so on. By the 1990s these sizes had become typical, and the earlier standard sizes were being referred to as 'jazz' sizes. However, in the latter half of the 1990s there has been a trickle back to the shallower sizes. Some drummers (like Dennis Chambers) always preferred shallower toms, and the retro-movement to 1960s kits has of course helped this trend.

■ *Bernard 'Pretty' Purdie, who has played on countless sessions from Aretha Franklin on, is synonymous with the funky use of hi-hat 'barks.' Purdie even has a beat named after him, the 'Purdie Shuffle,' as played by Jeff Porcaro on Toto's 1982 hit 'Rosanna.'*

■ *Japanese classic (inset): The Pearl Export is the definitive budget kit, and has reputedly become the best-selling drum kit of all time. The Export kit has remained in production for nearly 20 years, and is now a model for dozens of Taiwanese clones.*

Fashions moved from birch shells back to maple, the traditional warm and bright material of the American drum industry. The retro-shell movement sung the praises of thin shells, and reinforcing rings made their re-appearance. Such attention to detail and craftsmanship would never come cheap. But drummers were prepared to invest in quality. This allowed a small return in the fortunes of American drum craftsmen. Drum Workshop (DW) launched its range based on the Camco designs of the American drum guru George Way. Back in Europe Sonor spared no expense, and in Britain Premier finally produced a Rolls Royce kit, the Signia: its first all maple drum kit.

The Modern Drummer

Today many rock bands carry enough hardware for a recording studio on each gig and some drummers have live set ups which could stock a drumstore – unfortunately for their overworked drum techs. Neil Peart had a revolving riser with three drum sets, and Tommy Lee with Motley Crue had a gantry which turned a full circle vertically while he was playing. Hand painted customized kits are back – for example Charlie Morgan's Versace-designed Signia kit for Elton John, and Bobby Rock's Peavey kit decorated in Renaissance art. (Tasteful? Keith Moon would have loved it.) After a decade of machines, programming and sampling, rock emerged with a tougher but more professional slant in the 1990s. Unsurprisingly, many drummers rebelled against kits getting bigger each year and rediscovered simplicity. In America the grunge bands demonstrated this with straight ahead beats and hard hitting players like the Daves Grohl (Nirvana) and Abbruzzese (Pearl Jam), using four or five piece kits and concentrating on the beat rather than the flashy fills of HM. In the U.K. – where grass roots rock never dies – new bands not only happily flaunt their 1960s influences but actively seek out 1960s kits. Hence there's a brisk trade in 'vintage' Ludwig and Gretsch. The implication is that the basic four piece kit – which is where we started – is the definitive drum kit the drummer will always return to. Who knows? What's not in doubt is that practically any combination of drums imaginable is available today: if someone wants a huge kit with solid hardware they can get it; if the preference is for light stands and small shells, they are available too. The choice for drummers has never been wider.

■ *Chad Smith of The Red Hot Chili Peppers (below) is a prominent Pearl endorsee. Known for his funky but hard-hitting style, Smith and bassist Flea mix funk, rap and grunge styles – Smith's versatility was illustrated by his ability to drum one-handed for several club dates after breaking his wrist in 1995.*

■ *This Pearl Masters Series kit (right) illustrates current thinking in drum manufacture, with several typical late 1990s features: the rack system was designed in conjunction with the late Jeff Porcaro, while a second hi-hat to the drummer's right is operated by remote cable. All shells are of relatively thin maple ply with reinforcing hoops, isolation mounted with no tom tom arms, in pursuit of a more open, resonant sound. Note how Simon Phillips' Tama kit (inset) uses a similar racked layout with second hi-hat.*

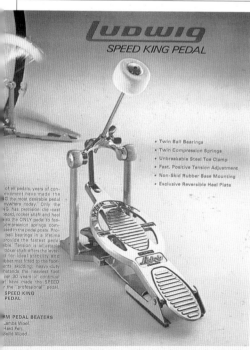

KICK DRUM PEDALS

Kick drum pedals, like drum sticks, are personal items of equipment which can make or break a drummer's performance. Drummers sometimes use the same pedal throughout their career. Basic designs haven't changed substantially over the years. Some drummers still use Ludwig Speed Kings – the first versions of which date back to 1937 – or 1960s Premier 250 pedals.

One element that has changed is the drive action – the inflexible metal link plate of the Speed King and the leather straps of earlier pedals have given way to tougher flexible nylon straps, or, more often today, a single or double chain drive. Chain drives were popularized by Tama, who

successfully re-introduced the original Camco chain drive pedal (leading eventually to their Iron Cobra), and Drum Workshop with their 5000 series Turbo pedals. D.W. followed up with the acclaimed 5002 double pedal, which really started the double pedal fashion and led to double pedals being offered by all the manufacturers.

Kick drum pedals have several parameters which can be adjusted to improve action and comfort. Tension is adjustable by a single or double spring which alters the weight and return of the stroke, in combination with the variable length of the beater shaft. Beaters themselves are made from different materials, including felt, wood and plexi-glass, and in different shapes.

LUDWIG
SPEED KING PEDAL

- Twin Ball Bearings
- Twin Compression Springs
- Unbreakable Steel Toe Clamp
- Fast, Positive Tension Adjustment
- Non-Skid Rubber Base Mounting
- Exclusive Reversible Heel Plate

Springs compress rather than stretch, so each stroke of action gets stronger and faster.

Spring tension is adjustable with screwdriver from bottom of pedal.

5002A "ACCELERATOR"

Bass Guitar

> "James Jamerson at Motown and Brian WIlson of The Beach Boys were my two biggest influences: James because he was so good and melodic, Brian because he went to unusual places. I started to realize the power the bass player had within the band. Not vengeful power – it was just that you could actually *control* it."
>
> **PAUL McCARTNEY,** THE BEATLES

Bass is the most subversive component of modern rock music, unique in its capability not only to drive the rhythm but to undermine the harmonic development and reflect the melody – and all, potentially, at the same time. The greatest rock music has exploited these qualities with devastating results.

No one particularly noticed when the world's first fretted electric bass guitar, the Fender Precision Bass, was put on to the market in 1951 by a small California company. Up to that point there was no such thing as a commercially available electric bass guitar. There were acoustic tenor guitars with four strings – quite different in purpose – and a few experimental electric 'upright' basses such as Rickenbacker's Bass Viol. But the bass stringed instrument generally used was the acoustic double-bass, which to some seemed bulky and cumbersome, and was often barely audible in raucous musical settings.

Leo Fender figured that certain players would welcome a louder, more portable instrument that offered precise pitching of notes. During the 1950s his company's ground-breaking Precision Bass helped spread the Fender name among bassists, who were also attracted by a new amplifier designed for the new electric bass player, the Fender Bassman. At first this unit came as a 26 watt combo amp with a 15" speaker, but it's the slightly later 40 watt version with four 10" speakers that's now considered the classic. Ironically, it's recognized today as a great guitar amp, too – and in fact was the basis for the Marshall company's first amp design.

Leo Fender never played an instrument: his interest in electronics grew from a boyhood fascination with radios and gadgets. But he clearly developed a great ability to listen to what players wanted, and to adapt those needs into mass-produced, commercially viable products. Guitar parts were fabricated, machined, screwed down, bolted together. Capitalism and guitars joined hands in the California of the 1950s, and rock'n'roll was just around the corner.

Despite the fact that the Fender Precision Bass was first marketed in 1951, with other American makers like Kay and Gibson quickly adding bass guitars to their lines, popular use of the electric bass guitar remained scarce at the time, and it wasn't until the second half of the 1950s that the inestimable power of the low-pitched bass guitar really started to be heard publicly with any kind of frequency.

The emerging rock'n'roll music stayed at first in the hands of double-bass players, such as Al Rex with Bill Haley's Comets ('Rock Around The Clock' hit number one in the U.S. in May

■ *The unprecedented demands on amplifier technology made by the Precision Bass resulted in the concurrent launch of the Bassman combo, later produced in a novel four speaker configuration.*

■ **Fender Precision Bass**
Introduced: 1951

Leo Fender's Precision bass was a radical innovation, launched where no proven market existed. As this

1952 example demonstrates, the double cutaway design, scale length and general layout set precedents which are followed by practically every major production bass today.

■ Although guitar hero Duane
Eddy was associated with the
Gretsch Chet Atkins guitar, Eddy
also used both a Danelectro Long
Horn bass, and the UB2 shown in
the 1962 sleeve below.

■ **Danelectro Long Horn Bass**
Introduced: 1958

*Nat Daniel's design offered excellent
top-fret access, and eccentric looks.
This example is Duane Eddy's own.*

1955), Joe B. Mauldin with Buddy Holly's Crickets ('That'll Be The Day' 1957), and Bill Black with Elvis Presley ('Heartbreak Hotel' 1956). Black got a Fender Precision around 1957: photographs show one in the MGM studio during the filming of *Jailhouse Rock*, and Presley's title track recorded that April sounds as if the King's bassman is playing his new Fender.

The Fender Bass Takes Off

By 1957 Fender basses were being seen more frequently on stage – contemporary photos reveal a Precision among the live bands of Jerry Lee Lewis and B.B. King, among others. Around the same time the bass guitar began to infiltrate American studios, too. Duane Eddy's instrumental hit 'Rebel Rouser,' recorded in March 1958, featured two bass players: Jimmy Simmons playing double-bass to give depth and tone to the bassline, and Buddy Wheeler playing the same notes on electric bass guitar to add a percussive, attacking edge – what Eddy's producer Lee Hazelwood called 'click bass.'

This technique turns up on other records made at the time, notably in Nashville where it was termed 'tic tac bass,' for example on Presley's 'Stuck On You' (March 1960) with Bob Moore on double-bass and session guitarist Hank Garland on six-string electric bass, or Patsy Cline's 'I Fall To Pieces' (November 1960) with Bob Moore once again on double-bass and Harold Bradley on Danelectro six-string bass.

Around 1956 the New York-based Danelectro company had been the first to introduce a six-string bass, the UB2. Nathan Daniel started Danelectro in 1954, building many instruments with the Silvertone brand for the Sears, Roebuck mail-order company. Daniel also made his own lines with the Danelectro brand, and while his instruments were boldly styled using cheap and basic materials, they worked surprisingly well.

The Dan'o six-string bass was effectively a guitar tuned an octave lower than usual, and guitarists were the target for this instrument, judging from from Danelectro's catalog description: "A six-string guitar with extra-long neck and fingerboard, and extra-long strings."

A great up-front example of Danelectro six-string bass can be heard on Duane Eddy's 'Because They're Young' (recorded January 1960), or a little later on Glen Campbell's 'Wichita Lineman' (1968). Session bassist Carol Kaye, known for her work with The BEach Boys and many others, says she loaned Campbell her six-string Danelectro bass for the gorgeous solo. Kaye also played on Ritchie Valens' 1958 hit 'La Bamba,' with what sounds suspiciously like a Dan'o six-string bass holding the ensuing chaos together. Later in the 1960s Jack Bruce in Cream would briefly use Fender's six-string bass model, the VI, before moving on to a regular four-string Gibson EB-3.

107

■ *The traditional double-bass or 'viol' offered scope for on-stage clowning, exploited to the full on early Elvis shows by Bill Black (right), but was bulky and difficult to amplify. The significant practical advantages of the Fender electric bass and its derivatives resulted in accelerating popularity. Black bought a Fender bass around 1957, and by 1960 the electric bass had in effect completely supplanted its acoustic forebear.*

The general design and through-neck construction of the 4000 was used by Rickenbacker for many of its other bass models in years to come, including the fancier two-pickup 4001 (introduced 1961) and the export version with dot markers, the 4001S, used later by Paul McCartney and by Chris Squire in Yes.

At the close of the 1950s, the bass guitar was slowly edging out double-bass and beginning to make a stand on its own as, potentially, the primary bass instrument for the new rock music. In the States, Guybo Smith added a trebly bass guitar contribution to Eddie Cochran's 'Summertime Blues' hit of August 1958, while in Britain Brian Gregg created a pleasing throb below Johnny Kidd & The Pirates' wild 'Shaking All Over' (1960). A rash of instrumental pop tunes began to feature bass guitar players like Nokie Edwards on The Ventures 'Walk – Don't Run' in 1960, and Jet Harris on The Shadows' 'Apache' of the same year. Such pioneering players underlined the bass guitar's emerging role as the natural partner to the lead and rhythm guitars in these new pop groups, defining the now-classic rock line-up of two guitars, bass and drums.

Today, bass playing is a specialized job. Back at the birth of rock, however, many musicians became convinced that providing the steady root-note plonk of the average bass part was an easy job, barely above drumming on the evolutionary scale of musicianship. The bass was seen as a lesser guitar – a sort of guitar for the slow-witted. Paul McCartney says that in the early 1960s, as the pre-fame Beatles found their musical feet, he like many fledgling beat musicians of the period felt the stigma of the bassman. "None of us wanted to be the bass player," McCartney says, remembering the time when he was still a Beatles guitarist and Stu Sutcliffe filled the bass playing role. "It wasn't the number one job: we wanted to be up front. In our minds it was the fat guy in the group nearly always played the bass, and he stood at the back. None of us wanted that, we wanted to be up front singing, looking good, to pull the birds."

But, as we shall see, things changed. The level of skill required from a bassist has increased spectacularly, and bass players today have to know what they're doing. Bass guitars themselves have improved, too. Nevertheless, suspicion still lurks in some quarters that guitarists, keyboardists, vocalists – even drummers – have some innately 'correct' vision of music, advanced from that of the humble, plonking bassist. Equally dangerous for some bassists is a reaction to all this that sends them off into their own obsession with dazzling if largely unusable technique, a sort of defense against the charge that the bass might be somehow less worthy than other instruments.

The Rickenbacker Bass

Back in the 1950s, another small California company added a bass guitar to its line. In 1953 Adolph Rickenbacker sold his company to Francis Hall, who set about modernizing and revamping the Rickenbacker product line, principally through the efforts of German-born guitar maker Roger Rossmeisl who joined the California outfit early in 1954.

Rickenbacker's first bass guitar, the 4000 model of 1957, is a typically unusual Rossmeisl design bearing a large body with angular horns. It was the earliest electric bass guitar to be constructed in the 'through-neck' style: the neck is not bolted (like Fender) or glued (like Gibson) to the body, but extends right through the length of the instrument, with 'wings' attached either side to complete the full body shape. This unusual configuration had first appeared on the Bigsby/Travis guitar of 1948. A purported benefit of such a design is that the strings and their associated bridge, nut and tuners are all located on the same piece of wood, enhancing sustain and tonal resonance. More likely Rickenbacker found this an efficient and straightforward production technique; Rossmeisl had already tried it out for the company's innovative Combo 400 guitar of the previous year.

As the 1960s got underway, makers began to react to the new popularity of the bass guitar. Some who had already tried a bass in their line added more – Fender, for example, waited until 1960 to introduce its second model, the Jazz Bass – while others who had been waiting to see what happened now jumped into the bass market – the enormously successful Harmony company, for instance, did not add a bass guitar to its list until 1962.

British pop groups defined the sound of the 1960s for many listeners, and the bass playing that drove them could not have been more varied. Bill Wyman in the Stones provided solid, safe and rather reserved basslines. "The straightest rhythm section in rock'n'roll, they called us," Wyman recalled in his autobiography. "Yet if Charlie Watts and I hadn't been so understanding, forgiving, conscientious and tolerant of other people's excesses, the Stones wouldn't have existed for more than the band's first five years. The greatness of the front line is beyond question, but living with them hasn't been easy," he explained.

Much more adventurous was John Entwistle, whose most famous bass moment in the Who comes as a series of spluttering, twangy solos in the group's 1965 single, 'My Generation.' "So as to get the right effect, I had to buy a Danelectro bass, because it has thin little strings that produce a very twangy sound," Entwistle told Dave Marsh. But the strings broke easily and, as no replacements were available in London, Entwistle simply went and bought two more Dan'o basses after breaking strings during the recording of early takes. Eventually he gave up, and the final version that is heard in such splendor on the record was made with a Fender Jazz Bass.

Paul McCartney had come along in leaps and bounds as the Beatles' bassist, and gradually his basslines became more melodic and were pushed further forward in the Beatles mix. He started using a Rickenbacker on the *Rubber Soul* sessions in late 1965, and from then on would alternate between that and his original Höfner 'violin' bass. But by the time McCartney came to record the superb 'lead-bass' parts for the *Sgt. Pepper* album at the end of 1966 and into 1967 he was using the Rickenbacker as his main studio instrument.

McCartney remembers that he started to experiment with basslines, moving away from the simpler efforts of earlier recordings based on the root notes of chord sequences. "I wondered: what else could you do, how much further could you take it? *Sgt. Pepper* ended up being my strongest thing on bass, the independent melodies. On 'Lucy In The Sky With Diamonds,' for example, you could easily have had root notes, whereas I was running an independent melody through it, and that became my thing. So once I got over the fact that I was lumbered with bass, I did get quite proud to be a bass player. It was all very exciting."

On the other side of the Atlantic a player from a different background was also beginning to make a mark. In Detroit, James Jamerson began in 1959 to play double-bass sessions for a record company in Detroit owned by Berry Gordy. The company would soon be known throughout the world as Motown. With remarkable foresight Gordy christened his company of black musicians 'The Sound of Young America.' Motown's fresh merger of pop and R&B from artists such as The Supremes, The Four Tops, Smokey Robinson, Marvin Gaye and Stevie Wonder became just that, attracting a huge audience of both black and white fans during the company's heyday from 1964 to 1967.

■ *Rickenbacker was one of the first US companies to introduce a viable alternative to the Fender bass; their distinctive through-neck 4000 range debuted in 1957, and has since become a mainstay of Rickenbacker production. The 4001S shown here dates from 1964.*

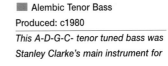

■ Alembic Eight-string
Produced: 1976

*This bass was custom made for
ELP bassist Greg Lake, and
illustrates the typical Alembic
features of exotic woods, multi-
laminate through-neck construction,
XLR output and 'dummy' middle
pickup which reduces interference
from external noise sources.*

ALEMBIC

■ Alembic Tenor Bass
Produced: c1980

*This A-D-G-C- tenor tuned bass was
Stanley Clarke's main instrument for*
*over a decade, and formed the basis
for a later Alembic Clarke signature
series. Clarke is shown using this
bass in the shot below right.*

Jamerson switched to electric bass in 1961, buying a Fender Precision and an Ampeg 35 watt Portaflex combo amp when Gordy asked him to go on the road with Jackie Wilson, and three years later Jamerson became a full-time member of Motown's fluctuating team of studio musicians, unofficially known as the Funk Brothers. Jamerson shines out on Motown hits like The Supremes' 'Stop In The Name Of Love' (1965), The Four Tops' 'Reach Out' (1966), and Stevie Wonder's 'I Was Made To Love Her' (1967), among many others. His powerfully rhythmic basslines were often beautifully melodic, and Jamerson's recorded work with Motown helped to change the perception of the electric bass guitar's role in pop music from root-note machine to an important part of the overall musical picture – even if, uncredited, Jamerson's stellar playing would for years remain anonymous to the many bass players whose ears pricked up on hearing the latest Motown 45. Jamerson died in 1983, only 47 years old.

By 1964, well over ten years after Fender's Precision had first appeared, the electric bass was at last becoming established as the modern bass instrument. In their different ways, McCartney and Jamerson personified this new acceptance. McCartney was an unschooled pop musician, originally a guitarist who was 'lumbered' with the bass, but who made the instrument his own and showed it off to the world, mainly on-stage through Vox amps, including the famous AC-100 head and T-60 bass cabinet. Jamerson came from a jazz background playing double-bass,

but found pop studio work with an electric bass more lucrative, and soon discovered that he could make wonderfully expressive music on bass guitar, proving to many session players that the electric bass was a legitimate musical instrument.

Improvements to stage and studio equipment during the 1960s made the bass guitar increasingly audible, and vital musical steps were taken by players such as Jack Bruce in Cream, Phil Lesh in The Grateful Dead and Jack Casady in Jefferson Airplane, along with studio bassists like Tommy Cogbill (Wilson Pickett, Aretha Franklin, Percy Sledge), Carol Kaye (Beach Boys, Glen Campbell, Monkees), Joe Osborn (Simon & Garfunkel, Mamas & The Papas, Fifth Dimension) and John Paul Jones (Dusty Springfield, Herman's Hermits, Donovan... and later, of course, Led Zeppelin) among many others.

Guitar makers too were reacting to the changing musical atmosphere around the bass guitar in the 1960s, although some still viewed the instrument as a kind of lesser version of the guitar. Fender, however, was on a roll, and in the mid 1960s 'Fender Bass' became a generic expression, synonymous with electric bass guitar. In January 1965 Fender was sold to CBS (Columbia Broadcasting System) for $13 million and became the Fender Musical Instruments division of Columbia Records Distribution Corporation. CBS poured millions of dollars more into Fender and increased its output dramatically, but as a result quality gradually declined into the 1970s; the original team that had built up Fender grew disenchanted and one by one left the organization.

California Dreaming

California was also the birthplace of the next significant development of the bass guitar – but in a set-up that was about as far removed from the orthodox business environment of a big-league organization like Fender's new CBS parent as it was possible to get. Alembic started out as one observer put it "as more of a concept and a place than a company." The place was San Francisco, the time was 1969, and the motivating force was one Augustus Stanley Owsley. Part of the community of roadies, friends and acid freaks that gradually grew up around the Grateful Dead was a sort of electronics workshop known as Alembic, named after an apparatus used by distillers (and also apparently by alchemists) "to convey the refined product to a receiver," as the dictionary defines it.

Owsley had created Alembic in the warehouse where The Grateful Dead rehearsed north of San Francisco. At first the idea was for Alembic to come up with new ways of providing clear, accurate recordings of Dead concerts so that the band could improve their live performances. This developed into a general interest in the improvement of studio and live sound quality, primarily by examining and refining all the different elements of the musical process, working from the PA systems and recording equipment that came at the end of the musical chain back to the microphones and instruments that provided the initial source of the band's sound.

With this focused interest in drawing good sound from rock instruments, Alembic quickly developed a guitar repair and modification workshop. The combination of the woodworking talents of Rick Turner, a one-time Massachusetts folk guitarist and guitar repairer, and the electronics knowledge of Ron Wickersham, who came to Alembic from the Ampex recording equipment company, soon turned the workshop into a full-fledged guitar making operation.

Alembic started to customize instruments, a process it dubbed 'Alembicizing.' Some Guild Starfire hollow-body basses were Alembicized for Phil Lesh of the Dead and Jack Casady of

Jefferson Airplane in 1970 and 1971, and the very first official Alembic instrument made to the new company's own design was a bass guitar built for Jack Casady in 1971. Slowly – or at least as quickly as the various recreational sideshows of San Francisco at the time would allow – Alembic started to standardize a regular line of short-scale, medium-scale and long-scale basses. The Alembic basses featured a unique combination of features: high quality, multi-laminate, neck-through-body construction; attractive, exotic woods; heavy, tone-enhancing brass hardware; and complex active-electronics systems with external power supplies. Combined with the newly introduced benchmark bass amp, the Ampeg SVT that combined a 300 watt head

■ *Motown session bassist James Jamerson was perhaps the most significant early figure in establishing the art of the bass guitar; his melodic, rhythmic basslines, played on a 1962 Precision, powered many hits such as 'Stop In the Name Of Love' and 'Reach Out.'*

with massive 8x10 cabinets, the bass guitar had reached a new level of sound quality and power that would be matched by fresh playing styles and novel musical fusions.

The turning point for the popularity of Alembic's bass guitars came when Stanley Clarke started to play the company's high-class, expensive basses. As the 1970s progressed, Clarke came to personify a new breed of bass player, helping to elevate the bass guitar to the role of soloing instrument and an equal partner to the other frontline instruments.

Clarke had joined Return to Forever with keyboard player Chick Corea in 1972, and the group forged a highly successful fusion of jazz, rock and Latin flavors through the early-1970s. Clarke's first solo album to feature prominent electric bass appeared in 1974, the first of a long line, and these more than any other records established the idea that a virtuoso bass guitarist could become a star. Bass players were clearly becoming more willing to accept new instrument ideas and designs than were guitarists, and some bassists were beginning to pay a high price for the privilege. Thanks to Alembic, the specialist, high-quality, high-price bass guitar had arrived.

Other bassists helped to shape the bass sound of the 1970s, few more so than a pair of funk pioneers, Bootsy Collins and Bernard Edwards, who defined funk bass at either end of the decade. Bootsy did a spectacular job in James Brown's band (he played the impossibly convoluted bassline on the 1970 single 'Sex Machine') as well as in George Clinton's wild P-Funk projects, using a strange star-shaped custom bass made by Larry Pletz. Bernard Edwards provided the solid, undulating grooves at the heart of the smooth disco-funk of Chic, exemplified by the 1979 track 'Good Times,' primarily on Music Man and B.C. Rich basses.

Slapping and Fretless

Seventies pop was becoming more elaborate in the hands of groups like Swedish sophisticates Abba, whose bassist Rutger Gunnarsson would weave beautiful basslines through hits such as 'Money Money Money' and 'Knowing Me, Knowing You' (both 1976). Rock too was growing up during the 1970s and turning progressive, as Chris Squire provided surging, bright, melodic lines for Yes. It was also in the 1970s that Larry Graham in Sly & The Family Stone (and in his own group Graham Central Station) used his Jazz Bass to popularize the 'slap' style of percussive funk playing.

'Slapping' had been used for decades by some double-bass

■ *Larry Graham, bassist with Sly And The Family Stone, helped define the art of funk bass, bringing the 'slap' style of playing to the world's attention with 1973's 'Thank You* *(Fa Lettin Me Be Mice Elf Again,' plus a string of other Stone and solo releases. Graham is pictured here using his trademark natural finish Fender Jazz bass.*

was in his hands during the late 1970s that the instrument came alive for the first time. Not that Pastorius was by any means the first player to use fretless bass, but he popularized its sound by bringing it right up front, playing it in a virtuosic manner as a featured instrument.

players, who would literally slap the strings with their picking hand in order to get more volume from their acoustic instruments. Many bass guitarists first noticed Larry Graham applying a modern version of the idea: using his right-hand he would bounce the edge of his thumb off one of the lower strings of his bass guitar while also pulling higher strings, in various rhythmic combinations, generating a powerfully percussive sound. With its roots in 1970s funk, the bass guitar slap style also crossed over into jazz and fusion, but really took hold in the 1980s when it infiltrated all manner of musical styles and became required knowledge among bassists, even generating instructional books and videos dedicated entirely to its practice.

Jazz-rock fusion also supplied one of the greatest electric bass guitarists of recent times. The name of Jaco Pastorius has become almost synonymous with the fretless bass guitar, for it

■ *Bootsy Collins' complex rhythmic bass patterns revitalized James Brown's recorded output from 1970's 'Sex Machine' onwards, before Collins went on to join George Clinton's Funkadelic outfit in* *1972. Here Collins is pictured with one of his trademark star custom basses made by Larry Pletz, which is usually teamed with a complex 10-cabinet custom-made amplification system.*

Electric Bass: The Pioneers

1951: Leo Fender's Fender Electric Instrument company launches the first commercially successful electric bass guitar on to the market in October.

1952: Roy Johnson of the Lionel Hampton Band is one of the first bassmen publicly to

play the Fender Precision Bass, described in Down Beat as "this sensational instrumental innovation." Johnson's replacement, Monk Montgomery, continues to use the Fender bass, heard on low-fi live Hampton recordings of the time such as Live In Sweden 1953.

1956: Danelectro issues the

first six-string bass, the UB2, triumphantly emblazoned across Duane Eddy's later 'Because They're Young' 45.

1957: Rickenbacker launches its 4000 model through-neck bass; Bill Black enlivens the Elvis band with a Fender on tracks such as 'Jailhouse Rock'; Fred Kirk with the John Barry Seven is among the first

The fretless bass, with its smooth, unfretted fingerboard, enables bassists to achieve a sound that is completely different when compared with the fretted instrument: notes 'swell' with a beautifully warm tone and fretless players can easily execute an impressive slide or incorporate longitudinal string vibrato into their sound. To obtain similar sounds, some players had tried electric upright basses of the early-1960s, such as the double-bass-shaped Ampeg Baby Bass or the more skeletal German-built Framus Triumph Bass, nicknamed the 'pogo stick', but neither proved very successful.

The first fretless bass guitar had been marketed by Ampeg in 1966. Among the earliest well-known players of fretless bass guitar was Rick Danko of American folk-rock pioneers The Band. Danko was primarily a fretted Fender player, but around 1970 had been given an Ampeg fretless, which can be heard on a good deal of *Cahoots* (1971) and some of the live *Rock Of Ages* album. Another early exponent of the fretless bass was Ralphe Armstrong, who used a hybrid Fender with John McLaughlin's Mahavishnu Orchestra (on *Apocalypse* 1974 and *Visions Of The Emerald Beyond* 1975) and later with Jean-Luc Ponty. While it was primarily in jazz-rock that the instrument first took hold, the distinctive sound did spread to other styles, and a striking, influential appearance of the instrument in pop music occurred on Bad Company's summer 1974 hit single 'Can't Get Enough,' with Boz Burrell's fretless Precision well to the fore.

But it was Jaco Pastorius who came to define the sound of fretless bass when in 1976 he joined the jazz-rock group Weather Report, staying for six eventful years. The band had been formed in 1971 by keyboardist Joe Zawinul and sax player Wayne Shorter, both of whom had been members of the experimental jazz-rock line-ups of the Miles Davis band in the late 1960s, where they'd acquired a taste for the fusion of rock's amplified rhythms and the moody freedom of modal jazz. They developed this combination in Weather Report, and turned it into a commercial success.

Jaco used a fretted Fender Jazz Bass that had been modified by removing the frets, and on-stage popularized the newly developed 200-watt solid-state Acoustic 360 amp, revolutionary because its 18″ loudspeaker was contained in a 'folded-horn' enclosure, a design borrowed from cinema and PA systems and which helped it deliver devastatingly powerful bass sounds.

Jaco's pioneering use of the fretless bass with its singing, sustained quality and his tremendous harmonic and melodic skills on the instrument coincided with some of Weather Report's finest recorded compositions and daringly improvisational live work, nearly always with Pastorius's bass prominently positioned in the mix. The band became one of the most successful jazz-rock outfits, and probably their best known piece from the period is 'Birdland' from *Heavy Weather* (1977), an intricate weave of sounds and textures enlivened by Jaco's strong bass work.

However, most bass players had their earliest encounter with the sounds of Jaco's playing when they heard his first solo album, *Jaco Pastorius*, released in 1976 and including the captivating double-tracked 'Continuum' that characterized the Jaco fretless sound. He played a regular fretted Fender as well, which appeared on just two tracks: 'Come On Come Over,' and the much-imitated 'Portrait Of Tracy' that demonstrated Jaco's remarkable use of high-pitched harmonics.

Ampeg was one of the few companies to address the more rigorous demands made on bass amplification by the late 1960s. The 300 watt SVT system was popularized by Bill Wyman, who started using both an Ampeg bass and SVT stack after the Rolling Stones arranged an endorsement deal with the Ampeg company.

British bassists to record with electric bass, on 'Every Which Way' (seen in the film Six Five Special).

1958: Dave Myers plays the loudest Fender in Chicago, adding an electric bottom to Little Walter's driving Chess material.

1960: 'Tic tac bass' breaks out in Nashville, a percussive studio duet of double-bass and electric bass that underlines hits like Patsy Cline's 'I Fall To Pieces.' The clicky bass sound also turns up on easy 1960s hits such as Bert Kaempfert's 'Wunderland Bei Nacht.'

1961: James Jamerson switches to Fender electric bass for a Jackie Wilson tour, paving the way for his great later Motown recordings; Jet Harris emphasizes the electric bass's melodic potential on Shadows tracks like 'Kon-Tiki.'

1962: Duck Dunn riffs away under Steve Cropper and Booker T's 'Green Onions' jam.

Despite Jaco's post-Weather Report band Word Of Mouth as well as his notable contributions to Joni Mitchell's *Hejira* (1976) and her live *Shadows And Light* (1980), his career was to be tragically shortlived, and following drug-related problems he died after a brawl outside a bar in summer 1987, just 35 years old. Jaco opened many players' ears to a whole new world of possibilities from the fretless bass guitar, and any number of bassists could be heard in the 1980s 'doing a Jaco' by playing conspicuous and melodic fretless basslines. One of the most individual contributions was Pino Palladino's lyrical fretless that featured prominently on Paul Young's 1983 hit 'Wherever I Lay My Hat (That's My Home).'

Losing Your Head

Meanwhile the Fender blueprint for the bass guitar continued to supply most players with their needs, sometimes amalgamated with Alembic-derived ideas such as active electronics, or with a new variation like a fretless fingerboard. But a more radical redesign was taking place in New York. Ned Steinberger had worked as a cabinet maker and furniture designer, and met guitar-maker Stuart Spector when they both shared a workspace at a woodworkers' co-operative in Brooklyn. Steinberger became intrigued by instrument design, helped Spector develop his 1977 NS-1 bass model, and started to experiment with ideas for a further bass guitar design.

Steinberger was uneasy about the relatively unbalanced weight of the neck and tuners of a typical bass in relation to its body. This led him to a creative leap: why not take the tuners off the peghead and put them on to the body? He wasn't the first to think of this option, but nobody had made anything

approaching a commercial impact with such a design. Following a number of experiments with 'headless' guitars, Steinberger went further. Aiming for a rigid structure to enhance the sustain and tone of the conventional instrument, he came to the conclusion that the optimum material was a reinforced plastic composite of graphite fiber and resin.

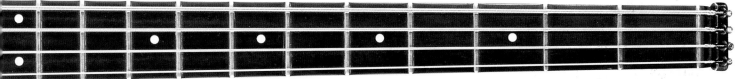

■ **Steinberger L-2**

Introduced: 1981

Ned Steinberger's radical redesign of the bass represented the culmination of his earlier attempts to improve bass ergonomics with the Spector NS-1. Note the differences in body shape and bridge design from the 1979 prototype (back and front, below).

Eventually Steinberger produced his first all-composite bass, which was probably the first solid composite musical instrument molded in one piece, and showed it to the trade in 1979. It had an all-composite construction, a tiny rectangular 'body' with tuners on the end, a headless neck, and active pickups. Initially, Steinberger's intention was to sell the design to one of the big guitar companies, but after a negative response he decided to make the bass himself.

A company was formed, and the Steinberger Bass was launched during 1981. While many industry people remained skeptical, some musicians warmed to the unusual new bass. The first Steinberger bass, a fretless model, was sold to session bassist Tony Levin, best known then for his work with Paul Simon and King Crimson. Several other notable and conspicuous bassists began to take up the diminutive Steinberger, including Sting with the Police, Geddy Lee of Rush, and the Stones' Bill Wyman.

The Steinberger design was enormously influential in the early-1980s – not so much in the use of graphite and plastics, the expense and complexity of which put off most mass-market manufacturers, but more in the immediate visual characteristics, the small body and headless elements of the design. For a year or two the buzzword among electric bass makers was 'headless.' Active pickups, supplied to Steinberger by California company EMG, also became widely used on other instruments, providing a more open tonal response, and unlike the headless concept proved an enduring option for bassists.

115

■ *One of the most noticeable stylistic movements of the late 1970s was the popularity of the fretless bass, largely brought about by the lyrical fretless work of Jaco Pastorius. Pastorius used a Fender Jazz bass with the frets removed. Although not the first player to use the fretless style, Pastorius's memorable work with Weather Report and Joni Mitchell helped popularize the fretless bass; his presence on the cover of the six-string oriented Guitar Player magazine (opposite) demonstrates his influence.*

Take Five

During the 1970s a number of bass players began to think about changing and extending the tuning of their instruments to suit particular musical styles and requirements. Minneapolis freelance bassist Jimmy Johnson, best known for his recent work with James Taylor, ordered a custom five-string bass from Alembic in 1975. Alembic intended its five-string to be fitted with an extra high-C string above the usual E-A-D-G strings. The high-C was not in itself a new idea for bass guitar: Fender had used it on their ill-judged and therefore shortlived Bass V of 1965. But Johnson modified the five-string to take a specially made low B-string, giving a B-E-A-D-G tuning. Johnson's Alembic arrived in 1976, and was probably the first low-B five-string bass guitar. With increasingly wider string-spacing, the low-B five-string bass would become an important addition to the bass player's kit during the 1980s.

Session player Anthony Jackson, who has worked with artists such as Paul Simon and Steely Dan, came up with the idea of a six-string bass. However, this was not like the earlier Danelectro, which was more of a guitar than a bass. Jackson's six-string bass extended both upwards and downwards by keeping the standard four strings tuned E-A-D-G and adding a high C-string and a low B-string, resulting in a six-string bass tuned B-E-A-D-G-C that could command a much bigger spread in the musical picture. Jackson's first six-string bass was made in 1975 by New York maker Carl Thompson, and further custom models have been built for him by makers Ken Smith and Vinnie Fodera.

Jackson blazed a trail for the six-string bass, but of greatest significance for the general development of the bass guitar was the additional low string, employed and popularized during the 1980s in the shape of the five-string bass guitar (tuned B-E-A-D-G). Whereas the six-string bass has principally been put to use by players in the jazz and fusion fields, the five-string became an essential addition to the instruments carried by many touring and recording bassists from all styles of music, and by the end of the 1980s a five-string model appeared on most bass-makers' pricelists.

As the 1980s dawned, it was clear that a revolution was taking place among players and manufacturers, as the bass guitar became the hip instrument of the moment and a glut of successful bassists highlighted its new-found versatility and prominence. In Europe it was Mark King, the talented bass-playing frontman for Level 42, who personified this fresh cult of the bass, center-staging a funky slap style that led a whole new generation of players to take up the evidently enjoyable, popular and hugely fashionable bass guitar. In the U.S. Billy Sheehan came to prominence in the pop-metal band of singer David Lee Roth, where he cheerfully battled it out with Roth's guitarist Steve Vai, and Sheehan established himself from the mid 1980s onward as a bass hero, much in the mold of the guitar hero of years past.

MTV, the music satellite-TV channel, started to broadcast a series at the very end of 1989 called *Unplugged*, capitalizing on the rise in popularity of acoustic music at the time. As more programs followed, 'unplugged' quickly became a catchphrase that summed up a musical trend. The idea was that rock bands better known for loud, amplified work would unplug their electric equipment and play a concert with acoustic instruments. This proved surprisingly successful: many musicians clearly reveled in the opportunity to unplug and go acoustic, even if only for the

Classic bass years

1963/64: *Paul McCartney slams his Hofner violin bass into great early Beatles tunes such as 'I Saw Her Standing There' and 'I'm Happy Just To Dance With You.'*

1964: *James Jamerson puts the bottom in Motown's house band, the Funk Brothers, weaving lowdown melodies through 45s like The Supremes 'You Keep Me Hanging On' and The Isley*

Brothers' 'This Old Heart Of Mine.'

1965/66: *McCartney gets a Rickenbacker and makes Beatle bass marvels like 'Rain.'*

1970 *Bootsy Collins gets down for James Brown's 'Sex Machine,' later refining the lowly funk groove with Parliament and Funkadelic; Andy Fraser puts the melody in white soul for Free's Fire & Water.*

1971: *Chris Squire twangs progressively on The Yes Album and Fragile.*

1974: *Stanley Clarke's eponymous solo album defines the electric bass player as flash frontman; Larry Graham slaps that bass on Graham Central Station's 'Hair.'*

1976/77: *Jaco Pastorius shows how to play fretless bass on his own solo album*

and Weather Report's Heavy Weather.

1977: *Chuck Rainey is Mr. Session as he fills Steely Dan's Aja with effortless grooves.*

1983: *Peter Hook demonstrates that bass guitar is relevant in the sequencer age with New Order's 'Blue Monday.'*

1985: *Mark King slaps and funks on Level 42's World Machine.*

one gig, and fans welcomed the appearance of a new slant on well-known material. As far as the musical instrument industry was concerned, the popularity of acoustic music in general and *Unplugged* in particular gave a new lease on life to the sales of acoustic instruments.

Acoustic was in vogue, and air began to appear inside all manner of guitars – including basses. One of the earliest acoustic bass guitars had been the vast Earthwood Bass of 1972, and other models made by Guild and Eko followed. In order to increase their volume, both companies offered optional versions with bridge-mounted pickups to provide a novel amplified-acoustic sound. It was primarily this type of 'electro-acoustic' bass that became popular as the *Unplugged* acoustic boom began to reverberate around the early 1990s – when in fact 'acoustic' often meant acoustic only in looks and feel, because in reality amplification still had to be used to project most performances. The new breed of electro-acoustic basses had thin bodies and bridge pickups. The first to appear had been the Kramer Ferrington in 1986, and the model was used to fuel *Unplugged* shows by bands such as Fleetwood Mac and The Cure. Kramer's Ferrington was quickly followed on to the market by electro-acoustic basses from many other makers, including Washburn and Ovation.

In sharp contrast to the acoustic trend, some manufacturers began to link together the bass guitar and the synthesizer during the 1980s to make a new instrument, the bass guitar synthesizer, but these experiments foundered as the first electronic circuits were largely unsuccessful in accurately sensing and reproducing the lowest frequencies of a bass guitar's strings. Later, the MIDI Bass system developed by Steve Chick in Australia overcame many of the earlier problems, and was incorporated into basses by makers such as Wal in England, Valley Arts in the U.S., and the Peavey Midibase and CyberBass.

In the late 1990s the bass guitar remains an important and largely irreplaceable component of modern rock music making. Some players prefer the retro feel of an old or made-to-seem-old Fender, underlining the 45-year heritage associated with their instrument. Other bassists choose a modern instrument from the newest makers, perhaps combining graphite technology, state-of-the-art electronics and exotic woods. But as Steve Harris, long-standing bassman for heavy-metal merchants Iron Maiden, points out, it's the way a bass is used and the context it works in that counts the most. "I'll listen to the bass player if I like the band," Steve says. "But I won't listen to the bass player just because he's good if I don't like the songs."

GUILD ACOUSTIC ELECTRIC BAS

■ Seattle grungers Nirvana, Hole, and Alice In Chain's have all gone acoustic for MTV's *Unplugged*. Alice In Chains bassist Michael Inez plays a Martin B series acoustic bass for the band's performance, recorded in April 1996 and released as an album later in the year.

■ The Guild company was one of the first makers to introduce acoustic basses, and has benefited from the *Unplugged* boom. Clapton bassist Nathan East endorses the company's B500C in this 1990s advertisement in *Bass Player* magazine.

1986: *Baghiti Khumalo lends arresting African basslines to Paul Simon's* Graceland.

1995: *Bass Player magazine's bassist of the year is Marcus Miller (Miles Davis and others); other honors go to Geddy Lee of Rush (rock), John Patitucci (jazz), Flea of Red Hot Chili Peppers (funk), veteran sessioneer David Hungate (country), Lincoln Goines (Latin) and Aswad's Tony Gad (reggae).*

Recording and Production

"At Beach Boys sessions I watched Brian Wilson work as I imagine Orson Welles must have looked when he directed and performed in his early films. Like a team coach instructing his batters, he would whisper changes to be played on the next take to each musician. Brian composed and produced musical effects like the first viewing of a sunrise to a once-blind person."

NIK VENET, CAPITOL RECORDS EXECUTIVE

In the 50 years since the tape recorder was introduced, the process of making records has undergone a technological transformation. Some modern recordings owe more to computer equipment than they do to musical instruments. And yet many of today's engineers and producers continue to use techniques – and even equipment – that date back to the dawn of the tape era. They are looking to a return to simplicity, focusing on musical creativity rather than technological expertise.

In the early days, of course, there was no choice. The pioneers of record production could do no more than record, unchanged, the sound of music as it happened. The first rock'n'roll records arrived just as direct-to-disc recording was being abandoned in favor of tape. Recordings had previously been made by cutting discs on a lathe in the studio as the music played. Tape recording arrived immediately after World War II. The Germans had developed it in the 1930s, and used it in their war effort. The technology was brought back from Germany for British and American companies to develop. The Ampex Corporation of Redwood City, California, introduced its first machine in 1946.

In the 1950s, most pop recording was done in the studios of the major record labels. These were large, purpose-built facilities, with the best and most expensive equipment available. A typical studio of the era was that built by Capitol Records at the base of the famous Capitol Tower in Hollywood, California. This had three recording rooms, the largest measuring 60 feet by 40 feet, and four purpose built echo-chambers beneath to allow the addition of natural-sounding reverberation to recordings that had been made in the 'dead' acoustic of the main rooms.

At the same time, the Abbey Road studios of EMI in London boasted three large rooms, designed for both classical and popular music, which tended to mean light orchestral and dance band music. Like the American studios of the major labels, Abbey Road was a formal place in which to work. Engineers came to work in white coats with collar and tie beneath. And recording had to be fitted into strict three-hour sessions: 10am-1pm; 2pm-5pm; 7pm-10pm. Few people at this time used the studios in the evenings.

The Sun Sound

All this was to change. The impetus for musical innovation came from outside the major record labels and their studios. The independent studios and labels of America were welcoming to those excluded from mainstream pop – black musicians, hillbillies, the young – and much more open to experimentation.

World War II had brought a great impetus to the radio industry. Afterwards, electronic equipment was plentiful and trained technicians were in great supply. Most of the small studios of the early 1950s had strong radio connections. For instance, the Memphis Recording Service, where Elvis Presley made his first recordings, was started by Sam Phillips while he was still an engineer with one of the city's radio stations. His business cards declared "We record anything – anywhere – anytime. A complete service to fulfil any recording need." This was no exaggeration. Phillips' studio survived by recording school speech days, weddings and conferences as well as organizing PA equipment for outdoor events. But its owner's real concern was with music, particularly the blues, which he

1877: Thomas Edison patents the Phonograph – a tin foil-covered cylinder which records sound by embossing variable grooves as the apparatus is rotated by hand. Later versions utilize reusable wax cylinders.

1888: Emile Berliner demonstrates disc recording and reproduction; this will form the basis of sound recording for 50 years.

1897: First recording studio opens in Philadelphia, recording on disc.

1899: Danish engineer Valdemar Poulsen demonstrates a machine using steel wire as the recording medium. Although performance is poor, wire recorders will still be in use 50 years later.

1925: Electrical (tube-based) recording era begins, allowing the use of multiple microphones, ability to adjust sound levels and simple signal processing. Musicians no longer have to crowd round a single recording horn, fighting to be heard.

1928: First condenser microphones manufactured outside the laboratory. The CMV 3 or 'Neumann Bottle' is the first product of Georg Neumann's new company.

1929: The Blattnerphone is demonstrated. It records sound on ¼"-wide steel strip.

■ Gene Vincent's first demos were recorded in a Virginia radio station; once he signed to Capitol in 1956, the label opted for recording him in Owen Bradley's Nashville studios, rather than its own recording complex. The lack of studio interference and use of Vincent's own band, including Cliff Gallup on guitar, helped preserve the Blue Caps' natural exuberance on tape.

recorded and licensed to record companies in Los Angeles and Chicago. Only after those records had succeeded did he decide to start his own record label: Sun.

The way Elvis Presley's first sessions were recorded was typical. Sun's studio consisted of a single room, about 30 feet by 18 feet, with a control room at one end. No more than five microphones could be used at any one time, and all fed into a five-into-one RCA radio-type mixer with rotary faders. There they were mixed, live, into an Ampex mono tape recorder. There were no baffles to prevent leakage between the microphones, as is considered essential today. Instead of worrying about the separation between the individual instruments, Phillips concentrated on getting a good sound – and a good 'feel' – in the room and capturing that on tape. The only effect available was Phillips' distinctive tape echo. A recording session consisted

simply of placing the musicians in the room and inviting them to play a song for as long as it took to create a version worth putting on tape. A small number of takes would be recorded, and one chosen for release. The independent studios had little in the way of sophisticated equipment, but they did have time to experiment, and were free of the petty restrictions about session times and musicians' hours that were an important part of life in the big studios. At the same time, the owners of the independent studios were at liberty to break as many rules as they liked. Because mixing was 'live,' taking place at the same time as recording, the process was active and energetic. As the song was underway, Phillips would be adjusting the mix, altering the level of echo, riding the volume of the singer's microphone and allowing individual instrument channels – notably guitar and later drums – to distort where he thought it added extra bite.

■ *Although Sam Phillips' work with Elvis, Jerry Lee Lewis and Carl Perkins helped pioneer rock'n'roll, Phillips had already amassed much experience recording Jackie Brenston, B.B. King and Howlin' Wolf for the Chess and Modern labels. Phillips' blues records concentrated on feel over technique; similar priorities would characterize his rock'n'roll productions.*

■ **Elvis Presley Sun Singles**
Recorded: 1954-1955
One major technical aspect of Phillips' production for Presley's early singles was the 'Sun tape echo'; Phillips used a second microphone on the vocals, feeding it to a second tape recorder. The sound was then monitored off the tape a fraction of a second later, and reunited with the direct sound at the mixing desk. The result, much copied on later 'rockabilly' records, was a hard 'slapback' sound quite unlike the smooth reverberation of sophisticated studios' echo chambers.

This legacy created difficulties when Presley was signed by RCA, and his recording sessions transferred to its big studios in Nashville. Here things were much more formal. Sessions began in the afternoon, whereas in Memphis they had started in the evenings. The RCA engineers called out take numbers, rather than simply shouting, "Do it again." And for all their technical facilities, they could not initially work out a way of duplicating Phillips' tape-echo sound. In the end, they used the crude acoustic echo of a long corridor outside the recording room. But otherwise, things proceeded as usual, with the song perfected through rehearsal and repeated takes, rather than through anything being done to it later. Presley, at least at the beginning of his career, seems to have been a perfectionist. 'Hound Dog,' a number he had been performing live for some months, took 31 takes to get right when it was recorded in July 1956.

Sam Phillips was a believer in simplicity, as were many of the other pioneers of rock'n'roll. Cosimo Matassa, owner and chief engineer of the J & M studio in New Orleans, was faced with the task of using the same rudimentary equipment to record bands which might include brass sections and large vocal groups. Record companies such as Specialty and Modern sent artists like Ray Charles and Little Richard to Matassa's studio for his trademark sound, which was a result of absolute simplicity in equipment and method. His technique was to go into the recording room, listen to the band, and then return to the control room and attempt to duplicate that sound as far as possible. He was aided in this by a small, clean-sounding room. Unusually for a studio of this type, it had been the subject of professional acoustic treatment. Starting with only four microphone inputs, he had to use the physics of the different types of microphone to ensure all the musicians were covered. A ribbon microphone with a 'figure-of-eight' pattern picks up equally at front and back, but not at the sides. Thus horn players could be deployed on either side of the microphone's 'live' faces. In some cases, microphones were even moved during songs: for instance, during a saxophone break, a microphone might have to be swung away from the drum kit and towards the horn. This was clumsy, but with only four microphones to play with there was little alternative. The result of such simplicity, however, was good, strong sound.

For some producers and engineers, however, the simple methods of Phillips and Matassa were not enough. This was particularly the case with those who had been able to set up their own primitive 'home studios.' Les Paul, the electric guitar pioneer,

started his own home studio in the 1930s and used it both to record his musical contemporaries – Gene Autry, Bing Crosby, the Andrews Sisters – and to develop recording techniques.

Overdubbing Takes Over

Les Paul started experimenting with overdubbing as early as his 1948 release 'Lover.' At that stage, the only way this was possible was by making a backing track on one tape recorder, then copying it to a second while adding new voices or instruments at the same time. The process could be done several times, but the loss of quality was considerable.

Similar experimentation was crucial in the career of Buddy Holly. Norman Petty, Holly's producer, was a pianist and organist who formed an instrumental trio with his wife and a friend. After a couple of hits in the early 1950s, Petty invested their earnings in a studio, initially for their own recordings and then for wider hire. Petty was a stickler for musical quality, stopping recording when Holly went off-key, for instance, but initially he worked in the same way as the other producers mentioned, recording the sound exactly as it was audible in the room. Unusually, his studio benefited from having two recording rooms. Holly would sing in one, while the rest of the band played in the other, and this separation helped with the clarity of the recordings.

Early on in Holly's career with Petty, a decision was taken to produce two sets of releases, one labeled "Buddy Holly," the other "The Crickets." Sessions could produce either type of record: the difference was the addition of a vocal backing, which would be added later by over-dubbing, just as Les Paul had done it. This practice thus became commonplace in Norman Petty's studio. The breakthrough came with 'Words of Love,' recorded in 1957, when Holly himself was overdubbed, adding successively a second guitar part and two extra vocal lines to an original track consisting of drums, bass, rhythm guitar and a vocal. The effect of overdubbing in this way is that the original track rapidly loses fidelity, becoming distant and muffled. Here, though, it only adds to the song's strange, wistful air.

Heavy Stereo

Tape recording equipment improved throughout the 1950s. First, in 1951, separate record and replay heads made it possible to listen to the sound a fraction of a second after it was recorded rather than waiting until the end of a take. Stereo was demonstrated to the industry at the 1953 Audio Engineering

1934: *BASF develops the first recording tape, using a plastic base coated with iron oxide.*

1935: *German company AEG demonstrates the 'Magnetophon': the world's first tape recorder. It uses BASF's recently developed tape.*

1945: *Captured German 'Magnetophon' tape recorders taken to U.S.A. by U.S. army intelligence officers and developed further to form basis of U.S. tape recorder industry: Ampex and 3M.*

1946: *Les Paul develops overdubbing techniques using two disc cutting machines, copying between them while adding a new track.*

1947: *First variable pattern microphone appears: the Neumann U47.*

1948: *Tape recorders appear in studios; it is six years before they supplant disc cutting.*

1952: *Stereo recording introduced, using existing two-track machines.*

1956: *First stereo microphone, the Neumann SM2.*

1956: *The first 8-track machine, especially built by Ampex, goes to Les Paul. The huge hand-built machine is nicknamed the 'Octopus.' A year later Tom Dowd orders one for Atlantic records. It will be 10 years before these new eight track machines are mass-produced, and for a while there are no mixers available to match them.*

1958: *UK recording engineer/producer*

Society conference in New York, and the same year the first stereo tape machines became commercially available, offering two and three tracks. These were intended primarily for use in the major label studios big enough to accommodate orchestras. The third track provided a center channel, avoiding the 'hole in the middle' that bedevilled early stereo recording. The 'pan-pot,' which allows engineers to place a mono source within a stereo spread, had not yet been invented. Nor had the stereo record. Stereo recordings were issued only as pre-recorded tapes.

The early stereo machines had great possibilities for those who wanted to use them not for stereo but for twin-track or three-track mono recording, but they were not designed for this purpose. They had no facilities for 'sound-on-sound,' for instance – copying from one track to another, adding new sounds on the way, as had already been done with two tape recorders. Nor did they include 'sel-sync.' This system, using the record head of one channel as a temporary replay head so that an extra track could be laid down exactly in synchronisation with the original, was the key to true multitrack recording. It first became available in 1956.

Elvis Presley's move from Sam Phillips' Sun label to RCA in 1956 had a significant effect on his recording style. According to Presley's guitarist Scotty Moore RCA's engineers were more formal and less dictatorial in the studio than Sam Phillips, who would often insist on dozens of takes. The photo below, taken in the RCA studios some time in 1956, shows Presley discussing the session with RCA head of A&R Steve Sholes. Scotty Moore sits in front of Presley, whose Martin D-18 has now been flipped around, relegated from the role of playing rhythm to serve as an improvised bongo.

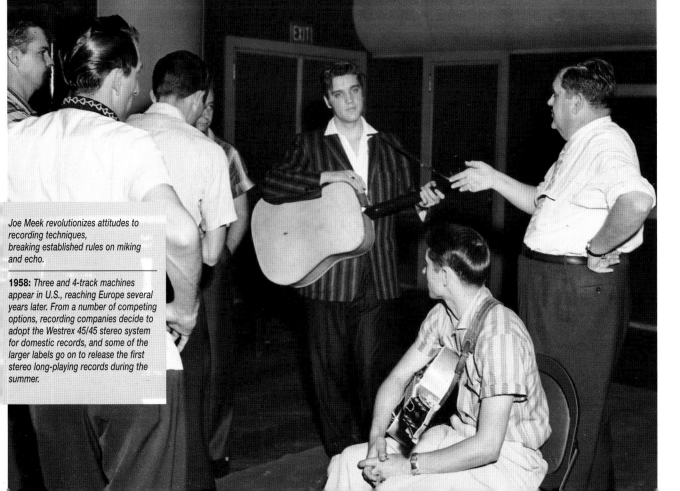

Joe Meek revolutionizes attitudes to recording techniques, breaking established rules on miking and echo.

1958: *Three and 4-track machines appear in U.S., reaching Europe several years later. From a number of competing options, recording companies decide to adopt the Westrex 45/45 stereo system for domestic records, and some of the larger labels go on to release the first stereo long-playing records during the summer.*

Nonetheless, despite their technical failings, the early two and three-track machines were welcomed by pop producers and engineers because of the possibilities they offered for adjusting a performance after the event. In the most basic set-up, the band would be mixed to one track while the singer went on the other: once 'sel-sync' had arrived it was possible for the singer to make numerous attempts after the backing track was completed. The two would then be mixed together on to a second machine. Three-track offered yet more flexibility: it was now possible to record rhythm on one track, vocals on another and strings and horns on the third.

Atlantic Crossing

The next breakthrough came from Atlantic Records in New York. The label had a tremendous roster of artists in the late 1950s, and coupled that with a purist attitude to recorded sound. That it achieved this in the conditions it did is something of a miracle. Its studios in New York actually served as the company's offices by day: furniture had to be moved every night to make way for the musicians.

Atlantic had an engineer of genius in the shape of Tom Dowd, who first started working for the company in 1948. He always sought instrumental clarity and separation, mainly by clever microphone choice and placement, even before he had the equipment truly to achieve it. From 1953, Dowd started recording to two tracks so as to be ready for stereo, even though stereo records were not yet available. But he resisted the pressure to go to three or 4-track, then just becoming available.

Listening to Les Paul's records, Dowd realised that there were too many overdubbed parts, recorded too cleanly, to have been done by simple 'sound-on-sound' copying. Then he discovered that Paul had acquired an experimental Ampex 8-track machine, which he had commissioned himself. Dowd immediately persuaded his Atlantic bosses to put in an order for a similar machine. Atlantic became the first record company to make it standard practice to record 8-track. In order to do so Dowd had to first rebuild his mixer, since no true multitrack mixers were then available.

This new equipment was put to good use by the producers Jerry Leiber and Mike Stoller in their series of records for the Coasters and the Drifters. The Coasters' recordings, miniature playlets of urban life, had always been meticulously contrived productions. Leiber and Stoller had been in the habit of spending hours working on the tapes, even in the mono and

two-track days, physically cutting the tape to remove prominent 'esses' in the vocal or to replace a badly sung chorus with a copy of one from an earlier take.

Multitrack vastly increased these possibilities, but Leiber and Stoller, under Dowd's guidance, used it with restraint. The Coasters records had always been recorded with a bare minimum of instrumentation, and unlike some later producers, Leiber and Stoller didn't allow the new technology to tempt them away from that pattern. A typical Coasters record, for instance 'Poison Ivy' or 'Along Came Jones,' would use only Mike Stoller's piano, guitar, drums, bass and King Curtis on sax. It was a different story, however, with their recordings for The Drifters, which were much more arranged, sometimes including prominent strings. 'There Goes My Baby,' their first Drifters production, set the pattern. Its peculiar orchestration, including strings and tympani, made it a nightmare to record and Atlantic had severe doubts about releasing it at all, even after Tom Dowd had done what he could to straighten up the tapes.

Later sessions were more controlled. Dowd recalls the recording of 'Up On The Roof,' a 1963 hit, as including up to 16 string players. He told EQ magazine recently that he put guitars on one track, bass on another, drums on a third, and piano and organ on a fourth. The fifth and sixth tracks would be occupied by lead and backing vocals, with horns and strings on

1967: *First practical noise reduction system introduced by Dolby. The Type 'A' noise reduction aids the use of larger numbers of tape tracks.*
First public demonstration of digital recording. The Japanese broadcaster N.H.K.'s Research Institute develops a PCM recording system based on a video tape recorder.
Accurate code for finding locations on tapes is developed based on NASA space techniques. This type of code is essential for synchronizing any two

tape machines. In 1970, with modifications, it becomes known as SMPTE Time Code.

1968: *Larger studios opt for 8-track tape machines. The multitrack standard moves to 16-track one year later.*

1970: *Japanese record company Nippon Columbia (Denon) starts using its own design digital recorders for some of its classical music record labels.*

1972: *The multitrack standard reaches 24-track. This remains the preferred size for analog multitracks although 32- and 40-track machines have appeared since.*
First studio designs built to meet needs of multitrack rock recording and high power monitoring systems. Not all are successful.

1973: *The very first digital effects units appear, starting with the Delta-T digital delay.*

the remaining two tracks. All would be recorded together in the main room, with a great deal of leakage from one track to another. Once again, mixing became an attempt to recreate the sound – and in stereo the disposition of the instruments – in the room.

The Wall Of Sound

The trend in the late 1950s and early 1960s was towards bigger productions, even at the expense of authenticity, and this played into the hands of the studios belonging to the major labels, many of which busied themselves with producing better sounding, professionally arranged cover versions of murky independent recordings. Musical leadership, however, was

■ *Les Paul (inset) was a pioneer of multitrack recording, at first dubbing across from one tape machine to another while adding a new part. In 1956 Paul took delivery of a prototype Ampex 8-track machine, which allowed him to overdub even more parts without the consequent loss in quality. The 8-track was used for many subsequent recordings.*

■ *Atlantic's Tom Dowd (below) was the first record company producer to spot the potential of 8-track machines, ordering an early Ampex example in 1957. Dowd produced classics by many Atlantic artists including Aretha Franklin (right), whose career previously seemed to have stalled with CBS under producer John Hammond.*

■ **Phil Spector:**
A Christmas Gift For You
Recorded: 1963
Spector used his favored studio band, 'The Wrecking Crew,' which included drummer Hal Blaine, guitarist Tommy Tedesco, and pianist Leon Russell as the basis of his sound. A total complement of around 18 musicians, not including the string section, was used to record A Christmas Gift For You on 4-track at Goldstar Studios, Los Angeles. As with all Spector recordings, the results were mixed down onto mono only, and the huge sound was obtained by having the musicians repeat the same arrangements, recorded onto spare tracks.

never in the hands of these major labels and studios. The most interesting work continued to come from independent labels and studios. This was even true in the era of the giant studio sessions, many of which were put together by independent producers. Of these none was more successful than Phil Spector. Spector started his career at 17, when he formed a group called The Teddy Bears with two fellow teenagers, taking them into Gold Star Studios in Los Angeles to record a number of songs he had written himself.

The Gold Star studio was later to become one of the city's most famous facilities, but in 1958 it specialized in recording demos for aspiring singers and songwriters.

One of the tracks Spector recorded then, 'To Know Him Is To Love Him,' went on to top the national charts for three weeks. A simple ballad, it is a classic example of the effects of 'bouncing' from tape machine to tape machine. Although the final lead vocal is clear, everything else is buried deep. The resulting misty, fuzzy sound is strangely haunting: Spector had learned that such imperfections can give a record character, and in later years he was always eager to give each disc he made its own individual and distinctive sound world.

The success of that single was not repeated, so Spector flew to New York, where he apprenticed himself to Leiber and Stoller, even playing guitar on some of their recordings with the Drifters. He was able to incorporate some elements of the Atlantic studio practice into his own productions for his own

124

label Philles. Starting with 'There's No Other Like My Baby' by the Crystals, these were, in the main, powerful-sounding and commercial girl group records.

The greatest of the Philles recordings were made in Los Angeles, at Gold Star, which by this time had improved its facilities. In 1960 it acquired new mono and two-track Ampex recorders and built a new desk offering 12 inputs and three outputs. Echo had been a problem in the past, but now the studio had two purpose-built chambers. It was here that Spector created what came to be called 'The Wall of Sound.' Larry Levine, the regular engineer at Gold Star, remembers working on 'Zip-A-Dee-Doo-Dah' with the Crystals (in this case an entirely different set of singers to those featured on the first Crystals recordings).

After spending several hours running through the song with all 12 channels open and their meters banging against the end-stops, Levine was beginning to despair of getting anything acceptable on to tape. So he turned all the 'pots' (rotary volume controls) off, and gradually faded them up one by one, working through basses, drums, guitars and so on. When he got to 11, Spector announced that he had the sound he wanted: the 12th, lead guitar, was left closed. This means that the lead guitar on the track came only from leakage into the other microphones. Again, this was not the 'right' way to do it, but it produced a compelling and original sound.

The key to the 'Wall of Sound' was the sheer number of musicians used to make it. A typical session would include at least 20 people and usually more. There would always be four or five percussionists, led by the drummer Hal Blaine, perhaps three bassists, four or five guitarists, plus horns and strings. Often Levine would run out of microphone channels, but even unmiked instruments would be allowed to stay in the room because of the contribution they made to the overall sound through leakage into adjacent mikes. All this would be mixed down to two tracks, or, as facilities became available, to three: rhythm, strings and vocals. Spector often dubbed parts in unison over the original track, sometimes several times, using the bouncing technique: the minute differences of timing and intonation between individual takes thickened the sound. And Gold Star's echo was another component of the sound. Spector enjoyed an incredible winning streak through the early 1960s, until 'River Deep Mountain High' which he created for Ike & Tina Turner in May 1966. Artistically, it was a magnificent achievement, but it was a commercial flop in the U.S., and

from this point Spector's career was never quite the same again.

All Spector's great recordings were in mono. The producer insisted on mono because it meant a production was 'finished.' Unlike stereo, mono is not dependent upon where the listener sits, the positioning of speakers and adjustment of the balance control. The same rationale was partly responsible for the rejection of stereo by Spector's greatest disciple, Brian Wilson of the Beach Boys.

Pet Sounds

The Beach Boys' very first recordings, in 1961, had seen them relying on their own musical and vocal resources. Their very first record, 'Surfin',' was recorded in an hour in a Beverly Hills demo studio, and is crude both musically and sonically. But it had character, and it was a modest hit.

Soon they moved far beyond that. A single session at Western Studios in Sunset Boulevard, Hollywood, with the engineer Chuck Britz

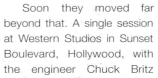
Recording Pet Sounds at Western Studios

behind the desk and Brian Wilson and his father Murry taking charge musically, produced a double-sided single, 'Surfin' Safari' and '409.' The sound was clean and strong. When the single was a hit, the group were put into the studios of their label, Capitol, to make enough tracks for an album. A single, day-long session is all it took.

But that was the last time the Beach Boys used the record company's facilities. In what would soon become standard practice for aspiring bands, they insisted on taking control of their own recordings. First they moved outside the studios, returning to Western Studios and the capable Britz, and then Brian Wilson began to produce the records himself, using techniques he had learned by practicing with the 'sound-on-sound' button of his own Wollensak domestic tape recorder.

Although the facilities of the time were still strictly limited (most of the early Beach Boys' records were made on three tracks), Wilson was learning how to get the most from them. From the time of 'Surfin' USA,' a national number three in 1963, he began double-tracking vocal tracks.

■ *Phil Spector was arguably the first personality record producer, famed for his 'Wall Of Sound.' Spector's production of 'River Deep, Mountain High' was credited to Ike & Tina Turner even though Ike, himself an experienced producer, was not involved in the session. The single's relative failure in the U.S. was a grave setback for Spector.*

■ The Beach Boys: *Pet Sounds*
Recorded: 1965-1966
Although Brian Wilson had used the new 8-track machines by the time he embarked on Pet Sounds in 1965, his favorite studios, United/Western and Gold Star, were both still 4-track. Hence most of Pet Sounds was recorded on

two Scully 280 4-track machines. Around one third of the tracks were mixed down to CBS Recording Studios' 8-track machines – in these cases Wilson would generally mix the existing 4-track instrumental backing direct on to one track, and leave the other seven for vocals overdubs only.

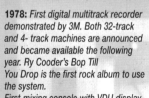

1978: First digital multitrack recorder demonstrated by 3M. Both 32-track and 4- track machines are announced and became available the following year. Ry Cooder's Bop Till You Drop is the first rock album to use the system.
First mixing console with VDU display and 'obvious' computer facilities shown. The Solid State Logic 4000 is initially the cause of much amusement but will come to dominate large studios, forever changing console design.

1979: Neve demonstrates first fully digital mixing console at trade exhibitions.

1982: AMS adds a 'Non-Lin' reverberation program to its RMX16 digital reverb, influencing a generation of drum sounds from Phil Collins onwards.

1983: First 'new' tube microphone for many years launched, meeting still-burgeoning demand for tube-based designs.

The Beach Boys would always record their vocals after the instrumental track. In the early days they would record the backing themselves, but increasingly the complexity of Brian Wilson's arrangements meant it was handed over to session musicians, many of them the same players Phil Spector used: as early as June 1963, Hal Blaine was replacing Dennis Wilson as studio drummer. For vocals, Chuck Britz would place Carl and Dennis Wilson and Al Jardine on one mike, Brian on another and Mike Love on a third, adding echo and mixing live on to one track. A single overdub would then turn five voices into ten, producing a rich and complex sound.

In 1965, Brian Wilson stopped touring with the Beach Boys, and a new musical pattern began to develop in which Wilson would record complex orchestral backing tracks, leaving vocals until the rest of the band returned. Studio bands and orchestras were hired, comparable in scale to Phil Spector's. Unlike Spector, however, Wilson did not use professional arrangers. Instead he would use his own 'head' arrangements, singing and playing the parts to the leaders of the respective sections – strings, brass, guitars – who would write them out and transpose them as necessary. Thereafter numerous run-throughs would be taped, the arrangements changing all the time, until an acceptable version came together. Even at the height of the *Pet Sounds* period, however, only a modest number of tape tracks were used for recording the backing: for that record, the music was recorded on either three or four tracks (two studios were used). These were then mixed to one or two mono tracks on an 8-track machine, and the remaining tracks were filled with vocals.

The disadvantage of this method of working is that artistic decisions have to be made 'live' in the session, rather than later. This was not something that worried Brian Wilson, then at the peak of his confidence. But it did sometimes have unexpected consequences. The *Pet Sounds* song 'You Still Believe In Me' has a prominent bicycle bell on its backing track. This is because the track started off with a different melody and lyrics as 'In My Childhood.' Once the initial mix of backing tracks had been made, it could not be removed.

Several tracks on *Pet Sounds* also contain stray studio chatter. On 'Here Today' for instance you can hear a half-buried conversation about cameras, the result of a hurried mix. Like many of the early users of multitrack recording, Wilson was not very interested in mixing. Nowadays the mix is a lengthy part of the creative process. In those days it was often seen as a chore and of little consequence compared to the process of creating great music in the studio.

During the making of *Pet Sounds* Wilson began work on a song called 'Good Vibrations,' then stopped, before returning to it once the album was complete. In the course of recording 'Good Vibrations,' four studios were used over six months. Countless instrumental arrangements were conceived, using cellos, fuzz bass, flutes, saxophones and a Theremin. It was the most elaborate session there had ever been for any single song: it may also have been the most costly. But in the end Wilson was able to unify the various elements, totalling, it is said, some 90 hours of tape, to create a classic 3:35 single. It was a hit, too, despite its outlandish sound.

The fragmentary way in which 'Good Vibrations' was created was now intended to be applied to a whole album. *Smile* was to

■ *Atlantic's success extended beyond the R&B and pop fields; Keith Jarrett, shown here recording in Atlantic's studios in 1971, was one of many jazz artists who made their name with the company.*

■ By the late 1960s recording techniques were becoming more sophisticated in all fields of music. One notable breakthrough was scored by bluesman B.B. King, who had signed to ABC Records in 1962. 'The Thrill Is Gone' in 1969 was claimed as the first blues record to feature strings, and became King's biggest crossover hit.

127

Sony starts selling PCM3324 24-channel digital multitrack. This forms basis for DASH digital standard supported by six companies. The alternative ProDigi standard is championed by Mitsubishi's 32-channel recorder. The standards are incompatible.

1984: German company EMT shows a system for recording sound on computer disks. The Digiphon is large, limited in ability and expensive, but a significant indicator of what is to come.

1985: First fully digital multitrack/digital desk signal chain at CTS studios, London. Audio results are excellent, but reliability is a problem. The first practical hard disk recorder/editor launched. The AMS AudioFile, initially conceived for obtaining very long samples, will later develop to become an industry standard.

Producer George Martin has frequently been described as 'the fifth Beatle.' Although the title is perhaps spurious, Martin, shown with the band in 1963, was integral to the Beatles' advances from 1966 onwards. Martin scored for strings or horns, contributed piano or harpsichord parts, and with EMI engineers helped overcome the studios' technical limitations. Martin translated the Beatles' sometimes vague descriptions into sounds, and although John Lennon in particular was reportedly not always satisfied with the realization of his instructions, Martin's influence would be sorely missed at the 'back-to-basics' Let It Be sessions.

be a revolutionary record created from tiny fragments: chord sequences, vocal chants, highly arranged orchestral sections, sound effects and so on. The fragments were recorded and dubbed on to acetate discs to enable Wilson to work out ways of combining and sequencing them. The one unifying factor to much of the work was a simple melodic theme, sometimes called 'Bicycle Rider' but best known as the chorus of 'Heroes & Villains': "Heroes and villains/ Just see what you've done." Sadly, at this point Wilson's creative command was fatally weakened by a combination of drugs, his own fragile mental health, frictions within the band and the increasingly circus-like nature of the sessions, which had become a popular place for Los Angeles' hip crowd to hang out.

In May 1967, Wilson scrapped *Smile*. Some of the material was saved, some crudely re-recorded for an album called *Smiley Smile*. The hours of improvisation around the central 'Bicycle Rider' theme turned into the 'Heroes & Villains' single, a hastily-assembled and truncated version of what should have been a masterpiece. 'Smiley Smile,' for the first time, was described as a 'Beach Boys Production.' It was the end of Brian Wilson's period of leadership.

Meanwhile, the most successful pop label in America was now Motown, in Detroit. Like Wilson and Spector, Motown was known for its highly-produced music, in which backing tracks could be produced before they were matched to singers. Originally Motown had recorded on three-track, like most of the major recording studios, switching to 8-track in the early 1960s. To save space in its tiny basement recording room, it had developed the technique of recording bass and electric guitars by feeding them direct into the mixing desk and letting the players hear the sound through the recording room's single monitor. In the room would also be drums, piano, organ and, at least at first, microphones for live vocals.

Motown had no pretensions to audio purism. Tracks were remorselessly limited and compressed, electronic techniques which even out variations in volume from inexperienced singers and produce a punchy sound. Extensive equalization was also employed, and output was tailored to sound convincing through a small monitor designed to simulate the sound of a transistor radio. Motown's producers would also regularly cut discs of work in progress, different mixes and edits. Berry Gordy, the company's owner, insisted that decisions about records should be made on the basis of their sound once they'd been cut.

With The Beatles

By the mid-1960s, American music had reached a considerable level of sophistication. But sophistication is not always what the audience requires. Sometimes it prefers 'authenticity.' This quality was present in the black music of the American south, simply and clearly recorded on the most basic equipment at places like Stax Studios in Memphis, which recorded on single-track mono until 1965. And it was detected in the music of the 'British Invasion.'

American industry observers hearing the first Beatles recordings were shocked at how musically crude they seemed. Technically, too, they were some years behind most of their American competitors, but this only enhanced their air of authenticity. The Beatles recorded at the Abbey Road studios of their record company EMI, which had always had excellent standards of engineering but was slow to make technological changes.

The first Beatles singles, and the first album, were done on two-track. Instruments would go on to one track and lead and backing vocals on the other. The vocal track could be replaced as necessary, and the instrumental track passed through a 'compressor,' to give it a tighter sound, before the two were mixed back together for mono release. Because recording was effectively just capturing the sound of the band's live act, it could be done at high speed. The *Please Please Me* album was recorded in a single 13 hour session.

It was becoming clear that extra tracks were needed. EMI looked at the American studios, which tended to use three tracks on ¹/₂″ tape, but opted instead for a system using four tracks on 1″ tape. It had acquired a Telefunken 4-track machine in the late 1950s, modifying it for use in classical sessions from 1959. Later it switched to standard Studer J37s, used for most of the Beatles' recordings.

The Beatles generally recorded in Studio Two, a rectangular room with a separate control room at the top of a flight of stairs. Later, when the Beatles' value to EMI became clear, the studio was handed over almost entirely to the band, who took to spending weeks on end in the studio as a way of escaping from the mayhem of Beatlemania. They began writing and rehearsing in the studio, as well as recording, and all this paid dividends as their work increased in complexity.

At first the Beatles' records featured just the band themselves. Then George Martin, their producer, began to play occasional piano parts. But the breakthrough came with

■ **Jimi Hendrix:** *Axis Bold As Love*
Recorded: 1967

Hendrix's second album was recorded at Olympic, London, produced by Chas Chandler. As Hendrix's last album on 4-track, the album relied heavily on bouncing down from one machine to another, to give effectively seven tracks. One extra problem arrived when Hendrix left the master tapes in a London taxi, forcing Chandler and engineer Eddie Kramer to remix the album overnight. Unable to duplicate 'If Six Was Nine,' they were forced to use a mixed copy which had been chewed up by Noel Redding's home tape machine, reputedly smoothing out the tape with a domestic iron.

■ *These 1967 shots show the Spencer Davis group in the London studios of Pye Records. The recording area is small, with no separate drum booth; Pete York's drum kit sits in the main area with one simple baffle at each side; a single Neumann is used to record toms, snare and cymbals.*

'Yesterday,' recorded in 1965 for the *Help!* album. Paul McCartney wrote the song, and it was recorded initially with just his guitar part. Then Martin suggested the addition of a string quartet, and composer and producer sat down at the piano and worked it out together. The result is extremely striking, far removed from the usual saccharine strings of the day.

Four-track was a step forward, but the Beatles were soon running out of space. The track sheet for the 1965 recording of McCartney's 'The Night Before' notes that drums, bass and rhythm were on one track, George Harrison's lead guitar on a second, vocals on a third, with the fourth for extra piano and

■ Willie Mitchell's Hi label was originally an offshoot of Sam Phillips' Sun records. By 1969 Mitchell had signed Al Green and assembled a studio band which included drummer Al Jackson, later of Booker T and the MGs, and the Hodges brothers on guitar, bass and organ. The small 4-track Ampex-based studio was used to record soul hits by Green and Ann Peebles up to the 1970s.

backing vocals. If any more space was needed, it had to be provided by bouncing down to a second machine. Usually all four tracks would be mixed to a stereo pair on the second machine. Two more tracks could then be added, and if necessary the four new tracks could be bounced back to the first machine. By this time, however, the losses inherent in the process would start to become noticeable.

Like Brian Wilson, George Martin had discovered the effectiveness of double-tracking vocals. But he resented using another track on his four-track machine for the purpose. One of EMI's great advantages was that it had an extensive in-house engineering staff, and Ken Townsend, a studio engineer, set himself the task of devising a way of doing it electronically. He came up with a system applied at mixing time that involved using

the recording head of the multitrack machine as a playback head (as in sel-sync) and, after delaying the sound by passing it through a second tape machine, reuniting it with the sound from the playback head as it made its way to the mono mix-down recorder. The delay between the two sounds could be adjusted for different effects, from echo through double-tracking to 'phasing.' The system was called Artificial Double-Tracking, or ADT, and was really the beginning of the vogue for studio effects that has remained with us until this day: nowadays, of course, such effects are achieved electronically rather than through the use of tape.

The four track restriction remained in place throughout the Beatles' glory years. It did not appear to cramp anyone's creativity. Indeed, it may have enhanced it, because it forced people to make creative decisions at the time rather than, as became common later, leaving everything until 'the mix.' The lack of standard electronic effects, too, brought out the ingenuity of the band, their engineers and their producer. And sometimes, of course, there were happy accidents, which more modern technology tends to militate against, because everything can be corrected.

One such bit of luck occurred during the making of 'Strawberry Fields Forever.' George Martin first recorded the song with drums, bass and John Lennon's electric guitar. Then Lennon announced he didn't like it, and asked for it to be re-recorded with a score for cellos and horns. This was duly done. Finally, Lennon decided he'd like half of one version and half of the other. Martin agreed in principle, but pointed out that not only were the two versions in different keys, they were at different tempos. In the end, though, the edit, performed by physically cutting the tape, worked. The slower version was a semi-tone lower than the faster version: speeding it up sufficiently to bring it to the right key also brought it to the right tempo.

The most elaborate recording of the Beatles' whole career was 'A Day In The Life' from *Sgt Pepper's*. John Lennon wrote the verses, and Paul McCartney contributed the "Woke up, got out of bed …" section. The song was recorded in the usual way, but a 24 bar gap was left between the two sections, with nothing but Paul McCartney banging out the same piano note to mark time. Mal Evans, the band's faithful roadie, counts out the bars to remind everyone when to come back in: his voice is still faintly audible on the finished recording, as is an alarm clock he set off at the end of the gap.

To fill the gap, Lennon asked for an orchestra to "freak out." Pressed for further explanation, he indicated that he wanted a gradual increase in volume from nothing to extreme loudness. He thought it could be done by hiring a symphony orchestra and asking the players to do what he wanted. George Martin pointed out that this wasn't likely to work, and instead he hired a half-sized 42-piece orchestra and wrote a very basic score, indicating that each instrument should move, over the 24 bars, from the bottom of its range to the top, at the same time increasing in volume.

It became apparent that the normal four tracks were not likely to be enough this time. For the first time, Ken Townsend devised a way of linking two four-track machines together. A

50 Hz tone was recorded on one track on the first machine and this was amplified to provide the mains power for the second. Seven tracks were thus available for simultaneous recording, although the machines proved somewhat reluctant to start together when it came to remixing. Martin then recorded his orchestral crescendo four separate times: in the final recording they are superimposed on one another slightly out of synchronisation. The section appears twice, once in the middle of the song, when it is cut short by a tape edit, and once at the end, where it is followed by a huge chord, played on four pianos and again overdubbed numerous times. Nothing the Beatles did after that was ever quite so creative, although 'I Am The Walrus' comes close. The Beatles decamped to Trident Studios in London to record 'Hey Jude' because they wanted to use its 8-track machine. EMI eventually saw the necessity of following suit. Its first 8-track machine was installed in 1967, and the Beatles returned to use it for *Abbey Road*, the last album they recorded.

By the beginning of the 1970s, the shape of commercial recording had become established. Studios would continue to add tracks, sessions would take longer, particularly for mix-down, and the experimentation that had so enlivened the Beatles' sessions would increasingly be replaced by the products of the new studio effects industry.

With the ever-increasing time and cost of studio recording, it became fashionable for the most successful artists to build studios of their own, either at home or elsewhere. There was nothing particularly new in this: Les Paul claims to have built his first home studio in the 1930s, and the Beach Boys had retreated to Brian Wilson's home after the bruising experience of recording *Smile* in 1966. But now it became a common pattern and it was imitated right down the scale, with the arrival of cheap semi-professional four- and 8-track equipment, starting with the Teac 3340, which cost less than $600 in 1973. Subsequent cassette-based multitrack systems were cheaper still.

Olympic engineer Eddie Kramer, shown above in the studio, engineered early Jimi Hendrix albums, and went on to co-produce Electric Ladyland. Kramer and engineer George Chkiantz created some of the first phasing effects put on record, notably on Axis Bold As Love.

U.K. band Cream became one of the first British bands to record on 8-track, after signing to Atlantic and flying to the U.S. to use the company's state-of-the art studios.

■ Police drummer Stewart Copeland was a home studio pioneer. His 24-track setup was used for solo projects such as his 1982 soundtrack for Francis Ford Coppola's Rumblefish movie.

■ Mike Oldfield's Tubular Bells album originated from a home recording, and helped establish the Virgin record company. Oldfield would return to the home studio approach for later albums.

Down Your Manor

Much home recording equipment was used for unreleasable doodlings. Some artists, however, produced precise demos that were copied in their subsequent studio sessions, saving time and money. Others managed to produce albums for release, often playing all the parts themselves. The motivation for these efforts was the success of Mike Oldfield's *Tubular Bells*, which started life as a demo, done by sound-on-sound overdubbing on a domestic Bang & Olufsen tape recorder, but was actually recorded in a commercial studio, Virgin Records' The Manor.

The Manor was one of an increasing number of studios to be built out in the country: it was becoming more and more common for bands effectively to live in the studio while their records were being made, and the country meant both cheaper property and more appealing surroundings.

Those who continued to use commercial studios were

creating ever more elaborate and grandiose productions. As early as 1968, the American heavy rock band Iron Butterfly had smashed the normal song-structure of pop music, giving their album *In-A-Gada-Da-Vida* a 20-minute title track. Others followed this lead, with the culmination coming in Yes's *Tales From Topographic Oceans* of 1974, a double album consisting of four side-long tracks. Such massively arranged pieces of music pushed even the standard 24-track recording system to its limit. It became common to lock two 24-track machines together electronically, to allow 46-track recording.

The arrival of quadraphonic recording, which mesmerized the recording industry for much of the 1970s, added to the complications. Inevitably, there was a backlash. Punk rock meant faster, shorter, simpler music and its do-it-yourself ethos brought basic independently-made recordings into the charts. But it is interesting to note that the most famous punk band of all, the Sex Pistols, made their one album in a professional 24-track studio with Chris Thomas, a highly experienced producer who had worked with the Beatles, at the helm.

One of the things the punks disliked were synthesizers, but their arrival, at around the same time as punk, was to have much greater long term consequences. At first they were treated as just another instrument to be recorded, usually by direct-injection into the mixing desk. But the introduction of the sequencer, a device used for recording and playing back sequences of notes on one or more synthesizers, made things more complicated. Ways were sought to integrate the sequencer with the tape recording process, usually by the incorporation of a synchronizing pulse on one track. With the replacement of the early analog synthesizers and sequencers with digital equipment, the possibilities increased. One unit that soon became ubiquitous was the Harmonizer, a digital device which allowed the engineer to change the pitch of a recorded

The Home Studio

The 1970s was a time of tremendous wealth and expansion for the record industry: when it came to making records, money was no object. The technology, too, had reached a certain level of maturity. This was a great time to be a studio owner. All you had to do was buy a huge Solid State Logic mixing console, a Studer 24-track tape recorder and a pair of massive JBL monitors, surround them with shagpile carpet and smoked glass and await the arrival of the Indulgent Ones.

The party was still in full swing when, in 1978, Teac slipped in the back door with its 144 Portastudio, an all-in-one mixer and multitrack recorder for under $800. It was small, cheap and attracted little attention. Few realized that the very thin end of a very fat and steeply raked technological wedge had been knocked quietly into place. The demise of the professional recording studio had begun.

Many manufacturers soon jumped on the portastudio bandwagon, to give a wide choice of machines, dominated by Fostex, Yamaha and Teac, who later renamed its musicians' and professional equipment division Tascam.

In 1980 the functionality gap between the $800 Portastudio and the $800,000 studio complex was vast. The Portastudio had just four tracks, the sound quality was mediocre and there was no prospect of being able to record drums, brass or string in an acoustically treated space with lots of microphones. But a new generation of low cost reel-to-reel multitrack recorders soon arrived, as high precision engineering techniques and effective low cost noise reduction systems meant that the number of tracks feasible on a given width of tape increased dramatically. Teac had its 8-track $\frac{1}{2}$" tape format, but newcomers Fostex captured the mass market with the A8, offering eight tracks on $\frac{1}{4}$" tape. Then, from both Fostex and Tascam, came 16 tracks on $\frac{1}{2}$" and 24

tracks on 1" tape, delivering sound quality approaching that of professional 24-track machines on 2" tape.

Early attempts to squeeze eight tracks on the humble $\frac{1}{8}$" cassette format to create the 8-track portastudio met with indifferent audio quality, and hence limited success. But the advent of Dolby S noise reduction meant the format was more than adequate for demos. Dolby S was the semi-pro spin off of Dolby SR, a stunningly effective system that lent analog tape recorders a performance comparable to digital. Both Fostex and Tascam were quick to add Dolby S to their 16-track $\frac{1}{2}$" and 24-track 1" machines to produce a new level of

track without altering its speed. Thus an out-of-tune instrument could be painlessly tuned to match the others after it had been recorded.

Even more profound was the introduction of the sampler, which, for the first time, allowed the electronic recording of sections of music and speech so that they could adjusted before being introduced into a track. The first important device in this area was the Fairlight CMI (computer musical instrument), which offered sampling as part of its facilities. But the Fairlight was much more than a more reliable Mellotron. In 1982, it was upgraded with Page R, the first sequencer for sampled sounds as well as synthesizers. Musical notes were recorded and presented as events in time, capable of adjustment. By allowing sequences of bars to be copied, repeated and modified, it was made possible for non-musicians to produce music. A new class cf person, the 'music programmer,' soon became common on the recording scene. Soon all the various electronic devices could be linked together using the MIDI system. At first, electronic instruments and acoustic instruments rarely met, but as sampling improved, the new machines began to have consequences for other musicians. It became common practice, for instance, to sample other people's drum sounds. Recording drums had long been an obsession for engineers. George

Roxy Music's Brian Eno experiments with a Teac 3340-based home set up. Eno's later work would retain the do-it-yourself ethos, not least his productions with Daniel Lanois for U2. Although the band worked in established studios such as Hansa, Berlin, U2 also rented tape machines and mixing desks to record in a Dublin castle.

affordable recorders with truly professional results.

Mixing console manufacturers also attacked the new budget multitrack market. For several years now it has been possible to buy a desk with basic mix automation, capable of 24-track recording and mixing, for a few thousand dollars – as opposed to the $250,000 of an S.S.L. or Neve console. A moderately successful musician, composer or management information clerk can therefore now convert the spare room into an automated 24-track studio for under $10,000.

By 1990 the gap between the $100 an hour studio and the $10,000 home studio had substantially narrowed. It became commonplace for professional musicians to start a project at home and then transfer to a larger studio to add the strings and brass and to mix using the big studio's superior mixing consoles, monitoring, effects processors and, let's not forget, professional engineers. Another leveling influence was the introduction of the DAT (Digital Audio Tape) recorder. This was a relatively affordable stereo mixdown format which was capable of truly top professional results. That was the beginning of affordable digital recorders and the digital audio revolution that continues today, with machines such as the Alesis ADAT.

Martin had recorded Ringo's kit with no more than four microphones, mixed live to one track along with bass and rhythm guitar. But the increasing number of tracks available on multitrack tape machines meant greater possibilities for the "perfect" sound. It became common to use at least 15 microphones on the kit, mixing them down to at least four tracks, including separate tracks for snare and bass drum, and often more. All the extra possibilities meant it became common to spend whole days just getting a drum sound. The early drum machines were scorned because of the inadequacy of their synthesized sounds, but once they began to incorporate sampled sounds, the days of the drummer in the studio were numbered. Sampled sounds were always perfect and needed no miking up: the whole process was instantaneous, although the machine still had to be programmed.

More recently, drummers have made something of a comeback in the studios, but they don't bring their kits. Instead, they play pads which trigger the digitally-stored samples. That way the drummer's feel is combined with the required sound.

All this meant that by the 1980s it was possible to make successful records quickly and efficiently in studios that were physically much smaller than had been necessary in the past. This was certainly true of the studios used by Stock Aitken & Waterman, who made a string of hits with such artists as Kylie Minogue and Rick Astley from a modest facility near London Bridge. The only 'real' instrument that was regularly used was the guitar. Even the rhythm track was constructed rather than played. A single bar of perfect rhythm guitar would be copied over and over again to make up the track. Everything else, bass, drums, piano and so on, was programmed in from a keyboard. Only vocals remained to be recorded in the traditional way.

Since those days, there have been two further technological developments. The first was digital recording to tape. The second, still in its early stages, is recording direct to computer disk. By the end of the 1970s, analog recording had gone as far as it could. There were plans for a monster 32-track machine using 3″ tape, but the tape costs were frightening, and all analog recording continued to suffer from tape noise, despite the ingenuity that had gone into noise reduction.

Digital recording, developed in the late 1970s, has no such problems. The new equipment was fantastically expensive at first, and restricted to two tracks, often on modified video recorders. But by 1979, 3M had developed a 32-track digital multitrack and that was used for Ry Cooder's *Bop Till You Drop*, a record that benefited considerably from the publicity of being the first commercially available digital rock album.

It does not seem to have been a particularly happy experience. The machine was effectively a prototype, and the recordings it made could not be edited by the time-honored razor blade method. 3M later withdrew from the manufacture of tape recorders. At first engineers found digital sound difficult.

■ Ry Cooder (right), a master of roots American music, pioneered new technology with his digitally-recorded Bop Till You Drop album. Cooder later reflected: "I'd still use digital for mastering, but I'm not convinced all-digital recording is the way to go."

■ As 1970s rock recordings became technically complex, jazz engineers retained a more purist approach. Rudy Van Gelder, who engineered influential works by John Coltrane and Miles Davis, is shown here recording Joe Farrell and Elvin Jones (far left) in his studio in Teaneck, New Jersey in 1971, with simple microphones and minimal EQ.

The Digital Revolution

The alternative to digital recording is analog recording – what we've all been doing for the past few decades. It's called analog because a continuous magnetic analog of the fluctuations in sound pressure that are the basis of sound are recorded on tape as fluctuations in magnetic flux. This recording process is vulnerable to all sorts of adverse outside influences: residual magnetic flux, radio interference and tape speed variations can lead to hissy, wowy, fluttery, muffled recordings. With digital recording, however, the sound is initially converted into 1s and 0s and is thereafter dealt with as such.

On tape, a high flux level is a '1' and a low flux level a '0,' so there's no room for confusion and hence no chance of distortion or tape hiss. Nor are wow and flutter any longer an issue because a digital chip regulates the rate at which the 1s and 0s are read, not the tape speed.

The first commonly used digital music recorders came from Sony in the late 1970s. The frequency response needed (44.1kHz as per CDs) was too high for existing analog audio recorders (max 20kHz) so the digitized sound was stored on Low Band U-Matic video cassettes. The box that performed the analog-to-digital conversion was called the PCM 1600. It and its successors, the 1610 and 1630, became the exclusive international standard for cutting CDs, and remains so to this day. For general use, however, it seemed clear that a dedicated digital format was required.

As the 1970s moved into the 1980s Sony came up with the DASH (Digital

Michael Tretow, who engineered Abba's *The Visitors*, told Studio Sound that he no longer needed to make allowance for tape losses. Not only that, but the dynamic range available was such that instruments he could hear perfectly well in the studio would disappear when he played the tapes on domestic equipment at normal listening levels. Digital sound in the studio only began to make economic sense, however, with the invention of a digital medium for home listening. The Compact Disc was first demonstrated in 1979. Since then, digital recording has generally become the standard, usually with up to 48 tracks.

The days of moving tape, however, may be numbered. Digital recording works by breaking sound into digital information. That digital information can be manipulated in various ways. Hard-disk recording replaces tape storage with computer-style storage. One advantage is that things are instantly accessible, with no winding backwards and forwards,

but there is much more to it than that. Direct-to-disk recording equipment, whether on a dedicated machine or a personal computer, allows sound to edited in exactly the same way as words are edited in a word-processor. The sound is displayed on a screen, and it can be cut, copied, joined, faded, filtered, turned backwards, turned upside down, changed in pitch and so on with the touch of a control knob or a mouse.

In practice, this means that acoustic instruments and voices can be modified as easily as if they were synthesizer or drum machine tracks. A couple of guitar strums can be duplicated and changed in pitch to form the rhythm track of a whole song. Tracks, including vocals, can be sped up or slowed down while the computer keeps the pitch the same; or the pitch can be changed while the tempo stays the same. Vocal tracks can be seamlessly compiled out of numerous takes and edited as appropriate. Similar effects can be achieved with a personal computer and suitable software.

Audio Stationary Head) 2-track and 24-track format, and Mitsubishi quickly followed with its Pro-Digi 2-track and 32-track format. All used a reel-to-reel tape format with the tape passing by a stationary head. They were hugely expensive (over $30,000 for a Mitsubishi X800 32-track) and once again set the big boys apart from the home players.

In 1982 Sony came up with the F1, a variant on the 1630 series using VHS rather than U-Matic and at a much lower price: intended as a domestic format, its quality meant it was widely used for professional work. Then came the DAT (Digital Audio Tape) recorder. In October 1987 Sony launched the DTC1000 studio DAT machine, delivering the death blow to all other stereo digital formats. Though not without its problems, this modest machine quickly became a studio classic.

The DAT format we know today is more properly known as R-DAT or Rotary Head DAT. This is as opposed to S-DAT or Stationary Head DAT, which was a parallel Sony R&D project in direct competition with the R-DAT team. There have been reports that the S-DAT prototype now resides at the bottom of Tokyo harbor.

The Sony 3324 and its 48-track stablemate, the 3348, won the battle of the giants, but finally both big formats were dealt a crippling blow a few years later in the shape of the Alesis ADAT. Although Akai had produced a 12-track digital portastudio back in 1984 with some success, the ultra-low cost ADAT brought digital multitrack to the masses. Using a standard S-VHS tape and transport Alesis managed to squeeze 40 minutes of 8-track CD quality audio into a compact rackmounting box for

around $4,000. An optional BRC remote allowed up to 16 ADATs to be run in sync to provide a theoretical 128-track maximum. Certainly it has become common practice to link three machines to provide a 24-track system for under $12,000. Although the big studios prefer the big Sony machines, top quality digital is now available to many serious musician and producers and the idea of moving between home and studio during a project has expanded.

Soon after the ADAT, Tascam came up with the DA-88, a similar looking digital 8-track based on the superior Hi8 video format. Operational details and the longer 117 minutes running time has made the DA-88 the choice for radio, television and film professionals, although the ubiquitous nature of ADAT has made it a winner for the project music studio.

Early in 1996, Tascam, Yamaha and Sony launched 4-track digital portastudios based on the MiniDisc format. Costing around $1,000 they offer basic editing facilities, digital quality audio and relatively cheap media for the price of an upmarket analog portastudio. Although the MiniDisc, along with its Philips rival, the DCC digital cassette, has seemingly bombed as a domestic format, perhaps its fortunes will be revived in the home recording market. Also released in early 1996 was the 02R digital mixing console from Yamaha. At $6,000 for a basic model, this compact device appears capable of matching other models costing several tens of thousands. This, together with the ADAT and DA-88, has brought the abilities of the home/project studio closer than ever to the top professional facility.

The Age Of Perfection

Elvis Presley's first recordings were made live, with a single pass of the tape. The Beatles' first album was recorded in a day. These days, however, things can be a little more complex. Consider the 1993 Donald Fagen album *Kamakiriad*.

It is not quite true to call *Kamakiriad* a typical album of our day. Fagen, and his producer Walter Becker, who formed the core of Steely Dan, are notorious for their perfectionism. It is, however, a fascinating example of what modern technology makes possible. Roger Nichols, Steely Dan's engineer, told the story in an article in EQ magazine.

Recording would begin with Fagen bringing a sequencer into the studio, programmed with tracks for snare drum, kick drum, hi-hat, bass and DX7 keyboards. The idea was for these to form a guide for live musicians to overdub. First, though, their timing was adjusted by putting them through a digital delay capable of moving the beats around in tenth of a second increments: the snare might be pushed back a little, for

instance, the hi-hat forward, and so on. When a drummer was brought in, however, it was soon discovered that while his timing was fine on the choruses, he wavered on the verses. The solution was to make samples of the sound he was making with his live drums and use them to replace the sounds of the machine drums. So the choruses continued to have real drums played by a drummer, while the verses had the sound of real drums played by a machine.

Next the overdubs began, again using real musicians. A decision was taken to use good performances, even with flaws, and then use technology to correct those flaws. In one example, a bass line by Walter Becker was found to have one note that buzzed and cut off short. The offending section of the track was transferred to the Macintosh computer. The same note from a similar passage was then substituted for it. The 'repaired' section was then transferred back on to the multitrack machine. When recording backing vocals, where a song had several identical choruses, it was decided that the

Nirvana, shown here recording a 1991 radio session in Holland, was just one of many bands whose sound was best captured on analog. Steve Albini, producer of In Utero, invariably records to analog.

1986: Dolby introduces Spectral Recording, which allows analog tape recorders to match and arguably exceed the performance of 16-bit digital recorders in many parameters. First totally automated mixing console appears. The Harrison Series 10 is analog, but digitally controlled and allows automation and resetting of every control.

1987: First professional DAT recorders appear – but adapted domestic

machines find wider studio use.

1991: The launch of the Modular Digital Multitrack. US company Alesis develops 8-track digital recorder using S-VHS tape shortly followed by similar approach on 8mm cassette from Teac. The user can add machines to meet track requirements.

1994: Compact and low cost digital consoles announced by Yamaha, but with analog interfaces.

1995: Fully digital low cost digital console from Yamaha, the O2R, threatens to revolutionize the pro audio market when matched with Modular Digital Multitracks.

best results would be achieved by concentrating on recording one perfect version and copying it as many times as was necessary. Something similar went on with rhythm guitar. The musicians would play the song through, and the passages with the best feel would be copied and used throughout the song.

By the time mixing came round, time was tight. Some of the tracks were still not complete, so a copy was made of the complete 48-track master. Mixing started in one studio while Fagen finished his lead vocals in another. On more than one occasion, Nichols had to mix a song before the lead vocal had arrived. What he did then was to take the vocal track recorded on Fagen's tape and synchronise it back into his original. The finished mixes, of which six different versions were made, were mastered to recordable CD, DAT (Digital Audio Tape) and optical disk. The whole process had taken three years.

No wonder there is something of a backlash, with bands and producers doing what they can to produce more spontaneous music. The Rolling Stones, for instance, produced their 1994 album *Voodoo Lounge* by forming themselves into a semi-circle in Dublin's Windmill Lane studio and playing live for producer Don Was. Speed is a matter of pride to Was. He aims to take no more than 15 minutes getting an acceptable sound before a band begins to play.

Modern technology, too, has its detractors. Tube and ribbon microphones from the 1950s and before are in great demand, as are tube limiters and compressors. Even digital recording is out of favour in some quarters. Stephen Street, producer of Blur and Morrissey among others is a devotee of analog. He prefers it because he still likes to edit tape by cutting it. And Steve Albini, who recorded *In Utero* for Nirvana as well as albums for The Pixies and The Wedding Present, shares his doubts. "I record and mix to analog," he says, "and I don't know of many serious engineers who do otherwise by choice."

■ **John Martyn:** *And.*
Recorded: 1996
Veteran Scottish folk singer John Martyn signed to the U.K. independent label Go! Discs in 1996. Martyn's album was recorded on the Alesis ADAT digital system, which gave high quality results at less expense than larger studios, and also offered some less predictable advantages. Phil Collins drums and sings on several tracks. According to Martyn, "We were never in the studio at the same time. I simply recorded on ADAT and sent him the tape. He recorded the drums and vocals and sent them back to me. That's one of the great things about ADAT – it's like playing postal chess."

■ *Martin Hannett, shown with Joy Division/ New Order guitarist Bernard Sumner, helped pioneer rock-dance crossover, working on influential electro works by Happy Mondays and New Order. One of Hannett's distinctive techniques was to overdub hi-hats separately from the rest of the drum kit for more separation. New Order would go on to produce their own commercially successful recordings, while Hannett's productions for Happy Mondays would help kick-start the U.K. acid house scene.*

Acoustic Related to sound or hearing; of instruments: generating sound without electrical amplification, e.g. acoustic guitar, piano; acoustic modeling: synthesis technique using performance algorithms based on acoustic instruments.

Action Of guitars, the distance between the strings and the fingerboard; of acoustic and electronic keyboards, the response of the keys to the player's touch, or the mechanical components of the key assembly.

Active electronics Pre-amplification circuitry in guitars generally allowing additional tone control, increased gain, or better impedance matching for lower noise.

ADA Analog-to-Digital-to-Analog; the process of 'sampling' the amplitude of an analog signal; storing it in the form of binary numbers which can be stored and manipulated by digital recorders, effects units, samplers or other devices; then converting it back into analog form.

ADAT Alesis Digital Audio Tape. Eight-track digital recording format using S-VHS videotape, developed by Alesis and adopted by Fostex and others.

Additive synthesis Creation of sound by combining harmonics of different frequencies.

ADSR Attack, Decay, Sustain, Release; the basic elements of a synthesizer's envelope section, controlling amplitude, filtering and so on.

ADT Automatic Double Tracking – an electronic chorus-type effect imitating the sound of double tracking.

Aftertouch The ability of an electronic keyboard to react to increased pressure on a key; typically, to add a modulation effect.

Algorithm A specific combination of operators as carriers or modulators in Yamaha's FM synthesis system.

Aliasing Distortion caused in digital systems when sampling frequency is not high enough to read the high frequency components of the analog signal.

Ambience The character of a recording environment, which can be reproduced synthetically; the background sounds of a recording.

Amplifier Electrical circuit designed to increase a signal; usually, an audio system for boosting sound before transmission to a loudspeaker.

Amplitude The level of an electrical signal, and most often the loudness of an audio signal.

Analog(ue) A system which reproduces a signal by copying its original amplitude waveform, such as the groove of a vinyl recording, the varying magnetic flux of a tape recording, or the voltage levels of an analog synthesizer. As opposed to digital, where the signal is recorded as a series of numbers.

Attenuation Reduction in amplitude of a signal.

Audio frequency Sonic range of human hearing, around 20Hz to 20kHz.

Auxiliary Mixer function allowing channel signals to be sent to an external device such as an effects unit or foldback system. See Effects.

Auto-locate System allowing reference points on a tape recording to be set so that the recorder can spool the tape directly to them.

Automation The facility of a computerized mixing desk or software system to record, store, edit and repeat settings and fader movements.

Backline Amplifiers and speakers used by band, typically the bassist, and guitarists' own combos or stacks, as opposed to the PA system.

Balanced line Connecting cable using two signal wires and a transformer to cancel interference, as used in most professional recording and PA setups.

Bearing Edge The edge of the drum shell which supports the head. Bearing edges should be flat, so that all the edge is in contact with the head, and slightly sharp so as not to restrict vibration of the drum head.

Bell Flared section of brass instrument. In cymbal terms, the bell or 'cup' is the central domed section, which gives a more distinct 'pingy' sound than the cymbal's outside edge.

Bin The bass component of a PA speaker system. 'W' bins are a folded horn design, the layout of which resembles said letter.

Bounce Multitrack recording technique by which several tracks are recorded, then copied to another so the original tracks are free to be recorded on again.

Bug Small transducer or contact microphone used on an acoustic instrument.

Cardioid Common heart-shaped frequency-response pattern for general-purpose microphones.

Channel An individual input path of a mixer, not to be confused with a recording 'track.'

Chorus Electronic effect using short varying delays to give a multi-instrumental sound.

Classical Small-bodied, nylon-strung guitar for classical music.

Clavichord Mediaeval piano-like keyboard instrument.

Clavinet Electric clavichord produced by Hohner, much used in funk music.

Combo Combination amplifier/speaker system used for electric guitars or keyboards.

Compression Sound processing effect reducing the amplitude range of a signal. Extreme compression is known as Limiting; the converse is Expansion.

Course A pair of strings running together but tuned apart, as on a 12-string guitar.

Cowbell Bell-like metallic percussion instrument.

Crash cymbal Cymbal designed to emphasize certain beats or crescendos within music; usually made of thinner metal than ride cymbals, for a faster response.

Crook Upper section of saxophone, onto which the mouthpiece fits.

Crossover Electronic circuit which divides a signal between frequency components, for example separating bass signals from treble signals.

Crosstalk Unwanted spillage of audio signals from one mixer channel or tape track to another.

Cutaway Curve into guitar body, near neck joint, which improves top fret access. Florentine cutaways are sharp. Venetian rounded.

CV Control Voltage; the system by which the parameters of analog synthesizers are set, and by which they can be controlled by external devices such as sequencers.

DAT Digital Audio Tape; high-quality stereo audio recording format designed for domestic use but adopted by semi-pro and professional markets.

DCO Digitally-Controlled Oscillator – a more stable version of the Voltage-Controlled Oscillator.

Decay The dying away of a sound immediately after its attack; the second stage of a synthesizer's ADSR envelope.

Decibel (dB) A comparative unit of power levels, in audio terms usually referring to sound pressure levels with 0dB as the threshold of hearing.

Delay Audio effect which retards a signal by a certain interval; an 'echo' effect using transistor, digital or analog (tape loop) technology.

Digital System which stores and processes analog information by converting it into a series of numbers, e.g. Compact Disc digital audio, Digital Audio Tape, digital sound samplers and so on.

DIN Deutsche Industrie Normenausschus; German standard for electronic connections, most familiar from the circular five-pin sockets used for MIDI equipment, and for some domestic hi-fi connections.

Direct injection (DI) Recording technique using level-matching boxes to connect guitars etc. directly to the mixer rather than via a microphone.

Distortion Signal degradation caused by overloading of audio systems. Can be used deliberately to create a harsher sound, especially on electric guitars.

Dolby Analog tape noise reduction system named after inventor Dr. Ray Dolby; variations include Dolby B and C for domestic use, S for semi-professional, SR and A for professional equipment.

Double tracking Multitrack recording technique in which the same part is recorded twice, usually to create a fuller sound.

Drawbar Harmonic tone control mechanism of a Hammond or similar organ.

Dreadnought Martin term for large-body flat-top guitar such as D-18, since used generically.

Drop-in Switching from play to record mode in the middle of a recording to re-record part of it.

Drop-out Coming back out of record mode after a drop-in; or, a signal loss due to lack of oxide on a magnetic recording tape.

Dynamics Musically, the variation in volume in a performance.

Dynamic Range Sound pressure range between a system's noise floor and its overload level.

Echo Distinct repetition of a sound, created by reflection from a surface or by analog or digital processing.

Effects Generic term for audio processing devices such as digital delays, reverbs, flangers, phasers or harmonizers. The effects return input of a mixer returns the processed signal routed to the effects unit by the auxiliary send.

Electret Inexpensive condensor microphone capable of running from a small battery.

Electric/Electronic Electric instruments transduce a mechanical phenomenon such as a vibrating string into an electrical signal via a pickup; electronic instruments produce sounds by purely non-acoustic means.

Embouchure The positioning, and interaction, of the player's mouth and wind instrument mouthpiece.

Envelope The amplitude shape of a sound; the settings of a synthesizer's ADSR controls; the envelope generator (EG) section of a synthesizer.

Equalization (EQ) Control of a sound's tone by emphasis or de-emphasis of specific frequency bands; on a mixer, commonly High, Mid and Low. Parametric ('swept') types allow specific frequencies to be selected; graphic types have several fixed frequency bands.

Erase Head The first head on a tape recorder, which wipes off any previous recordings.

Escapement The part of the mechanism of a piano which determines the action of the hammer on the strings.

Expander Keyboardless synthesizer module controlled by MIDI or CV.

Fader Sliding potentiometer control which on a mixing desk usually controls channel volume level.

Feedback Generally, the phenomenon of introducing part of the output of a system back to its input. Controlled feedback within electrical systems can be useful; uncontrolled feedback, such as when a vocalist's microphone picks up its own output from a speaker, causes a howling noise, or howlround.

'F'-hole F-shaped soundhole on hollow body guitar derived from violin design. Some electric guitars, such as the 1960s Chet Atkins Country Gentleman, sport dummy f-holes for visual effect only.

Filter Analog or digital system for controlling the frequency balance of an audio signal.

Flanging A variation of phasing using time-delayed filtering; the name derives from the original method of producing the effect, by restraining the movement of a tape spool by touching its flange.

Flutter Pitch variation caused by minor changes in tape speed.

FM Frequency Modulation. In synthesizer terms, Yamaha's digital sound synthesis system which produces complex tones by using sine-wave 'operators' as both sound sources and modulators.

Foldback Mixer circuit allowing musicians on stage or in the studio to hear their performance via backline amplification or headphones. Also refers to the monitor system in general.

Frequency The number of cycles of a carrier wave per second; the perceived pitch of a sound. Frequency response measures the ability of a system to reproduce the frequency of the original signal.

Fundamental The lowest note of a chord; the lowest frequency in a sound with many harmonics.

Fuzz Crude distortion effect caused by clipping of an overloaded signal; commonly produced using guitar footpedal effects boxes.

Gain Ratio of output level to input level; mixer control which increases the input signal level.

Gate 'Trigger' signal for an analog synthesizer marking the start or end of a note, or other event.

Guiro Latin percussion scraper instrument.

Grand Large-bodied piano with horizontal strings.

Hammond Electronic organ invented by Laurens Hammond in the 1930s, using spinning tone wheels to produce differently pitched signals.

Hard disk High speed, high capacity data storage system for digital recording or storage of computer or sample data.

Headroom Amount of volume above the optimum working level a system can sustain before overload distortion occurs.

Headless Guitar design with no headstock, popularized by Ned Steinberger.

Hertz, kiloHertz (Hz, kHz) Unit of frequency; 1Hz = one cycle per second, 1kHz = one thousand cycles per second.

Hi-hat Pair of matched cymbals operated by pedal.

Hoop Drum rim which holds down and tensions drum head, through which tuning lugs pass. Drum hoops are usually pressed steel, in a triple flanged configuration, or cast aluminum or alloy.

Horn High-frequency component of a PA speaker system; elongated projection of a guitar's body beside the cutaway.

Howlround See 'Feedback.'

Humbucker Gibson term, now in general usage, for electric guitar pickup normally using two coils arranged to reduce noise.

Interface Connecting device which converts one data standard to another,

139

such as MIDI-to-SMPTE, Analog-to-Digital.

Jack Mono or stereo connecting plug, usually (¼") used for unbalanced signals such as electric guitars. Jackfields (or 'patchbays') are used to make interconnection of synthesizer modules or studio devices easier.

Keyboard The mechanical key assembly of a keyboard instrument; usually described in terms of its length in octaves and note range (e.g. five octaves C-C); and for electronic instruments, its velocity and aftertouch sensitivity.

Keywork Mechanism which opens or closes openings in the body of a woodwind instrument.

LA Linear Arithmetic – Roland's sample-plus-synthesis technique.

Leslie A cabinet containing a rotating speaker, much used by players of Hammond organs.

LFO Low Frequency Oscillator; synthesizer circuit generating sub-audio frequency signals as a source for modulation effects such as vibrato or tremolo.

Loom Multistrand cable used to connect mixer to multitrack recorder.

Lug Drum shell fitting, also referred to as 'nutbox,' which accepts threaded rods, whose tension affects tuning of the drum head. Tubular lugs are a traditional design, consisting of simple threaded brass tubes, used on Slingerland Radio King snare drums, and recently reintroduced by Noble & Cooley.

Mastering The mixing of a multitrack recording, or live performance, to a final stereo recording.

MIDI Musical Instrument Digital Interface; the industry standard control system for electronic instruments, by which data for notes, performance effects, patch changes, voice and sample data, tempo and other information can be transmitted and received via five-pin DIN sockets.

Mixdown The stage before mastering where the multitrack recording is mixed and equalized, effects are added and a final stereo version created.

Mixer Or 'board,' 'desk,' 'console;' device used in live performance or studio recording which combines several channels of audio signals into one or more outputs. Usually offers equalization, stereo panning, effects channels and monitoring. Digital mixers process audio in the digital domain; automated mixers can memorize settings.

Modulation Regular variation in a sound such as vibrato (pitch modulation) or tremolo (amplitude modulation).

Monitor Speaker system used in recording studio's control room; speakers used in PA system via which performers can hear themselves, and hence 'monitor' their own performance; computer display screen.

Monophonic Capable of playing only one note at a time, such as a wind or brass instrument, or early analog synthesizer.

MTC MIDI Time Code – a form of digital time code used to synchronize MIDI sequencers with other audio-visual equipment.

Multicore Multistrand cable carrying several signals, used to connect stage equipment to PA mixer, or recording studio to control room mixer.

Multi-timbral Instrument capable of producing more than one distinct sound simultaneously; typically, a MIDI keyboard or module with different sounds assignable to individual MIDI channels.

Multitrack Audio recorder capable of recording on several individual tracks, while monitoring previous recordings.

Mute Facility of a mixer to temporarily switch off a particular channel, or of a MIDI sequencer to silence a particular track. In wind instrument terms, a device which fits within or over the instrument's bell, to reduce volume or, in the case of a 'wah' mute, alter tone.

Noise Undesirable audio artifacts such as mains hum, digital quantization, or tape hiss. 'White noise' is a signal containing equal amounts of all audio frequencies.

Noise gate Signal processing device which closes down a channel when sound levels fall below a specific amount, to silence unwanted system noise.

Noise reduction Any method of removing tape hiss from analog recordings; best known is that of Dolby.

Nutbox See 'lugs.'

Overdubbing The process of adding solos or replacing guide recordings 'over' the existing tracks on a multitrack recording.

Oscillator Electronic circuit which produces a geometric waveform of a constant frequency, in the audio or sub-audio domain. A sub-oscillator produces a harmonic, usually one octave below the fundamental.

PA Public address (system); the system of microphones, mixers, processors, amplifiers and speakers used to present a sound at high enough levels to serve a large audience.

Pan pot Panning potentiometer; mixer control which sets the stereo position of a signal.

Patch bay Studio accessory or part of a modular synthesizer via which different devices are routed using patch cords; hence 'patch' for a particular synthesizer sound configuration.

Passive Non-powered circuitry which can therefore only subtract from an existing signal, such as the tone and volume controls of most electric guitars.

Performance control Synthesizer feature such as a wheel, pedal, switch or slider for changing a sound as it is being played, for instance by adding vibrato, tremolo, glide, pitchbend etc.

PFL Pre-Fade Listen – facility of a mixer to listen to a solo channel in isolation, without EQ etc. Sometimes effects returns can be switched to pre- or post-fade.

Phantom power Facility for a mixer to provide a balanced 48V power supply for condensor microphones.

Phasing Doppler-shift audio effect created by phase cancellation; created by varying the speed of one of two tape recorders playing identical recordings, or using electronic notch filtering techniques.

Pickup Transducer which converts string vibrations into electrical signals.

Pinblock Part of the acoustic piano which carries the tuning pins.

Pitchbend Imitation of string-bending effect created using a synthesizer's performance controls, either a wheel, lever or touch-strip.

Polyphonic Capable of playing more than one note at a time, such as a piano, organ or guitar.

Potentiometer ('Pot') Variable electrical resistor controlling volume and tone on electric guitars, settings on analog synthesizers, mixers etc.

PPM Peak Program Meter – form of audio signal level monitoring designed to register transient peaks.

Preamplifier Circuit used before a power amplifier to boost low-level signals to a useable level.

Pre-delay Time delay between a sound and the resulting reverberation, giving the impression of a larger 'space.'

Print-through Unwanted transfer of recordings from one layer of a tape to another due to long periods of proximity.

Pulse-width The positive cycle of a rectangular wave-form; pulse-width modulation creates a phasing-type effect.

Quantization The reduction of an analog signal to discrete steps; the 'pulling' of the notes of a real-time sequence onto the beat.

RAM Random Access Memory – the digital 'workspace' of a computer, sequencer, sampler or other digital device, normally cleared when the device is switched off, though battery-backed 'Flash RAM' can retain data.

Real-time Method of recording notes into a sequencer exactly as they are played, as opposed to 'step-time.'

Record head Part of a recording device which transfers electrical signals to magnetic tape.

Release The final phase of a sound as it decreases in volume after the sustain stage; the last part of a synthesizer's ADSR envelope.

Resonance Or 'Q' – the amount of emphasis placed on frequencies near the cut-off point of a filter.

Reverberation Ambience effect (actually a combination of many short echoes) which can be imitated digitally or by analog techniques (springlines, plates).

Ride cymbal A ride cymbal is generally used to tap out continuous rhythms, and is usually made of thicker metal than crash cymbals, to give a defined beat which does not build up into a wash of noise.

Ring modulator Audio processor producing complex bell-like harmonics from the sum and difference of two signals.

ROM Read Only Memory; usually, system programming of a computer, sampler or other digital device which is retained when power is switched off.

Sampling Audio recording technique using ADA technology to record, store, edit and manipulate sounds, replaying them at varying clock speeds to create pitch changes.

Sequencer Device which stores note information for an electronic instrument. Analog sequencers use potentiometers to control CV/Gate synthesizers; digital sequencers store note information in RAM, and can be used with analog or digitally-controlled synthesizers. Software sequencers run on computers and offer extensive music editing facilities.

Shell Cylindrical surround of a drum, and the main determinant of a drum's sound. Usually made of wood (which may be solid, or ply), metal (including brass, steel and aluminum), or other composite materials.

Single-coil Simple, common form of electric guitar pickup using a single coil of wire wrapped around the transducer magnet.

SMPTE/EBU From Society of Motion Picture and Television Engineers, and European Broadcast Union; a form of digital time-coding used to synchronize picture and soundtracks.

Soundboard The part of a musical instrument on which the bridges are fixed, and which largely determines its tone.

Sound-on-sound A technique of building up 'multiple' recordings by 'bouncing' between two stereo recorders, adding additional tracks to one channel each time.

Stack Stage amplification system for guitars, usually combining tube amplifiers and enclosed speaker cabinets.

Stage box Interconnection point between the band's equipment and the venue's PA system.

Step-time Method of recording notes into a sequencer one at a time without timing information, as opposed to 'real-time.'

Tine Tuning-fork-like sounding mechanism of a Rhodes-style electric piano.

Tremolo Regular variation in a sound's volume; the vibrato arm of an electric guitar is often inaccurately called the 'tremolo arm' or 'trem.'

Track An individual recording path of a multitrack recorder, not to be confused with a mixer 'channel.'

Transistor Semi-conductor device used in amplification and most modern electronic circuits.

Truss rod Bar inside guitar neck which is adjustable to correct bending as a result of string tension.

Tube Vacuum tube or valve. Amplification device using terminals held in vacuum in a glass tube; superseded by transistors, but still used in some applications for its 'warm' sound.

Twin-neck Guitar with two necks and sets of strings, normally six- and 12-string, or six-string and four-string bass, or in the case of Spinal Tap's Derek Smalls, bass and another bass.

Valve See tube.

VCA Voltage-Controlled Amplifier. The 'sound-shaping' element of an analog synthesizer. Controls the loudness of a signal and can itself be controlled by an ADSR or LFO.

VCF Voltage-Controlled Filter. The basis of 'subtractive' synthesis. Controls the tonal character of a sound by filtering the frequencies produced by the VCO, using different cut-off parameters such as high-band, low-band, band-pass and notch. Can be controlled by an ADSR or LFO.

VCO Voltage-Controlled Oscillator. The basic building-block of the analog synthesizer; produces a pitch using a particular waveform and can be processed by a VCA, VCF, LFO, and so on.

Velocity sensitivity Ability of instrument to react to the hardness (actually the velocity) with which a key is hit, so higher velocity results in louder sounds etc.

Vibrato Regular variation in pitch.

Vocoder Electronic device which combines the pitch information of one signal with the harmonic spectrum of another, typically producing robotic voices or 'singing' instruments.

Voltage control The basis of analog synthesis, by which oscillator pitch, modulation rate, filter settings etc. can be controlled by the voltage of signals from the keyboard and other circuits.

VU Volume Unit – form of audio signal level meter designed to give an overall indication of signal levels. See PPM.

Wah-wah Narrow band tone-filtering effects unit, usually in the form of a guitar footpedal.

Waveform Pattern of motion of a sound wave, which determines its tone. Sine waves contain only the fundamental frequency and have a pure tone.

Wow Pitch changes caused by slow variations in tape speed.

XLR Sturdy three-pin locking connector used for balanced audio signals, mains connections etc.

Zero fret Additional guitar fret used just in front of guitar nut on some guitars including 1960s Gretsch designs, intended to match tone of fretted and open strings.

142

144

Bibliography

John Aldridge *The Guide To Vintage Drums* (Centerstream 1994)

Tony Bacon & Paul Day *The Fender Book* (IMP/Miller Freeman 1992); *The Gibson Les Paul Book* (IMP/Miller Freeman 1993); *The Gretsch Book* (IMP/Miller Freeman 1996); *The Rickenbacker Book* (IMP/Miller Freeman 1994); *The Ultimate Guitar Book* (DK/Knopf 1991)

Tony Bacon & Barry Moorhouse *The Bass Book* (IMP/Miller Freeman 1995)

Geoff Brown *James Brown* (Omnibus 1995)

Walter Carter *Gibson: 100 Years Of An American Icon* (General Publishing 1994); *The Martin Book* (IMP/Miller Freeman 1995)

Julian Colbeck *Keyfax 1-5* (Music Maker Books et al, 1988/95)

André Duchossoir *Gibson Electrics: The Classic Years* (Hal Leonard 1994)

Colin Escott and Martin Hawkins *Sun Records* (Omnibus 1980)

Peter Forrest *A-Z Of Analogue Synthesizers* (Susurreal 1995)

Nelson George *Where Did Our Love Go? The Rise And Fall Of The Motown Sound* (Omnibus 1986)

Albert Goldman *Elvis* (Allen Lane 1981)

Charlie Gillett *Making Tracks: The History Of Atlantic Records* (WH Allen 1975)

George Gruhn & Walter Carter *Gruhn's Guide to Vintage Guitars* (GPI 1991)

Peter Guralnick *Last Train To Memphis: The Rise Of Elvis Presley* (Little, Brown 1994)

Peter Guralnick *Sweet Soul Music* (Virgin Books 1986)

John J Goldrosen *Buddy Holly: His Life And Music* (Panther 1979)

Steve Howe with Tony Bacon *The Steve Howe Guitar Collection* (IMP/Miller Freeman 1994)

Colin Larkin (ed) *The Guinness Encyclopedia Of Popular Music* (Guinness 1992)

David Leigh *High Times* (Heinemann/Unwin 1984)

Mark Lewisohn *The Complete Beatles Recording Sessions* (Hamlyn 1988); *The Complete Beatles Chronicle* (Pyramid 1992)

Dr Licks *Standing In The Shadows Of Motown* (Dr Licks 1989)

Mark Linett *Beach Boys Pet Sounds 30th Anniversary Collection* (Capitol Records Sleeve notes)

Ian MacDonald *Revolution In The Head: The Beatles' Records & The Sixties* (Fourth Estate 1994)

Andy Mackay *Electronic Music* (Control Data Publishing 1981)

Dave Marsh *Before I Get Old* (Plexus 1983)

Bill Millar *The Coasters* (WH Allen 1975); *The Drifters* (Studio Vista 1971)

Jim Miller (ed) *The Rolling Stone History of Rock and Roll* (Random House 1976)

John Morrish *The Fender Amp Book* (IMP/Miller Freeman 1995)

Martin Newcomb *Museum Of Synthesizer Technology Guidebook* (MST 1995)

Robert Palmer *Deep Blues* (Viking Press 1981)

David Petersen & Dick Denney *The Vox Story* (Bold Strummer 1993)

Hugo Pinksterboer *The Cymbal Book* (Hal Leonard 1992)

Dafydd Rees & Luke Crampton *The Guinness Book Of Rock Stars* (Guinness 1989)

Eugene Rousseau *Marcel Mule: His Life And The Saxophone* (Etoile 1981)

Aspen Pittman *The Tube Amp Book* (4th Edition, Groove Tubes 1993)

Paul Schmidt *The History Of The Ludwig Drum Company* (Centerstream 1991)

Brian Southall *Abbey Road* (Patrick Stephens Ltd 1982)

John Tobler and Stuart Grundy *The Record Producers* (BBC 1982)

Paul Trynka (ed) *The Electric Guitar* (Virgin 1993)

Paul Trynka & Val Wilmer *Portrait Of The Blues* (Hamlyn 1996)

Tom Wheeler *American Guitars* (HarperPerennial 1990)

Joel Whitburn *Top Pop Singles, 1955-1993* (Record Research 1994)

Timothy White *The Nearest Faraway Place* (Macmillan 1995)

Bill Wyman with Ray Coleman *Stone Alone* (Viking 1990)

We also consulted back issues of the following periodicals:
Bass Player (US); *Down Beat* (US) *EQ* (US); *Clarinet and Saxophone* (UK); *The Guitar Magazine* (UK); *Guitar Player* (US); *Guitarist* (UK); *Keyboard* (US); *Lighting & Sound International Magazine* (UK); *Making Music* (UK); *Modern Drummer* (US); *Musician* (US); *REP* (USA); *Rhythm* (UK); *Rolling Stone* (US); *Sound International Magazine* (UK); *Saxophone Journal* (US); *Studio Sound* (UK).

Photo Credits

Big Briar & Robert Moog 52 (Lev Theremin), 53 (Bob Moog); Britannia Row 87 (3); Max Brown/Bob Brunning 80 (Fleetwood Mac); David Cairns/Gibson 28; Barry Carson 35, 38 (Clavinet & Cembalet); Columbia 117; Demon Records 130; Frank Driggs Collection 120 (Elvis at RCA); EMI Records 91; EMI/Apple Corps 128; Mark Jenkins 53 (VCS-3), 54, 55 (Stevie Wonder), 58 (Oberheim), 59, 64; CF Martin & Co 51 (00042-EC); Key Audio 66; Martin Audio 83, 84, 85; Peavey Electronics 116; PRS 26 (McCarty Model); Redferns and Michael Ochs Archives: Front Cover (Penniman, Van Halen, Felder & Peart) 5, 7, 10, 12, 17, 18, 19, 25, 26, 27, 28, 29, (SRV & Johnson), 30, 33 (The Animals), 36, 37, 39 (2), 41 (Presley), 43 (Everlys), 45, 46, 49, 51, 56 (Wakeman), 57 (Franke), 60 (Yazoo), 64 (Depeche Mode), 67, 68, 69, 70, 72, 73 (2), 74 (2), 75 (2), 76, 77 (2), 79, 82, 83 (Woodstock shots by Elliott Landy), 86 (2), 88 (2), 89, 90, 95 (Manfred Mann), 92, 95, 96, 97, 99, 101, 102, 103, 104, 107, 108, 111, 112 (2), 115, 119 (Gene Vincent), 121, 122, 123 (2), 124 (2), 127, 131 (Cream), 132, 133, 136 (Nirvana), back cover (Haley & Peart); Selmer Paris 71; Chris Taylor 66 & 67 (Orbital); WEA Records 135; Charlie Watkins 81; Val Wilmer 126, 129 (2), 131 (Eddie Kramer), 134 (2).

Instruments photographed came from the following individuals' collections, and we are most grateful for their help:
Terry Anthony, Scot Arch, The Bass Centre, The Chinery Collection, Stanley Clarke, Country Music Hall Of Fame, Bob Daisley, Paul Day, Duane Eddy, David Gilmour, Gruhn Guitars, Hard Rock Café London, George Harrison, Hap Kuffner, Lewingtons, Adrian Lovegrove, The Martin Guitar Company, Jacquie Martin, Paul McCartney, Musical Museum (Brentford), Martin Newcomb, David Noble, Geoff Nicholls, Bill Puplett, Hank Risan (Washington Street Music) Alan Rogan, Rose Morris & Co, Music Ground, Sensible Music, Paul Trynka, Yamaha-Kemble Music UK

Memorabilia photographed in this book came from the collections of:
Tony Bacon, David Burrluck, Barry Carson, Paul Day, Scott Chinery, Christies, Hohner UK, Mark Jenkins, The National Jazz Archive (Loughton), Geoff Nicholls, Rickenbacker, Alan Rogan, Selmer Paris, Steve Soest, Paul Trynka

Principal photography was by Miki Slingsby; a small number of additional pictures were taken by Garth Blore, Nigel Bradley, Steve Catlin, Matthew Chattle and Richard Connors.

In addition to those already named we would like to thank: Gwen Alexander; Jeff Allen; Tony Andrews & John Newsham (Funktion One Research); Ivor and John Arbiter; Tony Bacon; Britannia Row; Chas Brooke; Geoff Brown; Bob Brunning; Dave Burrluck; David Cairns (Gibson); Pete Cornish; Paul Day; Lou Dias; Gerry Evans; Don Everly; Larry Fishman; Bill Halverson; Linda Hancock; Tommy Goldsmith (The Tennessean); Steve Grindrod (Marshall); Bob Henrit; Tony Horkins; Mark Jenkins; Cliff Jones; Jan Kuch (Ampex); Mike Leonard (TGM); Cosimo Matassa; Ted McCarty; Scotty Moore; Ian Lewington; Dede Miller, Jon Wilton (Redferns); Roger Mayer; Sally Milne (Martin Audio); Paul McCallum (Wembley Loudspeaker Co); Barry Moorhouse (The Bass Centre); Martin Newcomb (Museum Of Synthesizer Technology 01279 771619); Bill Puplett; Ken Parker; Les Paul; Alan Robinson (Demon); Sally Stockwell; Charlie Watkins; Bazz Ward; Doug West (MESA/Boogie); Tom Wilkinson; Steve Yelding (Marshall).

"This is the big boys' corner. This is the hardware department."
Keith Marlon Richards, 1993.